Difference in Philosophy of Religion

Edited by
PHILIP GOODCHILD
University of Nottingham, UK

ASHGATE

Published by
Ashgate Publishing Limited
Gower House
Croft Road
Aldershot
Hants GU11 3HR
England

Ashgate Publishing Company
Suite 420
101 Cherry Street
Burlington, VT 05401-4405
USA

Ashgate website: http://www.ashgate.com

British Library Cataloguing in Publication Data
Difference in philosophy of religion
    1. Religion - Philosophy 2. Individual differences -
    Religious aspects
    I. Goodchild, Philip, 1965-
    210

Library of Congress Control Number: 2002103824

ISBN 0 7546 0847 6 (Hbk)
ISBN 0 7546 0848 4 (Pbk)

Typeset by Express Typesetters
Printed and bound in Great Britain by MPG Books Ltd, Bodmin, Cornwall

DIFFERENCE IN PHILOSOPHY OF RELIGION

Can difference be subordinated to identity, simplicity or diversity? Or does it make a difference to the entire way in which we think? This book challenges the dominant agenda in the discipline of philosophy of religion by exploring issues of difference that have hitherto been obscured. It draws together some of the most innovative work in philosophical thinking about religion by some of the most creative and radical new thinkers in the field. Moving beyond debates between believers and sceptics, the contributors draw on critical theory to address differences in rationality, gender, tradition, culture and politics, showing how it is possible to think differently. Assumptions about rational neutrality, belief, tradition, experience and identity that undergird the rational exploration of classical theism are deconstructed. Instead it becomes important to explore a critical ethical reasoning, religious performance, internal religious tensions, location in culture, and a relation to exteriority as the groundwork for a future philosophy of religion.

The challenging new directions for inquiry presented in this volume offer philosophers of religion, theologians, and critical and cultural theorists fresh insights into ways of addressing problems of religious difference.

Contents

Acknowledgments

Chapter 4, 'Beyond belief: sexual difference and religion after ontotheology', by Ellen T. Armour, has previously been published in a more extended form in John D. Caputo (ed.), *Blackwell Series in Continental Philosophy: The Religious*, Oxford, Blackwell, 2001. We gratefully acknowledge permission from the publisher and editor to reprint.

List of Contributors

Ellen T. Armour is Associate Professor and Chair of the Department of Religious Studies at Rhodes College in Memphis, Tennessee. She received her MA and PhD in religion from Vanderbilt University. Her research involves using deconstruction to address issues of racial and sexual difference in theology. She is the author of *Deconstruction, Feminist Theology and the Problem of Difference: Subverting the Race/Gender Divide* (1999). She is currently involved in two book projects. With Susan St. Ville, Dr Armour is co-editing a volume of essays by religion scholars using Judith Butler's work. Dr Armour's current book project involves developing resources for thinking the sacred that can sustain attention to racial and sexual differences.

Mark Cauchi is currently working on a doctoral dissertation on Derrida and biblical ontology in the Graduate Programme in Social and Political Thought, York University, Toronto, as well as co-editing a volume on the relation of biblical thought and modernity.

Paul Fletcher is Lecturer in Christian Studies at Lancaster University. He received his doctorate from the University of Durham, on the work of René Girard, and is a co-editor of *Religions in the Modern World: Traditions and Transformations* (2001).

Paulo Gonçalves is Lecturer in Religious Studies at the University of Derby, UK, where he teaches the philosophy of religion. He has studied theology, philosophy and philosophy of religion in South Africa, France, London, Warwick and Manchester. He has published on deconstruction and early Christian metaphysics and is co-editing, with Arvind-Pal Singh Mandair, a volume entitled *(Dis)Locations: Language, Autobiography and Identity in Dialogue with Jacques Derrida*.

Philip Goodchild is Senior Lecturer in Religious Studies at the University of Nottingham, UK. He is the author of *Gilles Deleuze and the Question of Philosophy* (1996), *Deleuze and Guattari: An Introduction to the Politics of Desire* (1996) and *Capitalism and Religion: The Price of Piety* (2002), as well as editor of *Rethinking Philosophy of Religion: Approaches from Continental Philosophy* (2002). He initiated and organized the conference on Continental Philosophy of Religion at Lancaster, upon which this collection is based.

Amy M. Hollywood teaches in the Religion Department at Dartmouth College. She is the author of *The Soul as Virgin Wife: Mechthild of Magdeburg, Marguerite Porete, and Meister Eckhart* (1995) and *Sensible Ecstasy: Mysticism, Sexual Difference, and the Demands of History* (2002).

Avron Kulak received his doctorate in Social and Political Thought from York

University, Toronto, in 1997. His dissertation was entitled *Origin and Critique: Reading Nietzsche's On the Genealogy of Morals*. He has published studies in the area of religion and (post)modernity.

Arvind-Pal S. Mandair is currently Assistant Professor of Philosophy and Religious Studies and Bindra Chair of Sikh Studies at Hofstra University, New York. He was formerly a Post Doctoral Research Fellow in the Department for the Study of Religions at the School of Oriental and African Studies, University of London. He is the author of *Religion, Language and Subjectivity: Translating Cultures Between East and West* (forthcoming).

Navdeep Singh Mandair is studying for a PhD in the Department for the Study of Religions at the School of Oriental and African Studies, University of London.

Brayton Polka is Professor of Humanities and Social and Political Thought at York University, Toronto, Canada. He is the author of *The Dialectic of Biblical Critique: Interpretation and Existence* (1986), *Truth and Interpretation: An Essay in Thinking* (1990) and *Depth Psychology, Interpretation, and the Bible: An Ontological Essay on Freud* (2001).

Jim Urpeth is Senior Lecturer in Philosophy at the University of Greenwich. He co-edited (with J. Lippitt) *Nietzsche and the Divine* (2000) and was the 'guest editor' of a themed edition of the *Journal of Nietzsche Studies* on 'Nietzsche and Religion' (*JNS*, **19**, Spring 2000). He has written on themes in the thought of Kant, Nietzsche, Bataille, Heidegger, Foucault and Deleuze and is completing a book entitled *Transhuman Aesthetics from Kant to Deleuze* for Palgrave's 'Renewing Philosophy' series. He is the UK editor of the *Journal of Nietzsche Studies*. His main research interests are in aesthetics and the philosophy of religion.

Youssef Yacoubi is currently the Procter Fellow in Comparative Literature at Princeton University, completing his PhD in Critical Theory and Cultural Studies at the University of Nottingham, UK. He has taught Postcolonial Studies at Nottingham Trent and Nottingham universities. He has published articles on representations of Islam in literature and on the fiction of Salman Rushdie. He is the co-editor of the e-journal, *Critical Theology* of the Postgraduate School of Critical Theory and Cultural Studies at Nottingham.

Introduction

Philip Goodchild

Contemporary Philosophy of Religion

Philosophy of religion is a thriving discipline. Yet what remains truly extraordinary is the extent to which it is ignored in modern life, for while its issues are of interest to many, few pay attention to its experts. This disjunction between the discipline and a wider culture is significant: if we are to believe some of its practitioners, contemporary arguments in philosophy of religion may not give us absolute certainty, but they are sufficiently strong to generate conviction on questions of fundamental importance for the conduct of most aspects of human life.

Why is not everyone deeply moved by the fine-tuning of the physical laws of the universe so as to afford the fragile conditions capable of supporting life (see Leslie, 1989; Swinburne, 1991)? Are people incapable of taking a reasonable stance on such issues? Why do people cling to competing convictions, whether religious or sceptical, when they are aware that apparently rational and sincere people hold opposing views? Why do so few rationally explore the claims of religious diversity (see, for example, Hick, 1989; Griffiths, 2001)? Why is it that, even among those few who are exposed to philosophy of religion books and lectures, so many leave with their opinions unchanged? Are we to despair of the human ability to listen to the voices of reason? Or is our power of reasoning insufficient to question our most basic beliefs?

For when it comes to the most fundamental questions of religion, it would seem that everyone is their own authority and can decide for themselves – as though the decades of patient, open-minded searching and questioning by gifted specialists were worth nothing, as though any possibly genuine insight into religious matters could only be communicated through preaching or example, but not through argument. Finally, when it comes to philosophers of religion themselves, how is it that there remains such a diversity of opinion, if arguments are intended to establish what is the case? Are such philosophers little different to the rest of humanity, merely clever in argumentation, but not interested in genuine inquiry? Or is genuine inquiry at all possible?

Such considerations indicate that it may be fruitful to pay some attention to questions of *difference* in philosophy of religion: differences in rationality, in gender, in tradition, in culture, and even in larger political commitments. What is philosophy of religion for? Whose interests might it serve? Now it is precisely such questions which appear to be irrelevant to the eternal verities considered by philosophy of religion: the discipline is not intended to be about the perspectives of its practitioners; indeed, part of its disciplinary practice is to bracket out such partial perspectives, so that a universal, rational discourse may be attained that could, in theory, be embraced by all, or even so that the eternal nature of God can be explained in the eternal concepts of human reason. Yet one may suspect that it is precisely the existence of such universal or eternal perspectives that philosophy of religion seeks to establish through its arguments, while the existence of such perspectives is then projected and presupposed as the condition of possibility of its own discourse and disciplinary practice, in a repressed circular argument. For philosophy of religion to proceed, it must assume that the conceptions of truth and reason informing its propositions and arguments are entirely independent of the actual truths that it is attempting to establish – an assumption that emphatically was *not* universal in the tradition of 'classical theism' up to Descartes. Then, by making such an assumption and distinction between thought and existence, reason may conclude that a given proposition is the case, but such a conception of truth does not carry with it the gravity of existence. Like the character 'Aristoteles' in Plato's dialogue *Parmenides*, the student of philosophy of religion may be persuaded to answer 'Most true' to self-contradictory conclusions – especially when, in a democratically dialectical and didactic manner, both sides of the case are presented – while not being persuaded that they have seen anything other than a dazzling display of sophistic argumentation.

The suspicion may develop that arguments in the philosophy of religion are 'justifications' of highly localized and particular religious opinions – 'justifications' which masquerade as public and universal judgments of what is the case, and thus attempt to entrap the interlocutors into abandoning their own local and different perspectives, so as to accede to the judgments of the master thinker. If this imperialist strategy does indeed underlie much contemporary argumentation, it would seem that in practice few people are entrapped in this way other than the philosophers of religion themselves, who, by their alchemical reasoning, transmute the particular into the universal in a quest, not necessarily to achieve mastery, but to believe in their own mastery. The result of such a master discourse is that different particular judgments can be safely ignored by the one who has already attained the universal. Then the very challenge of diversity itself – perhaps the challenge that inaugurated philosophy of religion as a modern discipline – evaporates through self-inoculation. If such suspicions are correct, we would have at least one possible answer to some questions raised earlier. Why do people cling to competing convictions, whether religious or sceptical, when they are aware that apparently rational and sincere people hold opposing views? Why do so few rationally explore the claims of religious diversity – as though the decades of patient, open-minded searching and questioning by gifted specialists were worth nothing, as though any possibly genuine insight into religious matters could only be communicated through preaching or example, but not through argument?

Simplicity and Diversity

Let us illustrate how such self-inoculation against difference is achieved through conceptions of simplicity and diversity, drawing from two exemplars of processes of concept formation that are widespread in the field. For Richard Swinburne's inductive argument for the existence of God, the *simplicity* of the hypothesis of classical theism makes it more probable than other explanatory hypotheses; it is utilized to set aside questions of difference. For the 'postulation of God … is the postulation of *one* entity of a simple kind (the simplest kind of person there could be, having no limits to his knowledge, power and freedom)' (Swinburne, 1991, p. 322). Simplicity, here, would seem to be understood as being specified by the least information, if we are to draw from the rejection of the complexity of the many-worlds hypothesis for explaining the fine-tuning of the universe (Swinburne, 1991, p. 322), or the rejection of the complexity of Hume's hypothetical polytheistic explanation of the order of the universe (Swinburne, 1991, p. 141). It does, however, have its roots in medieval conceptions of divine simplicity as the rejection of any real distinctions within God, such distinctions being limits threatening the mastery and pre-eminence of the divine being. Simplicity is an attribute of the 'monarchical' conception of a transcendent God (see Macquarrie, 1984, p. 31).

Now the concept of a simple God may be constructed by starting with the concept of a personal being, as characterized by views, intentions and powers, and removing all limits, so that the divine being is omnipotent, omniscient and perfectly free (Swinburne, 1991, p. 141). The sleight of hand in this monarchical conception of God is achieved by not specifying the culturally particular meanings of 'power, knowledge and freedom', which can later be brought in at relevant points of the argument. Then this simple conception of God is merely a projection of dominant conceptions of power, knowledge and freedom in Swinburne's particular culture and tradition: it is a divinization of his own way of life, and an eclipsing of difference. Simplicity conceals particularity. Moreover, the conception of a person as composed of views, intentions and powers may only be formed of a finite, temporal being in relation, for we only discover and enact views, intentions and powers as finite, temporal beings in relation. Thus, far from being a genuinely simple hypothesis, this conception of a 'simple' God is a metaphysical abstraction beyond the limits of experience. It is only achieved by separating thought from existence, by constructing a crude anthropomorphic model, by evading the meaning of the passage to the infinite, by sacrificing actual personal relations and by reformulating religious language as a set of truth claims about a projected entity. Thus the first five contributions below explore the reintroduction of these concerns into the field, respectively.

At the opposite pole of the contemporary field, a second technique for inoculating against difference is through constructing a conception of diversity. Paul J. Griffiths, who, unlike Swinburne, is deeply conscious of the cultural location of his own philosophical discourse and opinions, finds a resource against difference nonetheless. For in order to depict a world of non-compossible, diverse and competing religions, producing involuntary assent among their members, he defines a religion thus: 'A religion, then, I shall take to be a form of life that seems to those who inhabit it to be comprehensive, incapable of abandonment, and of central importance' (Griffiths, 2001, p. 7). Instead of pointing to divine simplicity, Griffiths, concerned here with the realm of human culture rather than divine nature, postulates a religion as a unitary whole of unsurpassable significance. A series of objections should arise: religious people are often much less concerned with their own form of life than they are with God, the supernatural or their ultimate end; a 'religion' may be comprehensive, in the sense of taking account of and being relevant to everything, if it is an isolated, ethnic religion, but no religion can make this claim credible in the changing forms of life of economic globalization; and, while religious forms of life may involve some degree of commitment, the history of religions shows continuing processes of adaptation, reform, renewal, translation, syncretism, divergence, self-improvement and internal conflict that make some apparently 'essential' elements of any religion open to reinterpretation or even abandonment.

The purpose of Griffith's artificial construction of religious identity is revealed by his quotation from William Alston: 'In the absence of any external reason for supposing that one of the competing practices is more accurate than my own, the only rational course for me is to sit tight with the practice of which *I am a master* and which *serves me* so well in guiding my activity in the world' (Alston, cited in Griffiths, 2001, p. 93; emphasis added). The reification of a religious tradition is, once more, part of a project of mastery, not necessarily over others, but over one's own life, so that one is not unduly affected by difference. Given such mastery, Griffiths is able to pass over the key problem of religious diversity, for one in his cultural location, as follows: 'I shall simply register, without further argument, the opinion that Christians ought to be moderately epistemically troubled by knowledge of deep religious diversity because this is not something easily predictable from properly Christian theological assumptions' (Griffiths, 2001, pp. 96–7). He registers a moderate degree of significance for exterior difference, without beginning to address it. The reification of a religious tradition is, once more, part of a project of mastery, not necessarily over others, but over one's own life, so that one is not unduly affected by difference, by means of a deliberate blindness to internal difference within one's tradition. This reification is only achieved by ignoring how the unitary Western category of 'religion' has been exported to other cultures and identities, ignoring how such an other identity is constructed by abstracting stereotypical features of other traditions from their proper context of understanding and replacing an actual form of life with an abstraction, ignoring how certain theological and political interests are invested in such a unitary conception of religious identity, ignoring how such a religious identity is abstracted from the polyvalent texts in which it is expressed, ignoring how contemporary cultural dynamics have changed the meaning of religious experience, and rejecting the possibility of a religious encounter with the exterior, material world apart from any cultural interpretation. Thus Chapters 6 to 11 explore the reintroduction of these concerns into the field, respectively.

Difference

The suspicion that motivates this volume is that there is a prevalent blindness to difference in philosophy of religion – not necessarily a blindness to the diversity of religious truth claims that could be uttered in a democratic site of representation and debate, but a blindness to the way in which differences may shape religious practice, attitudes, representations and sites of encounter so as to produce a field of thought that cannot be reduced to a space of representation in the service of mastery over what is the case. The sheer *difference* in questions, assumptions, style, argument and execution of the essays collected here from those of standard examples of the philosophy of religion is merely one piece of evidence of the significance of such differences. Although they differ from philosophy of religion, they are representative in the above respects of a range of contemporary critical discourses in the humanities and social sciences which emphasize the location of thought in respect of rationality, gender, tradition, embodied experience and politics. In general, such broadly termed 'critical theory', with its roots in the nineteenth-century 'masters of suspicion', Marx, Nietzsche and Freud, would appear to put aside questions of the reality of the objects of religious worship, practice and belief – criticism of the religion being the 'premise of all criticism' – so that religion can be studied as a temporal human product. The result is that religion may be subsumed into a mode of culture, tradition and identity, and philosophical questions concerning religion are ignored.

If such wider movements in the humanities and social sciences have had any impact on the philosophy of religion, it is usually under the label 'relativism', which is regarded as an opponent. Now it may be argued that the 'relativist' is an artificial construct which, while embodying dominant political attitudes towards religion as well as the *Zeitgeist* of contemporary permissiveness, bears little resemblance to the work of those who explore concepts of difference within the realms of philosophy, tradition, gender, culture and politics. When dialogue and debate is pursued solely within the conceptual framework provided by a dominant philosophy of religion, the result is a breakdown of communication between philosophy of religion and critical theory.

The purpose of this volume is to deconstruct a sharp dualism between philosophy of religion and critical theory, as well as between 'theism' and 'humanism', so as to indicate the possibility of a different approach. The aim is to explore some of the challenges and opportunities afforded by drawing the discourse of critical theory into philosophy of religion itself. The result is a set of arguments deeply involved in the discussion of specific theoretical texts and religious traditions, specificity being the antidote to generalizing abstractions. The contributors, far from being 'relativist', may be regarded as passionately committed to the spirit of truth, justice and spirituality – even if the spirit of such concepts can barely be stated appropriately. Instead of entering the debate on whether 'God' and 'truth' are absolute or relative, the contributors explore a set of related conceptual problems which bear on the shaping of the discipline of philosophy of religion.

First, considering conceptual difference, the propositional framework of contemporary philosophy of religion is challenged by questioning its separation of thought and existence prior to verification. In addition, the tendency to reify religious truth as an object of propositions is challenged by appealing to a critique of idolatry. In contrast to such 'ontotheology', an infinite process of critique and exploration is instituted instead.

Second, turning attention to sexual difference, the centrality of investigating belief claims in philosophy of religion is challenged by exploring what is sacrificed by formulating religion in terms of belief claims. On the one hand, emotional and bodily ties, pre-eminently to mothers, are sacrificed in favour of abstractions; on the other hand, the signifying and productive role of ritual and bodily practices is eclipsed, including its construction of gender and relations of power.

Third, turning attention to difference in religious traditions, a challenge is issued to the process of assimilating traditions to clearly defined cultural and religious identities for the purpose of representing religious identity. This challenges not only the way in which philosophy of religion tends to think about religious diversity, but also the construction of unitary cultural subjects who may be assumed to articulate certain clearly defined belief claims. In particular, it can be seen that the object of philosophizing is too often replaced by an artificial concept of 'religion', constructed in relation to concepts of 'truth' and 'identity', that render invisible some of the forms of life of actual religious traditions.

Fourth, locating experience in culture, one may differentiate between the aesthetic consumption of experience in contemporary capitalism, and the authority of experience in the practice of virtue in religious life and community. Alternatively, one may challenge the subsumption of nature into culture by much recent thought, and regard even the logic of contemporary capitalism as an expression of non-anthropomorphized processes that point towards a religious materialism.

Finally, returning to the political question of the relations between religious differences on the basis of the preceding deconstructions, it is possible to challenge the dominant contemporary paradigms: particular tradition-centred, pluralist and secular. Instead, all people are faced with something purely exterior, and it is the universal encounter with exteriority that may form a basis for the meeting of religions.

While there are certainly many differences among the contributors, all of them share a rejection of the dualism of the religious/secular divide as two opposing poles and modes of thought upon which much contemporary debate in the philosophy of religion is based. Conceptions of difference, whether explored in relation to philosophy, gender, tradition, culture or politics, provide a key to bringing to light what has been obscured.

The Contributions

The first three essays invert philosophy of religion into a 'religion of philosophy' by exploring concealed religious presuppositions in Western critical thought. Brayton Polka's essay, 'The ontological argument for existence', utilizes Anselm's ontological argument to explore a necessary relationship between thought and existence. The extraordinary claim Polka makes is that reason is intimately connected with the human thought demonstrating the existence of God. Anselm had shown this through the case of the fool: either the fool denies nothing, and no one takes him seriously, or else the fool denies God, and thus presupposes God. Polka explores a repressed tradition of modern thought that refuses the legacy of Ibn-Sina's separation of essence from existence, for although it is one thing to postulate a proposition, and a second thing that it should be true, it is a third thing to critically assess the truth of a proposition in order to affirm it. It is this dimension of thought – that it critically affirms – that necessarily involves a relation to existence as its criterion, as 'that than which no greater can be conceived', for to conceive without reference to existence is to conceive something lesser.

Polka's ingenious argument effectively issues a deconstructive challenge to all clear and distinct ideas in consciousness of finite identity or finite difference, for these are 'dead' insofar as they are proposed without reference to existence. Then the concept of God as 'that than which no greater can be conceived' is dialectically and paradoxically related to human thought, in mutual dependence and presupposition. This breaks with the Neoplatonic subordination of human thought to divine existence, which was later carried forward by Aquinas. Instead, a critical principle of justice as the standard than which no greater can be thought becomes the essence of this dialectic, expressed in the separate sovereignties of human and divine. Rejecting the quest for mastery expressed in subordinating the divine to human thought, or the human to divine existence, critical thought becomes love of God and love of neighbour. Then the Good is not external to thought, but the standard by which one distinguishes the true from the spurious.

Avron Kulak's essay, 'Divine and graven images: the contemporaneity of theory and the Bible', continues to explore the critical difference between divine and graven images in human thought. In the first three chapters of Genesis, the Bible declares that humans bear the image and likeness of God, before situating that likeness in the moral realm as knowledge of good and evil, as that which lacks any natural or immediate image. The result is a self-critical principle: the human is in the image of the divine as its principle of truth; yet the divine must be distinguished from all graven images. This is a critique of any image of truth that could be constructed as an image. Kulak then draws on Augustine to apply this self-critical principle to the temporality of the creation stories. To reduce the sequence of creation to the postulation of a prior, eternal, self-present God, juxtaposed to a posterior, chronological, created order is to compose a story of graven images, without addressing the dialectical and mutual dependence of creator and created. Kulak thus deconstructs the distinction of the eternal from the temporal, along with the reified concept of God dependent on it. Then creation has a history, while it becomes the principle in light of which all moments are equally first, original and created. Furthermore, drawing on Kierkegaard's narrative of the Fall as contemporary with each individual, the history of creation is less a fall from pure self-presence than a beginning with self-consciousness of sinfulness. It is a beginning without a pure origin. Opposing Augustine and Kierkegaard's thought to Greek understandings of origins, Kulak argues that 'contemporary' critical thought, addressing its own origins, is biblical, not Greek. The Bible, then, provides the basis for the critical principles of Western thought, and not Greek philosophy.

The critique of finite images is an infinite process. Mark Cauchi's essay, 'Traversing the infinite through Augustine and Derrida', explores the concept of the infinite as a passage through limits, rather than as a simple projection of the unlimited. Drawing from Augustine's *Confessions*, he finds the infinite God described as both omnipresent, because unlimited, and impermeable, because God alone is the infinite creator. Augustine thus does not know which comes first: to call upon God for knowledge of God, whom one does not know, or to know God, so that one may call upon God for knowledge. Cauchi compares this aporia with the logic of the event described by Derrida: on the one hand, an event crosses a dissymmetrical border in order to occur; on the other hand, an event crosses no border that is anticipated, or else it would bring nothing new. Both describe the temporality of creation, which differs from Aristotle's conception of the infinite. Moving on to consider knowing finitude – and thus the existence of thinking, not simply the thinking of existence – Cauchi argues that each finite limit must be known on both sides, paradoxically, by two infinites in a reciprocal relation. Only as such is it possible to think of another without confining them within imposed limits. Cauchi finds Augustine's concept of the Trinity as the most adequate exposition of this logic of the infinite as mutual relation.

Ellen Armour's essay, 'Beyond belief: sexual difference and religion after ontotheology', builds on the deconstruction of 'ontotheology' – this being the construction of conceptions of 'being' with the aim of maintaining a particular theological position, which is later unconsciously inherited by Western reason – by arguing that it is relevant not merely to philosophical conceptions of truth and reason, but also to the everyday religious practice of belief. For belief exhibits symptoms of sexual and racial indifference by asserting an account of what is in spite of what appears to be real: it thus hides the real from view, giving an illusory mastery, and sacrificing the actual relations that have made belief possible – including relations between sexes. As a desire for mastery, belief is believed in because it is not true. Drawing on Luce Irigaray's essay, 'Belief Itself', and Jacques Derrida's essay, 'Circumfessions', Armour shifts attention away from projected abstractions to the material realm of rituals and bodies so as to expose the sacrificial economy at work in belief itself. Where religion in the modern West has predominantly been a matter of a relationship between a normative subject and a transcendent God, founded on the sacrifice of difference in material and especially maternal relations, she suggests that religion may become an encounter with alterity in each other and beyond.

Amy Hollywood's essay, 'Towards a feminist philosophy of ritual and bodily practice', extends the critique of the attachment of philosophy to the justification of belief, and even to the discursive realm, by exploring ritual and bodily practices. Far from regarding these as divorced from the discursive dimensions of religion, or simply as forms of symbolic communication, she explores the role of ritual as performance, effecting performative acts in a manner parallel to speech acts. Drawing extensively on recent anthropological theory, ritual is seen as a productive and signifying activity: it produces ritualized agents, people who have a knowledge of ritual schemes embedded in their bodies, habits and sense of reality. Exploring the reworking of the concept of the 'performative' by Derrida and Butler, Hollywood shows how certain social realities are constituted by ritual action. Such constituted social realities, like that of gender, have a force that may then affect subsequent relations; they have an ontological status measured by their force.

The next four essays explore the significance of difference in relation to religious traditions. Arvind Mandair's essay, 'What if *religio* remained untranslatable?', challenges the situation of Indic traditions by modern Western thought as objects of academic study by means of translation under the category of 'religion'. The unity and coherence of such religious identities are created by responding to the Western need for systematic ordering and control. Mandair argues that this ordering is a strategy for protecting the philosophy and theology of the West from alien contamination by the East. Thus the construction of religious identities for the appropriation of Sikhs and Hindus repeats a colonial gesture, practised in the Anglo-Vernacular mission schools of the nineteenth century, of giving back to Indians their original religions and languages. The result is that the study of Indic cultures is confined to specialist reservations which do not impinge on the free play of critical thinking in the discourse of the humanities. Mandair explores the influence of

Hegel's strategy for ordering and confining Indic religions, and argues that the phenomenological positioning of the other as other is necessary in order for Western thought to distance its interlocutors. By contrast, he argues that cultural difference can be understood as a 'dislocatory practice' rather than sheer diversity or difference of identities. The result of historicizing the philosophy of religion, turning attention to its actual disciplinary practices, is that it can be shown to be founded on a fundamental repression of otherness.

Navdeep Mandair's essay, 'Virtual corpus: solicitous mutilation and the body of tradition', gives an in-depth analysis of the process by which the construction of a religious identity is incorporated within a dominant Western thought by means of an abstraction of stereotyped obvious features from their proper context of understanding. This is a thorough analysis of the unconscious repression of difference achieved through postulating a few propositions: it involves a suppression of the other's cultural background, its proper context or alterionomy, and a simultaneous foregrounding of its salient features or alteriography. Thus a few salient features or beliefs may replace an entire way of life and thought. The result is that others are restructured as virtual entities. Then religious pluralism that ostensibly affirms religious alterity may do so by means of a dissimulation that effectively erases alterity. Mandair describes the effects of this from a Sikh perspective, and explores from within the Sikh tradition the dimension of Sikh culture that is intolerable for modern Western thought: its celebration of violence. Exploring the role of violence in key devotional texts, he shows how the violent relation to the divine is excessive and incommensurable, resisting all acts of identification. Deconstructing the relation between interior religion and exterior identity, Sikh militancy is reconceived as resistance to tyrannical authority, and a condition for authentic love for the other.

Paulo Gonçalves, in 'Religious "worlds" and their alien invaders', considers certain contemporary trends in the theorization of religions and turns the deconstruction of religious identity back upon the Christian tradition. Postliberal theologies, under the influence of Wittgenstein, Ricoeur and MacIntyre, reject the isolation of propositional truth claims by the philosophy of religion on the grounds that religious discourse should be understood according to its form of life, tradition, narrative or community: they are meaningful in their religious 'worlds'. Gonçalves addresses the tendency to reify religious 'worlds' and traditions as diverse and incommensurable homogenies of discourse and praxis, showing how such constructs serve the theological and political interests of particular 'orthodoxies' and parties within traditions. Via a critique of the Yale School's postliberal theology and John Milbank's 'Radical Orthodoxy', he argues that the identity of the Christian tradition is itself a reified theological construct. Drawing on received scholarship of early church history, he shows how this construct is at odds with Christianity's history of differentiation and exclusion. He then draws on deconstruction in order to elaborate alternative ways of theorizing and representing religious identity beyond abstract and ahistorical structuralist homogeneity.

Youssef Yacoubi, in 'Thinking a critical theory of postcolonial Islam', introduces the question of difference within the Islamic tradition. Much recent engagement between critical theory and Islam has been shaped by Edward Said's influential *Orientalism*, yet Yacoubi reads a critical theory of Islam in the margins of this text by turning to what has been suppressed within it. Moving on from debates concerning 'Orientalism' in the West's construction of its other, and an Islamic reaction to these that wishes to articulate a proper Islamic theology in contrast to a purely humanistic discourse on Orientalism, Yacoubi explores the deconstruction of the Islamic theological tradition itself. He contrasts a purely theological appropriation of the Qur'anic text with a poetic reading in terms of its negotiation of the pre-Islamic tradition of Jahili poetry, where the meanings of the text cannot be entirely overcoded by a theological signifier. The deconstruction of Islamic ontotheology reveals the presence of a repressed yet properly Islamic other within its own tradition, such difference being manifested in Islamic mysticism. The result is the possibility of a critical theory within Islam itself, and Yacoubi introduces a Continental Arabo-Islamic criticism in the form of the work of Mohammed Arkoun to show the thinkability and historical operation of an Islamic criticism that comes from the periphery.

The final three essays in the volume move beyond the ambit of deconstruction that has informed the preceding ones. Paul Fletcher's essay, 'Fantasy, imagination and the possibility of experience', explores the role of fantasy in the contemporary formation of thought. Instead of concentrating on truth or existence, he explores the appropriation of experience by imagination. In capitalist consumer culture, experience is transformed from the authoritative wisdom of a cumulative tradition to become concerned solely with passing moments of the extreme and the extraordinary. He locates contemporary forms of religious life centred on a quest for having experiences in the context of the transformations of modern reason, which replaces the voice of authoritative experience with the need to master the world through science and the possession of experiences. In German Romanticism, in particular, once religion is reformulated in terms of subjective imagination and reduced to aesthetic categories, it becomes a quest for experience as consumption of the aesthetic. Religion, in order to prove itself authentic through experience, becomes a parasite of this quest. Yet the means of consumption is capital: hence Fletcher turns to Walter Benjamin's analysis of capital as a purely cultic religion, lacking beliefs, and contrasts such contemporary manifestations of religion with the life and practice of virtue.

Jim Urpeth's essay, 'Religious materialism: Bataille, Deleuze/Guattari and the sacredness of late capital', by contrast, affirms the experience of the sacred that can emerge from accelerating the material process of capitalism. He explores forms of religious materialism in recent philosophy that refuse the anthropomorphic subsumption of matter into the object of subjective mastery or cultural interpretation. Rejecting once more the dichotomy between anti-religious materialisms and anti-materialist religions, he finds transcendence in immanence in a self-sufficient material order, felt as affectivity. In direct contrast to Fletcher, he follows Bataille in gesturing towards a radical mysticism at the heart of late capital insofar as its self-overcoming though pure expenditure can lead to a self-consciousness in continuity with matter.

In the final essay, 'Politics, pluralism and the philosophy of religion: an essay on exteriority', I attempt to bring some of the implications of the preceding discussions together by formulating some new proposals for the thinking of difference in the philosophy of religion in a series of disparate sections that aim to draw attention to difference. Here, turning attention once more from thought to existence, I explore the political problem of how differences may be negotiated in practice in human relations. The philosophy of religion emerged as a modern discipline in reaction to problems of religious diversity, and three dominant paradigms have emerged for the negotiation of difference: religious pluralism, religious 'particularism' and secular critique. Tracing each of these to their philosophical roots, and accepting that the concepts and identities upon which they are based have been deconstructed, I call for a new ontology based on giving attention to a common experience of exteriority. I propose that religious differences meet in a space of exteriority where, as a supplement to their own practices and critical projects, they pay attention to the universal limits of experience, where nature, history and experience predominate over culture.

References

Griffiths, P. (2001), *Problems of Religious Diversity*, Oxford: Blackwell.
Hick, J. (1989), *An Interpretation of Religion*, Basingstoke: Macmillan.
Leslie, J. (1989), *Universes*, London: Routledge.
Macquarrie, J. (1984), *In Search of Deity: An Essay in Dialectical Theism*, London: SCM.
Swinburne, R. (1991), *The Existence of God*, rev. edn, Oxford: Clarendon.

I
RELIGION OF PHILOSOPHY

Chapter 1

The Ontological Argument For Existence

Brayton Polka

In *The Guide of the Perplexed* Maimonides writes, citing the ancient rabbis, that the Bible is written in the language of men (Maimonides, 1963, pp. 100, 140). It is, however, this seemingly obvious statement that perplexes believers. For in what sense is the Bible human, given that its subject, its very origin, is divine? What is the nature of the divine name? Is it (not) a human concept? Spinoza, a staunch critic of Maimonides, introduces the opening chapter of the *Theological–Political Treatise*, entitled 'Of Prophecy', with the declaration that 'Prophecy, or Revelation, is the sure knowledge of some matter revealed by God to man'. But he goes on to point out that 'natural knowledge' then qualifies as prophecy. 'For the knowledge that we acquire by the natural light of reason depends solely on knowledge of God and of his eternal decrees'. Indeed, Spinoza proceeds to claim that 'the nature of mind ... is the primary cause of divine revelation', given the fact that 'all that we clearly and distinctly understand is dictated to us by the idea and nature of God – not indeed in words but in a far superior way and one that agrees excellently with the nature of mind' (Spinoza, 1989, pp. 59–60).

Both Maimonides in the Middle Ages and Spinoza in the early modern era found themselves compelled to address philosophy in light of the perplexing status of biblical language. In a sense their position was the reverse of that faced by the ancient rabbis and church fathers who, indirectly or directly, had found it necessary to address the Bible in light of secular learning and philosophy. Neither Maimonides nor Spinoza denies the validity of biblical language or the truth of (its) revelation. Yet both, it is clear, suffer an enormous anxiety of influence. Is philosophical truth biblical (or, in other words: is biblical truth philosophical)? When Spinoza identifies mind or reason with prophetic (divine) knowledge, yet as superior to mere words, has he liberated philosophy from biblical religion or, rather, shown philosophy to be fundamentally religious; or, finally, revealed religion to be philosophical? What does Spinoza mean when he states in the *Theological–Political Treatise* that the fundamental aim of his work is to separate philosophy from religion (see Polka, 1990)? What, indeed, does he accomplish in the *Treatise*, given that he never flags in holding that, consistent with his claim that all knowledge is prophetic, the true object (subject) of knowledge is God?

Modern thinkers, from Hegel and Kierkegaard through Nietzsche to Heidegger, Levinas and Derrida, not to mention their postmodern epigones, have not fundamentally advanced beyond medieval and early modern thinkers. What does it mean to contend, with Anselm, that there is one thing that cannot be thought without existing; with Maimonides, that there is no truth other than God; with Descartes, that truth cannot be thought outside God's existence; with Spinoza, that truth is its own (philosophical or theological) standard; with Rousseau and Kant that there is no end outside rational (human and divine) beings; with Hegel, that spirit communicates only with spirit; with Kierkegaard, that no one can go beyond the faith of Abraham; with Nietzsche, that the critique of Christianity has its origin in Christianity; and with Derrida, that there is nothing outside writing (scripture)? In light of the perplexing relationship between philosophy and theology, between human and divine knowledge, I shall undertake to argue in this chapter that the ontological argument for the existence of God – the claim that there is one thing that cannot be thought without existing – applies no less to human than to divine existence. It is precisely this critical insight, which is no less philosophical than it is religious, that is the perplexing truth of biblical revelation. I shall thus argue for the position that, in order for thought to be self-critical, in our age as in any prior age, it must remain faithful to the insight that nothing – religious or philosophical – can be thought outside the ontological argument for existence.[1]

Dialectic and Paradox

There are a number of interrelated themes or perspectives involved in showing how and why critical thought involves and expresses the ontological argument, how and why it is that it is precisely the ontological argument that constitutes critique. Simply put, one asks for a presentation of the logic central to the ontological argument. That demand elicits both critique and history. We find ourselves then in the Hegelian world of dialectic: the critique of history is the history of critique. Critique is historical, and history is critical. The critique of the ontological argument involves its history, from Anselm to Hegel. The history of the ontological argument embodies its critique: one thinks of, above all, no doubt, Hume and Kant. But the history of the ontological argument is perplexing. It began with Saint Anselm, in the later eleventh century, and, with the *coup de grâce* delivered to it by Kant at the apogee of the Enlightenment, it largely vanished from critical thought in the past two centuries of modernity. Yet, precisely because our greatest thinkers made the ontological argument central to their critical philosophy, it has never been forgotten. It has lingered on like a bad nightmare whose repressed content indicates that there is more to be found of heaven and earth in the ontological argument than is dreamt of in the philosophy of its critics. Is the ontological argument not the unconscious of modernity?

But what is modernity? There's the rub. All conventional narratives telling the story of modernity as the emergence of rational, secular, human, scientific or even critical values fail to confront the problem of origins. So Freud, in his typical tale of modernity as the three blows of scientific truth in the name of astronomy (Copernicus), biology (Darwin) and his own psychoanalysis, is unable to explain how that which is secondary, science, can emerge from that of which it is the effect, primary religion. How can that which is (secondary) effect explain that which is its (primary) cause (origin)? How did that which is effect (science) become explanatory cause and that which is cause (religion) become explained effect?[2] Having posited religion as primary, and with it also the pleasure principle, primary process, and the unconscious (the id), Freud is then compelled to make science secondary, and with it also the reality principle, secondary process, and consciousness (the ego). But what this means is that the real is not primary and that the primary is not real. Or, to formulate Freud's impasse in Hegelian terms, the real, that is, actual desire, is not rational; and the rational is not actual (unconsciousness).[3] It is little wonder, then, that religion returns in Freud, as in so many of our significant modern and now postmodern thinkers, as the repressed, as that which is unconsciously originary and prior. But how do we make the unconscious conscious?

The movement from unconscious to conscious is not the linear movement from ancient to modern, from mythical to scientific, from illusory to real, from religious to secular, from divine to human, that is, from faith to reason. Indeed, we may recall that in his final psychical model Freud connects unconsciousness, that is, repression, with the conscious ego (secondary process) and consciousness (that is, self-critical insight) with the unconscious id (primary process).[4] Consciousness is dead (repressing unconscious life). We are reminded of Nietzsche's call for liberation: God is dead (repressing human life). But is the struggle with consciousness, with God, a struggle unto life or a struggle unto death, to invoke Hegel's analysis of the coming into existence of the process of mutual recognition: spirit recognizing spirit? If we deny, negate, annihilate – reduce to nothing – and do not appropriate that in and through which alone we can gain recognition, then our struggle debouches in death, in nihilism. If, however, we recognize that that which we criticize is the very origin of our critique, then our struggle will be unto life, the life of mutual recognition (see Kulak, 1997).

We may recall the passage from the Gospel of John that prefaces *The Brothers Karamazov*: 'Truly, truly, I say to you, unless a grain of wheat falls into the earth and dies, it remains alone; but if it dies, it bears much fruit.'[5] You have to lose your life, to sacrifice your life, to live your life in service to and in love, in recognition of others, in order to save it. Consciousness is dead. God is dead. Consciousness as one-sided, finite and rigid must be negated so that it is opened unto the larger life of the unconscious, of the other, of God. God as the teleological projection[6] of that which is one-sidedly, finitely and rigidly human must be negated so that it once again serves to enlarge what is human. Both Freud and Nietzsche – the first, generally blind to himself; the second, often in opposition to himself – belong to the prophetic tradition, initiated in and through the Hebrew Bible, of the critique of idols. Idols are images reflecting the reduction either of the divine to the human or of the human to the divine. In the language of contemporary critique, idolatry is the reification of otherness. The deconstructionist expression of idolatry is ontic presence, the reduction of plenitude to that which is finite, finished, at its end, perfect. There are two broad categories of idols involving the finite conflation of human and divine. Rendered in contemporary argot, we may call them finite identity and finite difference, each the mirror reflection of the other. Kierkegaard would call idolatry the commensurability of thought and existence, the betrayal of the ontological argument.

When Derrida says that 'deconstruction is justice' (Derrida, 1990, p. 945), he reflects the modernist convention of reversing the rhetoric of Isaiah, Jeremiah and Ezekiel in favouring critique over content, the human over the divine. For the biblical prophets and their heirs, including Jesus and the apostles, justice, the covenant binding the chosen people to God, that is, to existence, is the standard than which no greater can be thought, the standard that cannot be thought not to exist. Justice is the critique of idols, at once human and divine. Justice is the deconstruction of ontic presence, whether of God or of human beings. What the prophets mean is that, consistent with Kant, to think – critically of – existence is to exist in one's thought, to practise what one thinks, wills or desires. False notions of the human inevitably express false notions of the divine. The reverse of this formulation is equally true. False notions of the divine inevitably involve false notions of the human. The radical, paradoxical demand of the prophets is that we recognize that the sole law appropriate to human beings is the law true for God. But the prophets no less demand that we recognize that the sole law appropriate to God is the law true for human beings. Divine justice *is* human justice, and human justice *is* divine justice. Each is the infinite, eternal critique of the other. Divine law, without its embodiment, its enactment, its incarnation in the covenant of human beings, would be transcendental illusion as found in negative theologies of difference. Then divine law would not express love of neighbour as formulated in Matthew 22:39. It is equally the case that human law without its creation in the image of the divine covenant would be immanental illusion as found in positive theologies of identity. Then human law would not involve love of God as formulated in Matthew 22:37. 'On these two commandments' – to love God with all your heart and soul and mind and to love your neighbour as yourself – 'depend all the law and the prophets,' Jesus declares in Matthew 22:40. But is the law one or two? The law involves and expresses two commandments. Is the law divine or human? Of the two commandments on which the law depends one is divine and the other is human. The law, it turns out, is undecidably divine and human. One may choose, depending on the context, to favour the rhetoric of divine or human, of transcendent or immanent, of religious or secular. But one may not choose, one is not free to choose, one in opposition to the other. To choose either God or neighbour in opposition to and thus in order to dominate the other is to lose both. That is the way of idolatry, sin, perdition, damnation and nihilism. Then the struggle for existence is not to serve, to liberate, to upbuild, to love, but to dominate the other. The struggle is unto death, not unto life.

To make the unconscious conscious is to learn, to work through, the hard lesson, in fear and trembling, that the integrity (wholeness) of thought and existence involves both their unity and their difference. For, indeed, in making the unconscious conscious, we are at the same time expanding our consciousness by rendering it more profoundly, more aptly unconscious. As Freud comes to recognize and as Jung consistently indicates with real acuteness, the unconscious is not a finite reservoir that, once rendered conscious, is then emptied of its content. The unconscious, like the infinite itself, is a qualitative concept that articulates the self in the richness (or poverty) of its historical otherness. The richer our conscious life, the richer our unconscious life. In Hegelian terms, the conscious *is* the unconscious, and the unconscious *is* the conscious.[7]

Both Freud and Jung recognized that people whose lives were flat and dull, that is, simply present to themselves, were not apt subjects for therapy. This is why they often tended to magnify or celebrate (romanticize) neurosis, just as the Bible, both

Jewish and Christian, magnifies or celebrates (romanticizes) sin. It is only sinners who are accessible to the unconscious, to the other, to the neighbour, to God. Jesus says in Matthew 9:13 that he came to call not the righteous – those in whom consciousness and the unconscious, thought and existence, are commensurate or identical – but sinners. (The insane would then be those in whom consciousness and the unconscious, thought and existence, are absolutely different, completely disassociated from each other.) Adam and Eve are our foreparents precisely because, in sinning, in not remaining in the garden, they showed that their consciousness was not commensurate with their unconscious. They initiated the life of the spirit in which the relationship of consciousness and the unconscious, of thought and existence, is that of self and other, of identity and difference. Neither is (becoming the) one except insofar as it is (becoming the) other. (Adam and Eve also create the conditions both of neurosis, the partial dissociation of thought and existence, and of psychosis, their complete disintegration, dissociation or difference.) Thought and existence are one only insofar as they remain incommensurate with, different from, and irreducible to each other. Thought and existence are two only insofar as each *is* the other. Their relationship is dialectical and paradoxical. Dialectic and paradox are to be understood as the relationship of two (or more) concepts such that one can exist or be thought only insofar as the other exists or is thought.[8] The dialectic of paradox is that in order to begin with one we must begin with both, but that there is no beginning with two that does not exist or that is not thought as one.

Anselm's Argument

It is precisely the necessary relationship between thought and existence – two yet one – that constitutes the argument conventionally called (since Kant) the ontological argument. That the ontological argument constitutes and is constituted by the structure of dialectic and paradox shows us how uncanny it is. It is distinctly *unheimlich*. That with which we are at home always reveals us to be other than ourselves: Adam and Eve, wandering Jew, nomad, pilgrim, *viator* (the medieval wayseeker). The ontological argument vanished from conscious thinking in the past two centuries only to live on in the profound depths of our unconscious, shaping the very thought and existence of modernity. Is it not uncanny that at the precise moment the ontological argument disappears from conscious thought it reveals itself unconsciously as dialectic and paradox, the very hallmarks of modernity?

In order to see how the ontological argument bears the uncanny, unconscious structure of modern dialectic and paradox, we need to review key moments of its history. The ontological argument proving the existence of God begins as a litotes supporting the sovereignty of human reason independent of divine authority. Anselm explains in the Prologue to the *Monologion* and in the Preface to the *Proslogion* that he wrote his works in response to the request of fellow monks that he set down for them arguments proving the existence of God based on reason and not on the authority of Scripture. At the end of Chapter 1 of the *Proslogion* he famously formulates his enterprise, paraphrasing (the inaccurate translation of) Isaiah 7:9, as faith seeking understanding. But why or how did it occur to a group of cloistered religious in a Norman monastery in the Dark Ages, over which it would only subsequently become evident that the dawn of medieval enlightenment was just beginning to break, to desire rational proof of the existence of God? Why was Scripture not sufficient unto itself? What does it mean for faith to seek understanding? Would not to seek what you have not already found be to fall into the Socratic aporia that all seeking is undertaken in ignorance of the good? Or is there something about Scripture, about faith, about the love of God and neighbour, that demands rational articulation?

Such questions Anselm does not pose, let alone answer. Nor does he explain to us what reason, not to mention rational demonstration, is. Still, he clearly shows us what he means; and what he shows us – and doubtless this is something we have yet to learn today – is that reason is intimately connected with the human thought demonstrating the existence of God. God, Anselm argues, is that than which nothing greater can be thought. His second formulation of the rational proof of the existence of God is that God is that which cannot be thought not to exist. Anselm's presentation and elaboration of his proof rationally demonstrating the existence of God occupy only three extremely brief chapters (2–4) of the *Proslogion*, which is itself a short work. Yet it is precisely this proof that launches and contains the whole history of modern critical thought. For what Anselm demonstrates is that (divine) existence is directly bound to human thought. He equally shows that there is no human thought outside divine existence. For God is that than which nothing greater can be thought, that which cannot be thought not to exist.

To prove his case, Anselm invokes the fool, *insipiens*, of the Psalms who denies in his heart that God exists. But, just as sin presupposes the existence of the saviour[9] and doubt the existence of the doubter and ultimately of God,[10] so the fool, if he is not simply foolish in denying the existence of God, has to know what he says: he has to be saying something real. Either/or: either the fool is mouthing mere words, and then his denial of God is not serious but foolish, and no one pays the least attention to it, or the fool knows what he is saying: the whole of his heart and soul and mind is in his denial of God. But then the one thing that he cannot deny is that what he says is true, or otherwise he would fall back into the logical contradiction of the Cretan liar, for whom lie and truth are either identical or different but never at once, dialectically and paradoxically, identical and different. Either/or: either the fool is foolish, and then his denial of God, his thought of God, has no basis in existence, or the fool is serious, and then his denial of God has a basis in existence. To repeat: either the fool is contradictory, he is contradicted by having no basis to his denial, or the fool is paradoxical, his denial engages the dialectic that all negation (as thought) presupposes, by affirming, existence.

Anselm does not articulate the dilemma of the fool in this explicit either/or fashion. But he is pellucid in showing that either the fool is foolish, and then he is saying nothing (his denial is not serious), or the fool is serious, and then he is saying something (his denial is not foolish). Either the fool foolishly denies nothing, or the fool seriously denies something. Anselm's basic (Freudian!) point is that there is no denial, no thought, that is not the denial or thought of something existing. Thus we re-engage the paradoxical dialectic of the ontological argument: to think is to discover (to adopt the more modern formulation) that there is one thing that cannot be rationally thought – denied or doubted – without existing. That, for Anselm, is God.

There are two basic elements in Anselm's argument for the existence of God. (Actually, there are three, as we shall see.) All three are intimately interrelated. First, as I have already indicated, Anselm binds human thought to divine existence. But if there is no human thought, as he shows in his deconstruction of the contradictory position of the denying fool, that does not involve and express the existence of God, would it not also be the case that God does not exist outside human thought? Second, Anselm insists, both against the fool and against his critic Gaunilo in his exchange with him, that to think is always to think something existing. Anselm recognizes that we can think (that is, say) many things that do not exist: from a mountain without a valley to the imaginary, lost island conjured up by Gaunilo, not to mention the idols of thought and existence that are more numerous than the countless heads of the famous hydra. We can say and in that sense fantasize anything (contradictory). But we cannot think anything contradictory. The very notion of fantasy or idolatry, like denial, presupposes (affirms) the critical standard of truthful existence by which we recognize it. As Spinoza will say, truth is its own standard, the standard both of itself and of what is not true. (Insanity is precisely the inability to distinguish between fantasy, such as hallucinations, and existence. All difference becomes identical with itself; and all identify becomes different from itself.)

The two elements of Anselm's argument for the existence of God – that God is that which cannot be thought without existing and that to think is to think something existing – are dialectically, paradoxically, intertwined. It is clear that thought and existence (consciousness and reality, the rational and the actual, other and self, God and neighbour) are given together such that neither is the cause (or the effect) of the other. To begin with one, say with thought, is to find ourselves engaging existence (God). To begin with the other, say with existence, is to find ourselves thinking (desiring, denying, willing, affirming and so on). What is so engrossing about the argumentation advanced by Anselm is that we see how the dialectic of thought and existence – *human* thought and *divine* existence – undercuts the rhetoric of Neoplatonic[11] hierarchy subordinating the human to the divine. While always insisting upon the fundamental difference between divine being and human being, creator and creature, the supreme good in itself and the relative good through another, the immutable and the changing, Anselm never wavers in his commitment to the rational demonstration of the identity, of the relatedness, of divine and human difference: God is that which cannot be thought by human beings not to exist. Anselm does not cease repeating the fundamental element of Neoplatonism that God as eternal and unchanging can be known solely in himself. Yet he never relinquishes his radical insight into biblical ontology that human thought, human reason, human effort, human desire, human engagement, human denial, what Spinoza will call *conatus*, involve and express the existence of God.

That the proof of the existence of God presupposes human thought and that to think is to think something existing reveals the third basic element in Anselm's argumentation. This third element is the mutual interdependence of thought and existence. There is no thought outside existence, and there is no existence outside thought. That, we can say, is the 'philosophical' (or the rational) characterization of Anselm's argument. But we can equally say that that there is no human thought outside divine existence and no divine existence outside human thought. That we can call the 'theological' (or religious) characterization of Anselm's argument. But we can also double our model by indicating that thought and existence are, together, in their very relationship, equally human and divine. What, then, is philosophical and what theological, what rational and what religious? What is human and what is divine? The ontological argument is uncanny precisely because, as the systematic articulation of the biblical conception of the human–divine relationship, it makes critical, it throws eternally into crisis, the very meaning of both 'man'[12] and God. It is equally the case that, in rational (philosophical) contexts, the ontological argument makes problematic, always, how we are to understand our two primary concepts of thought and existence (and their multiple equivalents). Indeed, the ontological argument, in forcing us to ponder without surcease the relationship between, on the one hand, thought and existence and, on the other hand, 'man' and God, compels us to recognize that each of these terms (or pairs of terms) always involves the interpretation, the critique, of the other. God constitutes the truth of being human and thinking humanly. But it is no less the case that human thought and existence constitute the truth of God. For the moment the absolute that is God is not conceived as relationship and the relationship that is human is not conceived as absolute the absolute becomes absolutism (the thing known solely in itself) and relationship becomes the merely relative (a matter of fact known solely relative to others).

Kant characterizes the countless versions of the resultant dualisms, which are ontically present in every age, as those of rationalism and empiricism or of dogmatism and scepticism. The funny thing about these dualisms is that, as contradictory, they are inherently unstable and so constantly turn into (as they reflect) their opposite. Nobody is more sceptical than the dogmatist or more dogmatic than the sceptic. When thought and existence, 'man' and God, reason and faith, philosophy and theology, and the like, are understood as dialectically related and not as dualistically opposed to each other, they are neither sceptical nor dogmatic, neither empiricist nor rational.[13]

Notwithstanding the profundity of Anselm's insight into the dialectic of thought and existence, the ontological argument did not fare well in the Middle Ages. Twelfth- and thirteenth-century scholastic thinkers – Moslem, Jewish and Christian – became increasingly preoccupied with thinking through the corpus of Aristotle, newly translated. There was little understanding of the fact that what Anselm called the rational proof of the existence of God embodied a concept of reason, of human thought, whose relationship to the existence of God was dialectical, or paradoxical, and not hierarchical. In rejecting the necessary relationship between thought and existence, the human and the divine, St Thomas Aquinas, the greatest of thirteenth-century thinkers, made three concepts of Aristotle central to his rational demonstration of the existence of God. While the very basis of Neoplatonic metaphysics, these three concepts were utterly alien to biblical thought and existence: first cause, telos and reason understood as thought thinking itself.[14] In holding that God is first cause, unmoved mover, and final telos of that which in the world is moved as effect to its final end, Thomas argues that we humans can rationally prove or know that God exists. But he denies that we can prove on the basis of reason and thus know as human beings what God is in himself. What God is in himself is a matter of faith. In distinguishing between knowing by reason *that* God is and knowing by faith *what* God is, Thomas maintains the Neoplatonic hierarchy positing divine over human; first cause, active mover and final end over that which is passively moved as finite effect to its end; faith over reason; and *theologia*, as the queen of the sciences, over *philosophia*, its *ancilla*. In replacing Anselm's rational proof of the existence of God with an altogether different 'rational' argument, Thomas effaces, in subtle yet dramatic fashion, the radical concept of reason underlying the ontological argument.

It is critically important to grasp where Thomas agrees with and where he differs from Anselm (apart from their common commitment to what are, for them, the saving truths of Christianity). Both thinkers, consistent with patristic (if not with biblical) thought, continue to articulate the difference between God and 'man', creator and creation, and eternity and time in the Neoplatonic terms of whole and part, of the immutable and the changing, and so on. But it is precisely Anselm's ontological argument necessarily binding (human) thought and (divine) existence that makes (will make) it impossible – both logically and metaphysically – to conceive of the relationship between divine and human being as that between immutable and mutable, whole and part, perfect (infinite) end and imperfect (finite) means.[15] Anselm's concept of reason – of the rational proof of the existence of God! – is implicitly biblical and thus in enormous tension with the Neoplatonic terms of the *Proslogion*, together with the *Monologion* and the exchange with Gaunilo. In contrast, Thomas' concept of reason is explicitly Aristotelian and in fundamental agreement with the concepts of unknowable first cause and telos central to Neoplatonism. The future, however, lies with the Bible and its concept of reason, not with Aristotle and his concept of reason. The ontological argument uniting thought and existence will triumph over the teleological argument based on a first (divine) cause that is unknowable to its secondary (human) effect. Here we shall simply mention the Condemnation of 1277, in which the Aristotelian concept of reason is proscribed as falsely delimiting divine creation; the no-holds-barred critique in the fourteenth century of unknowable Aristotelian causes in light of *the potentia absoluta dei* by William of Ockham and his followers; and in the fifteenth century Nicholas of Cusa's radical rethinking of cosmology (eliminating all finite teleology) in light of the infinity of God.

Modernity and Biblical Hermeneutics

It is surely no accident that in the seventeenth century the resolute rejection of Aristotelian (Neoplatonic) teleology by philosophers and scientists as varied as Bacon, Descartes, Pascal, Spinoza and Newton occurs at the same time that Descartes, in the *Meditations*, and Spinoza, in the *Ethics*, launch modern philosophy in the name of the ontological argument proving the existence of God. Descartes begins famously with the 'I think, therefore I am' and arrives infamously at the proof of the existence of God. Indeed, in the dedicatory letter of the *Meditations* that he addresses to the theologians of the Sorbonne, Descartes magisterially declares that demonstration of the existence of both soul and God properly belongs to philosophy. He cites as a proof text for this claim Romans 1:20, a passage frequently invoked by Augustine, Anselm and their medieval successors. In this passage Paul excoriates those whom he calls the enemies of truth for refusing to acknowledge that 'ever since the creation of the world' God's 'invisible nature, namely, his eternal power and deity, has been clearly perceived in the things that have been made'.

Spinoza reverses the Cartesian trajectory. He initiates the *Ethics* with the ontological argument – substance as the cause of itself is that which cannot be thought without existing – and arrives in the end at the free individual who, conscious of self, God and things, does not perish. This is precisely the individual who, as sovereign, would be the true citizen of the democratic state of which Spinoza, in the *Theological–Political Treatise*, is the world's first systematic theorist. It is remarkable that Spinoza develops his concept of democratic sovereignty as the termination of the very work in which he earlier presents what is also our first, modern, comprehensive concept of biblical hermeneutics. He conceives of interpretation in terms of the relationship between sovereign text (the Bible is to be read faithfully from itself alone) and sovereign reader (who is to read the Bible rationally by himself alone). He shows us precisely what he means by this paradoxical concept of two sovereigns in relationship (text and reader, self and other, faith and reason, God and 'man') when he provides a trenchant critique of the one-sided, contradictory and diametrically opposed hermeneutics that he associates with Maimonides and his medieval critics. The 'dogmatic' hermeneutics of Maimonides subordinates the Bible (faith) to the (Aristotelian) reason of the reader. The 'sceptical' hermeneutics of the critics of Maimonides subordinates human reason to the (faith of the) Bible. In neither case, Spinoza shows, can errors, resulting from gaps, anomalies, corruptions and perversions, whether in text or reader, be accounted for, either faithfully or rationally.

It is striking that, just as Spinoza views both Bible and reader as sovereign, so he equally imputes error (sin) to both. Indeed, it is precisely with his concept of sovereignty – the sovereign good – that Spinoza resolutely eliminates all elements of the Neoplatonic hierarchy (the great chain of being) that had continued to compromise the thought of Anselm, not to mention that of Maimonides and Thomas Aquinas. The sovereign good, of God, of the Bible, of the reader, of the ethical citizen, of the democratic polity, cannot be that which, as unknowable, is separate from and opposed to the world of human beings. Rather, the sovereign good is that in whose name human beings struggle to overcome the sin, the errors, the injustices of the world. This explains why the principle that Spinoza makes central to biblical interpretation is love, *caritas*, the golden rule of loving your neighbour as yourself. It is precisely love – love as its own standard: God, the neighbour – by which human beings are to measure others and by which others are to measure them. It is solely in terms of the standard of love, Spinoza indicates, that we can sort out what is true from what is spurious in the Bible, as in our own lives. Indeed, the Bible is truly the loving standard for readers, as readers are the loving standard of the Bible.

We are now in a position to understand why the ontological argument initiates a work entitled *Ethics*. Spinoza is the first thinker who fully grasps that the ontology involved in proving the existence of God embodies ethical and democratic practice. To think God, to know God, involves not Neoplatonic contemplation of the good but love of neighbour. The sovereign good, than which nothing greater can be thought to exist, that which necessarily cannot be thought not to exist, is love of God that human beings infinitely articulate in the diverse practice of their lives. It is no wonder that Spinoza resolutely insists that the only true subject of knowledge is

God, consistent with Romans 1:20, whose author, Paul, he regularly cites as an authority in the *Theological–Political Treatise*. We can also understand why Spinoza indicates that the purpose of his *Treatise* is to separate philosophy from theology, reason from faith. For what Spinoza means by separation is no longer hierarchical subordination (in the medieval tradition of queen and handmaiden) but democratic equality, the paradox of dialectical relationship, where neither philosophy nor theology can be true unless both are true.

It is extraordinary that Spinoza, having demonstrated that the ontological argument for the existence of God articulates the ethical principles of love and justice fundamental to both biblical hermeneutics and democratic practice, had no real followers and created no school of thought. In the most fundamental sense, Spinoza is the first and last of our modern philosophers. There can be no critical understanding of modern and now postmodern thought without addressing the 'separation' between philosophy and religion, between reason and faith, and thus the ontological argument and its relationship to both democracy and the Bible.

It is interesting to recall that in the mid-nineteenth century Benjamin Jowett, the famous translator of Plato, struck a blow for the freedom and independence of secular scholarship with the declaration that the Bible is to be read like any text.[16] Jowett's hermeneutical call to secular arms was viewed as radical in both conservative and liberal circles, albeit for opposite reasons. But, just as much of the subsequent opposition to Darwin came from conservative scientists who remained attached, not to the truth of biblical religion but to its Neoplatonic distortions, so scientists and secularists, generally, were not to find in a hermeneutics such as Jowett's a principled defence of the superiority of reason over faith. The Bible, as Spinoza had demonstrated, is a text, like any text, presumably, whose errors – whose sinning! – readers must faithfully and rationally account for. But Spinoza had equally shown that the Bible is a text, like any text, presumably, whose truth, the loving doctrine of the golden rule relating self and other, self and neighbour, self and God, readers must faithfully and rationally account for. Spinoza understood, in other words, that the Bible articulates the story of error and truth, of fall and salvation, of idolatry and redemption that is the very story of its readers' lives. The necessary connection between text and reader is precisely the necessary relation between existence and thought – between God and 'man' and between neighbour and 'man' – that is demonstrated in, through and by the ontological argument.

When Jowett, reflecting the growth of secular biblical studies in the nineteenth century, declared that the Bible was to be read like any text, he failed, therefore, to grasp the truly radical implications of his claim. In fact, he continued to hold that the Bible was superior to (and so unlike) other texts. He did not see that the concept of the Bible as text implies that all writings are texts only insofar as they are biblical. This, however, leads to the truly radical implication of biblical textuality, which is that the canon of the Bible is closed (it is one) solely insofar as it remains open to (inclusive of) all texts that are true to its spirit.[17] The Bible, as divine cause of itself, cannot then be superior to its creations, for it cannot be superior to itself. Hermeneutics and ontology bear the same dialectical, paradoxical relationship as do God and 'man' or thought and existence. Jowett did not see that a text is not just any formally organized collection of words, however brilliant: for example, a work of Plato. He did not comprehend what St Augustine in *The City of God* had comprehended, which is that the ontology of the divine city is not to be found in just any formally organized collection of human beings, however brilliant. The Roman republic, for example, had not been a true state, for it had not know the principles of love of God and love of neighbour. Unlike Augustine and Spinoza, Jowett did not see that the Bible is to be read like every text precisely because every text is to be read like the Bible. The Bible demands of its readers that they articulate a principle of interpretation, at once ethical and democratic, by which both text and reader are to be held accountable. There is an absolutely necessary connection between thought and existence. There is no thought outside our existing in it; and there is no existence outside our thinking (willing, desiring, practising) it. There is nothing outside the text.[18] So Derrida rejoins Jowett. But the text is nothing outside the necessary relationship between thought and existence. So we rejoin Spinoza, together with Anselm and Augustine. That there is nothing outside the text, that there is nothing outside the love of God and neighbour, is the hermeneutical articulation of the ontological argument.

Refutations

Before concluding my study, I shall complete my historical sketch of the ontological argument with a brief analysis of its two most significant moments following Descartes and Spinoza: Hume's refutation of it and Kant's refutation of it in light of his refutation of Hume. Hume's refutation of the ontological argument, with the resultant contradiction that he acknowledges is thereby created for him, remains the classical topos of modern anti-metaphysical or non-metaphysical thinkers, both philosophers and theologians:[19] the impasse or aporia separating thought from existence. Kant's refutation of the ontological argument is commonly viewed as the final quietus of classical metaphysics. Indeed, it is, when classical metaphysics is understood as rooted in Neoplatonic hierarchy and so having fundamentally nothing at all to do with biblical ontology. We may recall Kant's abiding belief that humankind will never give up the great truths of metaphysics – freedom, immortality and God – as the postulates of rational practice and his trenchant demonstration that Hume's empirical scepticism is contradictory, consistent with Hume's own self-understanding of it as irrational. Just as Kant denies (appropriates) knowledge in order to make room for faith,[20] so, as we shall see, he equally refutes the ontological argument as demonstrating knowledge of God as a rational or an empirical object in order to save (liberate) it as articulating the practical reason of human subjects. It is perhaps the supreme irony of modernity that, in naming the ontological argument, Kant destroys it. Yet what he actually does is to save it as the ethics of sovereign individuals who constitute the kingdom of ends in the name of democratic practice. He banishes both Philosopher King and Queen Theology from the commonwealth, the *res publica*, insofar as it is thought (willed) as the kingdom of ends, the democratic city of God.

    It is at the very end of *An Enquiry Concerning Human Understanding* that Hume formulates his refutation of the ontological argument. Since 'the only proper objects of knowledge and demonstration,' he writes, are 'the sciences of quantity and number … all other enquiries of men regard only matters of fact and existence; and these are evidently incapable of demonstration. Whatever *is* may *not be*. No negation of a fact can involve a contradiction. The non-existence of any being, without exception, is as clear and distinct an idea as its existence.'[21] But Hume thus fails to recognize that there is one fact the negation of whose existence involves a contradiction, and that is the negation of the existence of a human being.[22] Human beings are not simply facts, among others. We cannot say, consistent with Jowett, whose hermeneutical principle simply updates Hume, that existing human beings are to be read (interpreted, treated) like other existent facts, things or objects. The fact of existing as a human being involves and expresses the self-reflexivity of mutual recognition: the absolute command that you relate to others as you would have them relate to you. There is a necessary relationship between thought and existence.

In the Conclusion of Part I of the *Treatise of Human Nature*, Hume sees, yet he sees no exit from, the contradictory aporia to which he has been led. He is caught, he says, between 'total scepticism', to which his philosophical analysis has led him, and the 'principle' of 'fancy' or 'imagination', by which 'you expressly contradict yourself', since he has no way of preferring one fancy over another. 'What party, then, shall we choose among these difficulties?', he asks. 'If we embrace this principle [of fancy], and condemn all refin'd [that is, philosophical] reasoning, we run into the most manifest absurdities. If we reject it in favour of these reasonings, we subvert entirely the human understanding. We have, therefore, no choice left but betwixt a false reason and none at all' (Hume, 1951, p. 268). Thus philosophy, in Hume's hands, leads to the annihilation of reason. The logical alternative to the irrationality of philosophy is fancy (that is, unself-reflexive opinion or habit) whose reason is simply false. This is not the place in which to ponder the peculiarly modern psychology of Hume that is so completely unlike the supremely indifferent (dogmatic) suspension of mind that characterizes the ancient sceptics. Unlike the ancients, he openly acknowledges his contradiction (error, sin); yet he cannot (or refuses to) account for it. It is surely clear, however, that at the basis of the aporia to which Hume is led by his reasoning is his failure to comprehend either the thought or the existence of human beings whose necessary relationship is the demonstration that we know as the ontological argument.

Kant tells us that it was Hume's empirical scepticism that aroused him from the dogmatic slumbers of Leibniz' rational dogmatism. He dedicates himself henceforth to justify the ways of God to man, to show that the true dogmas of metaphysics (freedom, immortality and God) cannot be known as the objects of either empirical experience or rational contemplation but are to be thought – willed (desired) – as the subjects of human practice. Kant demonstrates in his critical philosophy that the truths of metaphysics are neither rational nor empirical but practical. The concept of reason that overcomes the dualism between empiricism and rationalism is that of practice, of desire, of willing the good (the necessary relationship of thought and existence) true for all human beings. Kant agrees with Spinoza that we do not will something because it is good (as in all versions of Neoplatonism) but that something is good because we will it (Kant, 1956, pp. 59–60).[23] The only thing good (or evil), whether within the world or without it, is the will (either human or divine).[24] Truth involves and expresses the will, thought and desire of (divine and human) subjects. Truth is not something given in the nature of objects (outside human beings and inaccessible to them). In short, in the words of Kierkegaard, truth is subjectivity.

In his refutation of the ontological argument in the *Critique of Pure Reason*, Kant shows that being (God) is not an empirical object or a thing to be known. It is not a real predicate. So far, he agrees with both Hume and Leibniz. He also agrees with Hume, but now in opposition to Leibniz, in holding that being in itself, that is, the thing in itself, is, as a mere, logical predicate, empty of all content. Thus Kant, in his refutation of the ontological argument in the *Critique of Pure Reason*, shows that there is no necessary connection between (human) thought and (divine) existence when divine existence is conceived as an object, whether empirical or logical, to be known in itself. Yet, and this is the subtext of the *Critique of Pure Reason* which is then explicated in the *Critique of Practical Reason*, he agrees with Leibniz, in opposition to Hume, in holding that the thing in itself is the supreme good. But he critically opposes both Leibniz and Hume in showing that, while the thing in itself cannot be known as either an empirical or a logical object, it can and must be willed (thought, desired, loved) as a practical subject. Although Kant explicitly refutes the ontological argument, in the *Critique of Pure Reason*, as giving us knowledge of objects (whether empirical or logical), he silently embraces it, in the *Critique of Practical Reason*, as articulating the structure of reason. To reason is to will the necessary relationship between thought and existence in human life. Reason is the human practice of constituting the relationship between thought and existence as necessary. Kant thus joins Spinoza in showing that the very heart of the ontological argument, as originally formulated by Anselm, is ethics, the practice of the golden rule.

Conclusion

What the history of the ontological argument makes clear to us is that St Anselm, in undertaking to demonstrate the existence of God by reason, establishes the very conditions of modernity, of modern, critical thought. He shows that, just as there is no thinking outside the existence of God, so the existence of God is not given outside human thought. Thus the so-called 'secularization' of the dialectic of thought and existence, such as we find it in Descartes and Spinoza, the founders of modern thought, does not involve the displacement of God by 'man'. Rather, it is precisely the paradoxical relationship of the human and the divine, as articulated in the ontological argument, that allows Descartes and Spinoza, and finally Kant, to eliminate all elements of Neoplatonic hierarchy generating dualistic opposition between human beings and God, subject and object, reason and faith, thought and existence. It is these very dualisms that are called idolatry by the biblical tradition; Christendom as the rationalization of paganism in the name of Christianity by Kierkegaard; and ontic presence by contemporary deconstruction. When Anselm shows us that the fool who denies God in his heart cannot without self-contradiction deny existence – he must think (affirm) something, so long as his denial has significance – what he in fact indicates to us is the necessary bond between thought and existence. But it is only Descartes and, above all, Spinoza and Kant who demonstrate comprehensively that this necessity is not objective or natural: it is not given in finite space and time. Rather, the necessary bond between human beings is subjective: it is the product of subjects in relationship. The other name of this necessity, what Kant calls self-determination, is freedom. The necessary relationship between God and human beings, between the thought and existence of subjects in relation, is the product, the creation of will, desire or love. As Kant says, there is nothing – good or evil – outside the will, outside the relationship between thought and existence. What we will, what we desire, what we think: that is our good, our God. Our good, our God, is that which we will, desire, think or, in other words, embody in the practice, in the thought and existence, of our daily lives.

It is critically important to see that the concept of thought that is central to the ontological argument, what Anselm calls reason, is will, desire, love. The ontological argument is practice: willing the good such that both you and your neighbour mutually make it the standard of critique to which each of you is eternally subject. The ethical name of the ontological argument is the golden rule. To love God above all others and your neighbour as yourself is to articulate the necessary bond between thought and existence. To do unto others as you would have them do unto you is to locate your own existence in the thought of the neighbour and the existence of the neighbour in your own thought.

It is precisely the ontological argument that constitutes critical thought. The terms of its dialectic – thought and existence, human being and divine being, self and other, reason and faith, philosophy and religion – are constantly put into crisis by necessarily (freely) always being other than themselves. Indeed, it is uncannily paradoxical that it is the argument proving the existence of God that turns out to embody the critical dimension of human thought. One cannot be human without thinking, without proving, the existence of God. But it is equally true that God does not exist outside human thought (will, desire, love). Another way of putting this paradox is that it remains forever undecidable whether the ontological argument is metaphysical or ethical, religious or secular, divine or human, theological or philosophical. The paradox here is that it can be one solely by being both. In other words, it is the task of critical thought to engage, to work through, the crisis that is eternally engendered by the paradox that one can be two (different) only insofar as two are one (identical) and vice versa.

The ontological argument, in both its metaphysical and its ethical modes, must eternally confront the idols that result from the loss of the dialectical relationship between thought and existence, between human being and divine being. The paradox of the ontological argument is that the contribution it makes to critical thought in the new millennium, as in the former millennium, is precisely the fact that, because it is at once secular and religious, human and divine, it deconstructs the idols of both philosophy and theology. Critical thought, in embodying the ontological argument, brings philosophy and theology equally into crisis as it shows that each can be true only insofar as both are true. It is precisely the dialectical relationship of thought and existence, which is at once divine and human, both faithful and rational, that constitutes critique. The other name of critique is love, the affirmation of thought and existence, to which God and human beings are mutually bound. The ontological argument is the unconscious hermeneutic of modernity whose critical principle is to love God above all others and your neighbour as yourself. It is clear, then, that thought in the new millennium will truly be and remain critical, in its relationship to all modes of human existence, only insofar as it makes its uncanny, unconscious history at once canny and conscious. Nothing can be critically thought, insofar as it is rational and faithful, outside the ontological argument for existence.

Notes

1. The 'Heideggerian' claim on the part of Jean-Luc Marion that the ontological argument is not 'ontological' is to be rejected. In failing to make the dialectic of thought and existence, of 'man' and God, central to the ontological argument, he is unable to see that Spinoza and Kant, in addition to Descartes, are the true heirs of Anselm. See Marion (1999) and my critique (Polka, forthcoming).

2. I make this critique central to my analysis of Freud's metapsychology in Polka (2001).

3. It is important to note that Freud lacks a concept of desire (that which is at once primary and rational) in his metapsychology, although it is implicitly presupposed by the theory underlying his psychoanalytic practice (therapy).

4. Beginning with *The Ego and the Id*.

5. I cite from the RSV. This passage from John 12:14 is quoted twice in Book Six: 'The Russian Monk' (Dostoyevsky, 1990, pp. 285, 309).

6. I think here of Spinoza's brilliant critique, in the Appendix of Part I of the *Ethics*, of finite teleology as the human projection of fear and superstition.

7. We can say that Spinoza formulates the paradoxical relationship of consciousness and the unconscious in terms of the relationship between individuals and God in *Ethics*, Part V, Prop. 24: the more we understand individual things the more we understand God (the more individual things we understand the more [of] God we understand).

8. We think of Hegel as the master of dialectic and of Kierkegaard as the master of paradox. But Kierkegaard also embraced the language of dialectic. The section on Religiousness B, which the pseudonymous author of *Concluding Unscientific Postscript* views as the truth of Christianity, is called 'The Dialectical'.

9. In the *Recordare* of the Roman Catholic Mass the sinner says: 'Remember, sweet Jesus, that I am the cause of your way' (*Recordare, Jesu pie, / Quod sum causa tuae viae*).

10. In the Cartesian model.

11. I use the term 'Neoplatonic' to characterize that (highly amorphous, extremely widespread and hugely influential) amalgam of Greek metaphysics which, based on Plato and Aristotle, posits, beyond all human existence and thought, that which can be known only in and through itself. It is precisely the Neoplatonic conception of 'God' that is central to Christendom; that is, to what Kierkegaard calls 'rationalized paganism' (paganism rationalized in terms of Christianity) and that ultimately bears no relationship whatsoever to fundamental biblical notions such as creation, sin, covenant, law, love and freedom or to the notions of history and language presupposed (exposed) by these concepts.

12. In spite of, indeed, thanks to, our politically (sexually) charged times, 'man' (intended here as gender-neutral, like *homo*, as distinct from *vir*) is useful in allowing me to evade a term such as 'human being' which would appear, at least rhetorically, to favour ontology over epistemology (existence over thought).

13. Kant writes that 'all principles that can be taken from this [the heteronomous] point of view are either empirical or rational' (Kant, 1981, p. 46).

14. Thomas' distinction between natural and supernatural is ultimately true neither to the biblical distinction between creator (God) and creation ('man') nor to the Aristotelian (Neoplatonic) line dividing unchanging (finite) soul (form, substance) from changing (in-finite) body.

15. Indeed, while in Greek metaphysics the perfect, unchanging end is finite and the imperfect, changing appearance is 'in-finite' (that is, lacking in itself its own end) the fact that, for Christian metaphysicians, the creating end is infinite (without finite comparisons) and the created 'thing' is finite (yet human beings are made in the image of God, unlike all other finite things) completely disrupts and so destroys the economy of Greek metaphysics.

16. Jowett writes that the 'object [of the interpreter] is to read Scripture like any other book' (Jowett, 1970, p. 338). He goes on to observe, however, that, 'when interpreted like any other book, by the same rules of evidence and the same canons of criticism, the Bible will still remain unlike any other book ... and make for itself a new kind of authority by the life which is in it' (p. 375). He repeats: *'Interpret the Scripture like any other book*. There are many respects in which Scripture is unlike any other book; these will appear in the results of such an interpretation' (p. 377).

17. Note that Jean-Luc Marion writes with regard to Scripture that 'hence a sort of infinite text is composed (the closure of the sacred canon indicating precisely the infinite surplus of meaning)' (Marion, 1991, p. 156).

18. *'There is nothing outside of the text* [there is no outside-text; *il n'y a pas de hors-texte*]' (Derrida, 1976, p. 158).

19. One thinks of, for example, Emmanuel Levinas, Jean-Luc Marion and Richard Rorty.

20. So Kant writes in the Preface to the Second Edition of the *Critique of Pure Reason*, B xxx.

21. David Hume, *An Enquiry Concerning Human Understanding*, Section XII, Part III.

22. In analysing the contradiction that underlies the critique made by Hume of the ontological argument, one may equally emphasize his failure to acknowledge the unique role of self-referentiality in determining human existence. That is, Hume does not grasp the basis of Anselm's argument against the fool who denies the existence of God. He fails to see that to claim that there is no fact whose non-existence is contradictory presupposes (paradoxically) his own non-contradictory existence.

23. Spinoza, *Ethics*, Part III, Prop. 9, Scholium.

24. I paraphrase the opening sentence of Section I of the *Grounding for the Metaphysics of Morals:* 'There is no possibility of thinking of anything at all in the world, or even out of it, which can be regarded as good without qualification, except a *good will*' (Kant, 1981, p. 7). It is interesting to see that Descartes, too, makes the will central to his conception of human thought (cognition). He observes in the fourth Meditation that 'it is only the will or freedom of choice, which I experience within me to be so great that the idea of any greater faculty is beyond my grasp; so much so that it is above all in virtue of the will that I understand myself to bear in some way the image and likeness of God'. He goes on to say that, although the divine will is incomparably greater than his human will in virtue of its knowledge, power and object, 'nevertheless it does not seem any greater than mine, when considered as will in the essential and strict sense. This is because the will simply consists in our ability to do or not do something (that is, to affirm or deny, to pursue or avoid).' Because the will in its freedom is not externally determined, 'neither divine grace nor natural knowledge ever diminishes freedom; on the contrary, they increase and strengthen it' (Descartes, 1984, p. 40).

References

Derrida, J. (1976), *Of Grammatology*, trans. G. Spivak, Baltimore: The Johns Hopkins University Press.

Derrida, J. (1990), 'Force of Law: The "Mystical Foundation of Authority"', trans. M. Quaintance, *Cardozo Law Review*, **11** (5–6).

Descartes, R. (1984), *Meditations on First Philosophy*, in *The Philosophical Writings of Descartes*, vol. II, trans. J. Cottingham, R. Stoothoff and D. Murdoch, Cambridge: Cambridge University Press.

Dostoevsky, F. (1990), *The Brothers Karamazov*, trans. R. Peaver and L. Volokhonsky, San Francisco: North Point Press.

Hume, D. (1951), *Treatise of Human Nature*, ed. L. Selby-Bigge, Oxford: Oxford University Press.

Jowett, B. (1970), 'On the Interpretation of Scripture,' in *Essays and Reviews*, Westmead, UK: Gregg International Publishers.

Kant, I. (1929), *Critique of Pure Reason*, trans. N. Kemp Smith, Basingstoke: Macmillan.

Kant, I. (1956), *Critique of Practical Reason*, trans. L. Beck, Indianapolis: The Bobbs-Merrill Company.

Kant, I. (1981), *Grounding for the Metaphysics of Morals*, trans. J. Ellington, Indianapolis: Hackett Publishing Company.

Kulak, A. (1997), 'Origin and Critique: Reading Nietzsche's *On the Genealogy of Morals*', unpublished PhD thesis, York University, Toronto.

Maimonides, M. (1963), *The Guide of the Perplexed*, vol. I, trans. S. Pines, Chicago: University of Chicago Press.

Marion, J.-L. (1991), *God Without Being*, trans. T. Carlson, Chicago: University of Chicago Press.

Marion, J.-L. (1999), 'Is the Argument Ontological? The Anselmian Proof and the Two Demonstrations of the Existence of God in the *Meditations*', in *Cartesian Questions: Method and Metaphysics*, Chicago: University of Chicago Press.

Polka, B. (1990), 'Spinoza and the Separation Between Philosophy and Theology', *Journal of Religious Studies*, **16** (1–2), 91–119.

Polka, B. (2001), *Depth Psychology, Interpretation, and the Bible: An Ontological Essay on Freud*, Montreal and Kingston: McGill-Queen's University Press.

Polka, B. (forthcoming), 'Modernity in Light of the Ontological Argument', *Gregorianum*.

Spinoza, B. (1989), *Tractatus Theologico-Politicus*, trans. S. Shirley, Leiden: E.J. Brill.

Chapter 2

Divine and Graven Images: The Contemporaneity of Theory and the Bible

Avron Kulak

In the reflections that follow I undertake to show how the very notion of theory, insofar as it can make the claim to contemporaneity, involves a critical distinction between divine and graven images. It is precisely the distinction between divine and graven images as established by the Genesis stories of creation and fall that gives us a notion of temporality as contemporaneity. In addition to the stories of creation and fall, I shall call upon thinkers from St Augustine to Derrida in order to show that critical thinking has always been contemporary and, therefore, biblical.

The authors of the Bible make an enormous demand on both their readers and themselves when, within the first three chapters of Genesis, they twice invoke divine authority as the basis for holding that humans bear the image and likeness of God. 'Let us make man in our image, after our likeness,' God ordains on what is described by the biblical authors as the sixth day of creation (Gen. 1:26). Then, in the story of the fall, God judges of the fallen Adam that 'the man has become like one of us, knowing good and evil' (Gen. 3:22). Within the first three chapters of Genesis, therefore, the biblical authors transform the frame of reference for image and likeness by relocating it in the moral (the conceptual) rather than the sensory realm – by relocating it, that is, in that which has no natural or immediate image. They thereby pose, for themselves and for their readers, the question of the status of the images (the figures, the metaphors) that constitute not only divine but also human narrative. How, when there is no immediate frame of reference, is one to determine the truth of the image?

In separating both God and humans from their immediate images, the biblical authors are supremely conscious of the fact that, once the distinction is made between divine and natural images, it then becomes possible to confuse the likeness that unites God and humans with natural likeness. There are several possibilities here. Either the divine is reduced to the immediate reflection of the human or the human is elevated as the immediate reflection of the divine. Yet, not only is there the danger of conflating the divine and the human, but also there is the danger of reducing both to their own immediacies if the two are dualistically opposed. It is thus within the gap, the tension – the fear and trembling – of being both created in the image of the divine and commanded to have no graven images that the biblical authors situate themselves and their readers. Biblical thought, in other words, presupposes a double hermeneutic, each side of which acts as a control for the other:

the relationship of divine and human being on the one hand; the distinction between divine and graven images on the other. What is significant about this hermeneutic is that the relationship between divine and human being cannot be directly correlated with the distinction between divine and graven images. Rather, the distinction between divine and graven images cuts across the concepts both of the divine and of the human. The double hermeneutic that is central to the Bible provides, in other words, the self-critical, self-referential principle by which the truth of its and our images can be determined, continually requiring, while also making it possible, to rethink both text and reader.

Yet the very notion of a self-critical or self-referential principle, whether divine or human, is also subject to the distinction between divine and graven images. Is self-referentiality, for the Bible, to be correlated with the eternal self-presence of the divine and the corresponding loss of that presence for human beings? Is it the concept of a self-present, self-identical being that emerges from the claim that, in the beginning, God creates, for six days and nights before resting on the seventh? Is it the concept of lost presence or the absent origin that emerges as the human condition in light of the claim that, after the beginning, humans fall from the paradise in which they exist prior to knowing good and evil? What is the divine and what is the graven point of view for these stories? For when the very stories that provide images not only of a temporal, sequential creation but also of a temporal, sequential transition from innocence to sin already call into question the status of the natural image, the validity of reading these stories on analogy with natural, chronological time is also called into question. How, then, in light of the distinction between divine and graven images, do the stories of creation and fall deepen our comprehension not only of divine and human self-referentiality but also of the significance of biblical thought for contemporary theory?

When St Augustine takes up the biblical concept of creation in *The City of God*, he insists that, as he 'dare not say that there ever was a time when the Lord God was not Lord', he must 'shrink from making any assertion' when he considers 'what God could be Lord of if there was not always some creature' (St Augustine, 1950, p. 395). Augustine thus holds a double position: although 'time was created,' he writes, 'in all time time has been' (p. 397). For Augustine, just as the existence of God presupposes creation, there is no time when creation does not already exist. In the beginning, creation has a history. There is no literal, natural, first moment of creation. There is, therefore, no moment, for either God or creation, that is simply self-present, that is not already historical, deeply enmeshed in past and future. To reduce the logic of creation to the opposition between the prior, eternal, self-presence of God and the posterior, chronological, contingencies of human consciousness is precisely to reduce the story of creation to its graven images. God is then rendered the first cause of creation, known only in himself and, therefore, inaccessible to human consciousness, which then views itself as lost in the infinite regress of causes and effects. For since, in nature, there is no cause that is not the effect of a prior cause, there can be no natural, temporal regress (or progress) that culminates in knowledge of a first cause. But since, as Augustine indicates, God comes into existence with creation, the story of creation inaugurates an altogether different logic than that presupposed by the opposition between the first cause external to creation and natural time. Because creation is the logic, the principle, in light of which time and existence are rendered historical, it is creation that inaugurates the critique of presence in history. Rather than the Bible presupposing the existence of God as self-present being, it is the reduction of God or biblical ontology – the reduction of divine self-referentiality – to self-present being that constitutes idolatry.

Central to creation, therefore, is a concept of the temporal, whether divine or human, as neither merely eternal nor merely chronological, a concept of time as history. What, then, in light of the temporality of creation – and the distinction that it brings into existence between self-referentiality and self-presence, between divine and graven images – does it mean for humans that God knows (sees) all? To see all, for either the divine or the human, does not mean to see all of, to see the end or even beyond the end of, natural, chronological time. For chronological time has no beginning or end in itself. Rather, that God sees all, that God knows us before we are formed in the womb, liberates the self from viewing itself on analogy with chronological time, thus reconstituting the very origin, the very ground of human seeing. Either one sees, self-referentially and historically, with the eyes of the divine, or one's seeing reflects the contingencies of chronological time. As Derrida recognizes in *The Gift of Death*, the biblical conception of omniscience, properly understood, is inseparable from – it involves and, indeed, makes possible – the existence of the secret not as that which is known only by one, some or many but as the self-conscious, infinite recess of subjectivity that, shared by all, distinguishes truth from certainty, faith from dogmatism. It is precisely in light of omniscience – seeing (thinking) the distinction between divine and graven images – that the history of the secret, of the other, of the self as other, first emerges.

Descartes begins to explicate the structure of thinking liberated from viewing itself on analogy with chronological time when he writes, in the third of his *Meditations*, that 'the distinction between preservation and creation is only a conceptual one,' for 'it does not follow from the fact that I existed a little while ago that I must exist now, unless there is some cause which, as it were, creates me afresh at this moment – that is, which preserves me' (Descartes, 1984, vol. II, p. 33). In recognizing that creation eliminates the opposition between originally having been created and presently being created afresh, he points out that 'an infinite regress is impossible' when thinking properly engages the demonstration or explication of the existence of God (p. 34). Descartes is thus consistent with Spinoza, who, having explicated God as both one and infinite in the first part of the *Ethics*, goes on, in his critique of superstition, to separate the idea of God from any teleology that invokes a first cause or a final end. Descartes is also consistent with Hegel, who writes, in *Lectures on the Philosophy of Religion*, that creation 'is not an *actus* that "happened" once' in the past but is, rather, 'as an *eternal* moment, an eternal determination of the idea', the very structure of thinking rendered historical (Hegel, 1984, vol. 3, p. 275). What Descartes, Spinoza and Hegel together show is that, just as there is nothing anterior to the moment of creation, there is also nothing posterior to it. Once the ontology of creation is separated from its graven images, it becomes the principle in light of which all moments are rendered equally first, equally original, equally creative: the principle that allows, in Derrida's terms, for 'the very historicity that presupposes a tradition to be reinvented', to be created afresh, 'each step of the way, in this incessant repetition of the absolute beginning' (Derrida, 1995, p. 80).[1]

I bring together, along with the authors of Genesis, Augustine, Descartes, Spinoza, Hegel and Derrida not only in order to explicate the relationship between biblical thought and contemporary theory but also in order to complicate the question of what is meant by contemporary theory. For if, in fact, the history of theory presupposes a tradition that, in the beginning, enables its own reinvention – if contemporary theory expresses the reiteration of absolute beginnings – then all theory that reinvents or reiterates creation as the structure of each original moment is contemporary, whether it has already done so or whether it will do so in the twenty-first century or beyond. If, indeed, this is the case, then, just as one finds in the story of creation a truly historical basis for the critique of (divine) self-presence, one could equally expect to find in the story of the fall a truly historical basis for the critique of the loss of presence.

In *The Concept of Anxiety*, Kierkegaard indicates that the problem in comprehending the concept of original sin as a paradoxical account of origin is the temptation to read the story as presupposing a chronological structure. Kierkegaard holds that 'if the first [sin] means one sin in the numerical sense, no history can result from it, and sin will have no history' – it will not have come into existence – 'either in the individual or in the race' (Kierkegaard, 1980, p. 30). If the difference between Adam's sin and the sins of his heirs is that Adam's transgression, as original, conditions all other sin as a consequence – if Adam stands in relation to his heirs as a first cause – then history, the history of responsibility for each single individual, becomes an utter contradiction. For history would then have a beginning outside itself, a beginning that is ahistorical (irresponsible). Kierkegaard thus points out that to hold to the temporal antithesis between original and hereditary sin is to ignore the fact that, in depicting Adam as 'both himself and the race', the biblical authors thereby indicate that Adam's story is the reader's story, the history, both individual and universal, of the single individual (p. 28). Kierkegaard thus reiterates Hegel's recognition that the biblical story 'abstractly termed *the fall*' is 'not just a contingent history', not just an act that happened once, 'but the eternal and necessary history of humanity'. When, however, this history 'is portrayed' or understood 'mythically in the mode of a temporal process,' Hegel adds, 'then inconsistency is unavoidable' (Hegel, 1984, vol. 2, p. 527).

For both Hegel and Kierkegaard, then, to read the story of Adam and Eve as entailing either the fall from or loss of original presence is to reduce their (our) story to its graven images. Kierkegaard insists, in fact, that 'the Genesis story presents the only dialectically consistent view' of sin as original. 'Its whole content,' he writes, echoing Augustine's recognition that creation presupposes itself, 'is really concentrated in one statement', that 'sin presupposes itself, that sin comes into the world in such a way that by the fact that it is, it is presupposed' (Kierkegaard, 1980, p. 32). The concept of original sin, Kierkegaard shows, inaugurates an altogether different logic from that presupposed by the dualism between original and hereditary sin. For the biblical authors, all sin is simultaneously original and historical. Sin originates, it creates and preserves, human self-consciousness, human self-referentiality, by rendering it historical in the beginning. Kierkegaard is thus consistent with Kant, who, in turn consistent with the critical dimensions of biblical thought, expresses the significance for human consciousness of the biblical relationship between origin and history in *Religion Within the Limits of Reason*

Alone. 'No matter how early we direct our attention to our moral state,' Kant observes, 'we find that this state is no longer a *res integra*' (Kant, 1960, p. 50). What we rather find, he points out, is that 'the first really good act that a man can perform is to forsake the evil, which is to be sought not in his inclinations, but in his perverted maxim, and so in freedom itself' (p. 51). In the moment of beginning freely, historically, with the 'fall', what emerges for self-consciousness is the history of itself as other to itself, the history of its not having accounted for itself as the very gap or relationship between the divine and graven image.

What a consideration of the biblical stories of creation and fall shows us, therefore, is that, in beginning freely with itself, historical self-consciousness, both divine and human, has already begun, creatively, sinfully, with the other. Human existence is that in which divine existence is implicated in the beginning; divine existence is that in which human existence is implicated in the beginning. Thus what ultimately constitutes divine no less than human existence is the biblical paradox of love: in loving, in beginning with, the other as oneself, one finds that one must equally love, one must equally begin with, oneself as other.[2] It is the 'incessant repetition', the historical reiteration, of the hermeneutical, ontological and ethical implications of this paradox – the self can interpret itself, can be itself, only insofar as it recognizes its other in itself – that constitutes not only the history of beginning but also the beginning of history. This beginning is always absolute, always original, insofar as it involves what Kierkegaard alternately calls, in *Philosophical Fragments* and *Fear and Trembling*, genuine contemporaneity and the passion of beginning primitively.[3] To be genuinely contemporary, he shows, is to liberate the thought of the self no less than the other from its graven images, from the alternatives of immediate sensation (following at first hand) and immediate cognition (following at second hand), each of which but reflects the other and in light of which the self is never contemporary. For, in falsely believing that the immediate presence of the divine can be followed (witnessed) at first hand, the self finds itself always longing for immediate certainty but always in the position of following at second hand. The genuine contemporary, Kierkegaard shows, is the one who begins, primitively, originally, absolutely, to bring into existence, to reinvent, the divine beginning in light of which she or he is created. Central to biblical thought, therefore, is the paradox that it both begins, and begins with, us. The question of the significance of biblical thought for twenty-first century critical theory is thus the question of ourselves, the question of the history that constitutes us and that we in turn constitute.

That biblical thought is the (re)invention of the human – that the question of the significance of biblical thought is the question of ourselves – is evidenced in the fact that both creation and fall involve a concept of temporality that constitutes human thinking by opening possibilities for self-reflection that otherwise could not be conceived. For once thinking is liberated from viewing its origin and end, and thus the entirety of its content, as reflecting the oppositions and contingencies of natural, chronological time, in which, as we have seen through Augustine, there is neither origin nor end, the very structure of the moment, and thus of thinking, acquires a depth in light of which it is no longer merely self-present. Once the moment is no longer conceived chronologically, not only is the present no longer merely present (although it can be reduced to presence), but also the past is not merely past, not merely finished or fixed. The past is now open; it is subject to change. That is, in Kierkegaard's terms, the unchangeableness of the past can no longer be correlated with the unchangeableness of natural necessity. Rather, its unchangeableness is subject to the desire of the individual who wills the past as that which has come into existence on the basis of his or her freedom. It is precisely this that Nietzsche calls redemption, the transformation of every 'it was' into 'thus I willed it' (Nietzsche, 1961, p. 139). It is also this possibility that Montaigne calls repentance, the capacity for forgiveness, for preserving rather than losing oneself in light of discovering one's contradictions. What self-referentiality as historical means in biblical terms, therefore, is not that the self is capable of viewing itself in terms of a present certainty that would ground its existence but that it is the temporality of redemption and forgiveness that biblical thought brings into existence and that constitutes thinking created in the divine image of knowing good and evil.

In light of the above, it is important to note, in assessing the significance of biblical thought for the history of Western critique, that both Augustine and Kierkegaard develop their presentations of creation and fall in direct opposition to ancient Greek thought. Augustine initiates his consideration of the biblical concept of creation by opposing it to the extrabiblical conception of cyclical time, a conception that is modelled, he holds, on the constant, ceaseless repetition of the order of nature. From this cycle, he points out, not even the immortal soul that has apparently attained knowledge of the good is exempt. Rather, he insists, the soul is consigned to a ceaseless transmigration in which it alternates between delusive wisdom and real misery. Augustine thus evokes for us the myth with which Plato concludes the *Republic*, the myth of Er, in which the just and unjust life, the life of wisdom and the life of misery, are shown constantly to reverse into each other. When one has lived unjustly, Socrates instructs his interlocutors, one next chooses the just life. Yet, when one has lived justly, one chooses to live one's next life unjustly. Good becomes evil, evil becomes good. Whereas the critical dimensions of biblical thought preserve the self in its otherness by providing the principles in light of which the self can freely account for its history, the good as the end of thinking and desire in the Greek world provides no basis of critique. If one does not desire the good, one is unjust. Yet since, as Socrates argues in the *Symposium*, one can only desire what one does not possess, the good, as the end of desire, is always the end that one lacks.

It is in direct contrast to the Socratic conception of the good as the *telos* for human thinking and desire that Kierkegaard elucidates the biblical concept of knowledge of good and evil, together with its attendant concepts of freedom and love. For Kierkegaard, the knowledge of good and evil is posited 'only for freedom and in freedom', and thus 'never *in abstracto* but only *in concreto*'. Yet, Kierkegaard holds, because Socrates conceived the good only 'from its external side (the useful, the finitely teleological)', and thus as lacking for human consciousness, the Socratic concepts of morality, freedom and love remained speculatively – and practically – abstract (empty) (Kierkegaard, 1980, p. 111). What Socrates ultimately lacked, Kierkegaard insists, was the category of neighbour: 'He did not know that the neighbour existed and that one shall love him' (Kierkegaard, 1995, p. 373). Socratic thought, Kierkegaard shows, must be utterly distinguished from biblical thought. For Socratic thought is structured by two positions, lack and presence, that, while apparently in opposition, merely reflect each other: first, the finite teleology of the good that, in the end, is utterly external, unknown and other to human consciousness; second, the recollection that the truth that one lacks in existence is known in the eternal self-identity of the soul. Yet the very notion of the self-identity of the soul, as the myth of Er exposes to us, always reflects the lack of the good. The story of Adam and Eve, on the other hand, constitutes the self neither as that which lacks the good nor as that which is identical with the good but, rather, on the basis of the paradox of love that unites self and other in the knowledge of good and evil. Love of neighbour and original sin are inseparable.

What a consideration of the distinction between Greek and biblical thought through Augustine and Kierkegaard shows us, therefore, is that, when nature rather than God is viewed as the source of human imagery, neither self nor other can be preserved. In explicating the fate of consciousness that locates its end in the images of nature as reversal, delusion, misery and lack, Socrates can provide no critique of the images upon which his thinking is predicated. For, as we saw earlier, the very idea of the image as graven comes into existence only in light of the divine image. In lacking, as a hermeneutical, ontological and ethical principle, the concrete relationship of divine and human being, in not knowing that thinking can be preserved only when it is constituted as the relationship of neighbour by the biblical paradox of love, Socrates equally lacked the distinction between divine and graven images. There is no critique (of idolatry) outside the double hermeneutic of the biblical text. It is creation and fall, the creation and fall of humans created in the image and likeness of God, that separates the Greek and biblical worlds and that renders biblical thought contemporary.[4]

I thus return to my earlier claim that all thinking is contemporary that has its roots in biblical thought. Is it the case, then, to choose but two of the thinkers from among those whom I have invoked in making this claim, that the Cartesian *cogito* and Derridean deconstruction are equally contemporary?

At issue here is the question of how one reads, the question of the hermeneutical principles that the reader brings to the text and, equally, that the text brings to the reader. How, in light of his own hermeneutical principles, is Descartes to be read if the existence of both reader and text, self and other, is made the principle of interpretation? In indicating that the self's beginning in doubt both preserves (creates) and is only preserved by (created by) the strongest possible conception of the other – which Descartes calls God – and in also eliminating all natural, material images as inadequate for elaborating a conception of the other (self), Descartes formulates a notion of human origins and thinking that is consistent with the Bible. The hermeneutic that is central to Descartes' text, in other words, is the Bible's double hermeneutic: the relationship between divine and human being on the one hand and the distinction between divine and graven images on the other. It is in light of this double hermeneutic that the critical distinctions through which Descartes explicates what he calls his first principle – the problematic distinctions between God and human, infinite and finite, perfect and imperfect – must be comprehended. The origin and end of the thinking subject, for Descartes, is neither external nature nor the internal soul (human existence reduced to its graven images) but that power which, irreducible to either, reconstitutes and preserves both. In contrast to Socratic thought, and rather than instituting the self-presence of the self-identical subject,

Descartes' *cogito* comprises a conception of the human being as the creation (preservation) of the other.

How, then, is Derrida to be read if the existence of both reader and text, self and other, is made the principle of interpretation? Derrida in fact makes this principle his when he insists that deconstruction is justice. He goes on to acknowledge that deconstruction as justice is historical: it is at work in history, he holds, even before it becomes conscious of itself as deconstruction (Derrida, 1990, p. 965). Although he does not make clear precisely how he would construe this history, he does provide two deeply interrelated conceptions of temporality that together delimit it.

The just decision, Derrida holds, 'must rend time', thus remaining 'the very dimension of events irreducibly to come' (pp. 967, 969). In belonging to a future that is structurally always to come, justice belongs to a future that in principle never arrives – indeed, that *must* never arrive. This structural *différance* is understood by Derrida not to eliminate the possibility of justice but, rather, to preserve the possibility of the just decision by ensuring against 'all presumption of a determinate certitude of a *present* justice' (p. 965; my italics). Thus, because the concept of temporality central to justice functions as a deconstruction of presence, it has as its complement Derrida's earlier formulation of the deconstruction of originary presence, the idea that the text is always already subject to an auto-deconstruction that guards against the saturation of meaning by putting 'into question the authority of presence, or of its simple, symmetrical opposite, absence or lack' (Derrida, 1982, p. 10). As equally aimed at the opposition between presence and absence (lack), these two notions of *différantial* time, when held together, reinstitute the concept of temporality that is central to biblical ontology, the concept of temporality that presupposes the distinction between divine and graven images. Justice will never arrive – it is always to come, it will always have a future – only on the condition that it has always already arrived. Yet, in having always already arrived, in presupposing itself, justice presupposes not the finite reapplication of prior authority but always the rearrival, the reinvention, of its own absolute (primitive) beginnings. It thereby presupposes the time that Derrida calls messianic, a time that remains open to the coming of the other, but 'without the horizon of expectation' that is turned towards either a determinate future or a determinate past, a final end or a first cause (Derrida, 1996, p. 17). It is thus telling that it is to his biblical origins that Derrida alludes in describing, as both one and infinite, what he calls the aporetic interval that distinguishes the just decision from finite calculation. It is in this interval, he holds, that human will and desire fall.

Which of the two, then, Descartes or Derrida, is truly contemporary? Derrida, it is clear, is contemporary in a way that Descartes is not. But is Descartes not also contemporary in a way that Derrida is not? Descartes explicitly acknowledges his theological roots and, nevertheless, explicates the *cogito* through a now notorious series of oppositions that the principles of his own text allows the reader to rethink. Derrida consistently and brilliantly deconstructs those oppositions while nevertheless not explicitly recognizing, despite indicating, that the roots of deconstruction are biblical. Along with insisting that deconstruction is justice, Derrida acknowledges, consistent with Kierkegaard, that the Platonic conception of the good 'is not yet goodness', that an 'incommensurable inside of the soul or the conscience' is constituted only with the advent of biblical thought (Derrida, 1995, pp. 7, 101). Yet he also insists that he can discern 'fissures of "*différance*"' in Plato (Kearney, 1984, p. 117). But this cannot be – on terms that Derrida himself establishes. First, he understands *différance* not only as that which exceeds the opposition between presence and absence, an opposition that, as we have seen, structures Greek thought and from which Greek thought is unable to escape, since each of these opposites is but the reflection of the other, but also as the spacing (the differing and deferral) of temporality. Second, it is precisely because *différance* exceeds (calls into question) the binary relations between presence and absence that Derrida is subsequently able to develop his notion of the spacing of temporality as the aporetic interval of justice. The temporality central to *différance* is the temporality of justice. *Différance* and justice presuppose one another. If deconstruction is justice, there can be no deconstruction, no *différance*, in the Greek world, where freedom and responsibility have not yet been thought concretely but remain finitely teleological and abstract. *Différance* is responsibility – it is biblical – or it is nothing at all.

The critical principles of biblical thought constitute, I have argued, the very basis, the very origin, of Western critique. For it is only in light of biblical principles that the values that are central to explicating, to formulating as a problem, the dualisms that have riven human thinking and desire come into existence. Truth, as Nietzsche knew, comes into existence not as pristine, not as immaculate, not as unalloyed but conscious of itself as a problem. It is the existence of the divine, and of the human created in the image of the divine, that makes the idolatrous reduction of both possible. Thus the answer to the question of how the principles of creation, millennia after being formulated by the biblical authors, are always fully revealed and yet always still in the process of being revealed lies precisely in the freedom that is the very substance and subject of creation. Because each generation, each individual created in the image of the divine must begin again to reconstitute the history of absolute origins by accounting for the distinction between divine and graven images, because each must respond to having been chosen in advance, even before being formed in the womb, by God, the problem is always contemporary.

It is for this reason that the contemporary, too, must be freed from its graven images. The contemporary is not the present in opposition to either a past that we have outgrown or a future that will displace us in turn. The contemporary is the commitment to explicating, on the basis of the double hermeneutic that constitutes biblical thought – the relationship of divine and human being, the distinction between divine and graven images – the complex history of thought and desire. This hermeneutic, which is the very structure of contemporaneity, bears both a divine and a human signature. It is not a question, however, of whose signature is the original, whose the more necessary. All names that attempt to delineate and confront the dualisms, the graven images, into which thinking is prone to fall – God, substance, subject, reason, overman and *différance*, among others – are contemporary, both divine and human in the beginning. Thus to replace the name of God truly does not liberate one from responsibility, for creation, for sin, for truth conscious of itself as the problem of divine, human and graven images. As Nietzsche also knew, to replace God is an act that intensifies the burden of conscience, provided that it does not cut one off from redemption. For to replace bears the double meaning of both to substitute for and to restore. It is precisely in replacing God that the divine and human, as a problem, together remain contemporary.

Notes

1. Derrida's meditation on the paradox that only the absolute can be reinvented or re-expressed is made in the context of an analysis of the Epilogue of Kierkegaard's *Fear and Trembling* (to which we shall return later). After posing the question of whether the reiteration of the absolute beginning 'amount[s] to history, to a story', Derrida answers both 'Yes and no. The epilogue of *Fear and Trembling* repeats, in sentence after sentence,' he points out, 'that this highest passion that is faith must be started over by each generation. Each generation must begin again to involve itself in it without counting on the generation before. It thus describes the non-history of absolute beginnings which are repeated, and the very historicity that presupposes a tradition to be reinvented each step of the way, in this incessant repetition of the absolute beginning' (p. 80). In thereby making non-history central to history – in holding non-history and history together absolutely rather than refusing to allow them to be split dualistically (binarily) – Derrida not only differentiates his conception of history from any finite teleology and aligns it with faith but also indicates that central to the structure or principles of faith is the deconstruction of binary oppositions (that is, that it is precisely the critical dimensions of what Kierkegaard calls faith that initiate the deconstruction of binary oppositions).

2. In *Works of Love*, Kierkegaard writes that 'The concept "neighbour" is actually the redoubling of your own self' (1995, p. 21).

3. In *Fear and Trembling*, the problem of what it means to begin primitively engages the relationship between faith, ethics and aesthetics. Kierkegaard writes in the epilogue that, since 'no generation learns the essentially human from a previous one', that is, since 'no generation has learned to love from another', 'each generation begins primitively' when it comes to the task of faith (p. 121). Kierkegaard is clear, however, that there is nothing prior to faith, that faith cannot be the result of something prior. For to judge by the result, to justify one's existence on the basis of the result, is precisely what he calls the ethical, the sacrifice of the self to the other (the universal). There is no ethical beginning that has faith as its result. Neither, however, can what Kierkegaard means by beginning primitively be associated with what he calls the aesthetic, which he elucidates as the first interiority or spontaneous response to the immediacies of feeling and mood, the result of which is the sacrifice of the other to the self. To begin primitively to learn the essentially human is to begin creatively – lovingly, faithfully, absolutely – as the single individual responsible for preserving (reinventing) what is essentially human. To begin primitively is to recognize that one cannot, either in the beginning or in the end, go further than faith.

4. My analysis of the relationship of Greek and biblical thought to modernity is deeply indebted to that provided by Brayton Polka in *The Dialectic of Biblical Critique: Interpretation and Existence*. In engaging the tradition of biblical critique as developed especially by Spinoza, Kant, Hegel and Kierkegaard, Polka argues two interrelated points. First, Greek thought, in basing itself on what he calls the doctrine of contradictory opposites, is unable to develop either a conception of interpretation that does not contradict existence or a conception of existence that does not contradict the possibility of interpretation. Second, it is the ontological, ethical and hermeneutical demands expressed by the golden rule of biblical critique – so interpret the existence of the other as you would have the other interpret your existence – that provide the very basis for

rethinking the dualisms which haunt not only modern philosophy and theology but also politics, literature and art. See also Polka's *Truth and Interpretation*: *An Essay in Thinking*.

References

Augustine of Hippo (1950), *The City of God*, trans. M. Dods, New York: Random House.

Bible (1952), Revised Standard Version, Toronto: Wm. Collins Sons & Co.

Derrida, Jacques (1982), *Margins of Philosophy*, trans. A. Bass, Chicago: University of Chicago Press.

Derrida, Jacques (1990), 'The Force of Law: The Mystical Foundation of Authority', trans. M. Quaintance, *The Cardozo Law Review*, **11** (5–6).

Derrida, Jacques (1995), *The Gift of Death*, trans. D. Wills, Chicago: University of Chicago Press.

Derrida, Jacques (1996), 'Faith and Knowledge: The Two Sources of "Religion" at the Limits of Reason Alone', in J. Derrida and G. Vattimo (eds.), *Religion*, Stanford, California: Stanford University Press.

Descartes, René (1984), *The Philosophical Writings of Descartes*, trans. J. Cottingham, R. Stroothoff and D. Murdoch, Cambridge: Cambridge University Press.

Hegel, G.W.F. (1984), *Lectures on the Philosophy of Religion*, ed. P. Hodgson, Berkeley and Los Angeles: University of California Press.

Kant, Immanuel (1960), *Religion Within the Limits of Reason Alone*, trans. T. Greene and H. Hudson, New York: Harper Torchbooks.

Kearney, Richard (1984), *Dialogues with Contemporary Continental Thinkers*, Manchester: Manchester University Press.

Kierkegaard, Søren (1980), *The Concept of Anxiety*, trans. R. Thomte, Princeton, New Jersey: Princeton University Press.

Kierkegaard, Søren (1983), *Fear and Trembling*, trans. Howard V. Hong and Edna H. Hong, Princeton: Princeton University Press.

Kierkegaard, Søren (1985), *Philosophical Fragments*, trans. Howard V. Hong and Edna H. Hong, Princeton: Princeton University Press.

Kierkegaard, Søren (1995), *Works of Love*, trans. H. Hong and E. Hong, Princeton, New Jersey: Princeton University Press.

Nietzsche, Friedrich (1961), *Thus Spoke Zarathustra*, trans. W. Kaufmann, New York: The Viking Press.

Polka, Brayton (1986), *The Dialectic of Biblical Critique*: *Interpretation and Existence*, New York: St Martin's Press.

Polka, Brayton (1990), *Truth and Interpretation*: *An Essay in Thinking*, New York: St Martin's Press.

Chapter 3

Traversing the Infinite through Augustine and Derrida

Mark Cauchi

God's relationship to a human being is the infinitising at every moment of that which at every moment is in a man. (Kierkegaard, *Works of Love*[1])

It is perhaps fitting that the notion of the infinite has been a stumbling block on the paths of both philosophical and religious thinking. Both discourses, it seems, are bound together (united), and together bounded (limited), in this mutual impasse; that is, both discourses reach their boundary in that which is said to be unbounded. This situation is fitting, as I suggested, because perhaps it is precisely here, where each discourse is pushed to its limit and thus stopped dead in its tracks – pushed until its path is blocked – where we can see how each may in fact cross over, or pass over, to the other. The infinite, in this instance, would thus seem to have the dual vocation of being, in Derrida's terms, both an *aporia* for philosophical and religious thinking and the *passage* between them. (*Aporia*, recall, is Greek for non-passage, blocked path or impasse.) In both of these *missions* (vocations), to use more Augustinian language, the infinite would seem to be a border site: a place where things are *permitted* and denied passage, a site of *admission* and *dismissal*. In what follows, I will thus pass between, on the one hand, certain texts of the saintly Augustine, particularly those in which he describes relations within and to God, and, on the other, Derrida the *passable* atheist,[2] particularly those in which he thematizes the coming of the Other, all in order to determine the parameters of the infinite.

Probably the most intuitive or self-evident definition of the infinite, and one which originates in Anaximander, is as the unbounded or the unlimited (*to apeiron*). But above I depicted the infinite as itself a limit. Is it permissible to speak in this way of the unlimited as residing at the limit? Does not situating the infinite *at* the border or even *as* the border between, one assumes, two limited entities necessarily limit the infinite? It would doubtless seem more appropriate to describe the border as in itself finite, since, no matter how infinitesimally fine it is, a border is axiomatically bounded, confined or embordered on both ends. According to the more conventional notion, the infinite, as unbounded and disembordered, cannot be prevented or blocked from being anywhere. In fact, since there are not any delimitations within that which is infinite, it makes no sense to speak, topographically, of any-where, as if within the infinite one could differentiate between different places, between here and there. As absolutely or *wholly* every-where, it is no where in *partic*ular, and, as such, is atopical. Where this notion of the infinite reigns, there, there can be no aporia; there, there is no there.

Such, in fact, would be the literal definition of the omnipresence of that exemplary figure of the infinite, God. Thus, when Augustine opens his *Confessions*, this is the conception of God which he must confront. Far from finding this notion to be unaporetic, however (that is, far from finding God to be absolutely porous or permeable), Augustine finds, not simply himself, but God caught in an aporia.

> How shall I call upon my God, my God and Lord? Surely when I call on him, I am calling on him to come into me. But what place is there in me where my God can enter into me? 'God made heaven and earth' [Gen. 1:1]. Where may he come to me? Lord my God, is there any room in me which can contain you? Can heaven and earth, which you have made and in which you have made me, contain you? Without you, whatever exists would not exist. Then can what exists contain you? I also have being. So why do I request you to come to me when, *unless you were within me* [my emphasis], I would have no being at all? (Augustine, 1992, pp. 3–4)

A paradox, then. On the one hand, if Augustine denies God his omnipresence, God's absolute priority there wherever Augustine exists, he denies himself the possibility of calling on God (for he, Augustine, would not then exist). On the other hand, if Augustine simply presumes God's presence within himself, he then denies himself the need for calling on God, he denies that God is *also not* within him. Thus (1), as omnipresent, God's infinitude is impervious to blockage: he is absolutely permeable and lacking de-finition. And yet (2), precisely because God al-*one* is the infinite creator, he is totally impermeable, his borders cannot be crossed and, therefore, he is impervious to *at-one-ment* (God is the One that another cannot be one with). With the first, absolute passage; with the second, irresolvable aporia.

How is it that, within the *Confessions* at least, the infinite (God) may be characterized by both formulations? If only one of these formulations were put forth, would it still describe the infinite? Could the infinite ever be solely absolute passage or solely irresolvable aporia? In '*Sauf le nom*', Derrida asks, 'What would a path be without aporia? Would there be a way without what clears the way there where the way is not opened, whether it is blocked or still buried in the nonway?' (1995, p. 83) To paraphrase, does not a path, like a valley, presuppose something, like a mountain, through which it must pass or cross? On the other hand, in *Aporias*, Derrida writes, 'The "I enter", crossing the threshold, this "I pass" (*perao*) puts us on the path, if I may say, of the *aporos* or of the *aporia*: the difficult or the impracticable, here the impossible, passage, the refused, denied, or prohibited passage, indeed the nonpassage' (1993b, p. 8) Here, on the contrary, it is only once one begins the passage that one's path is blocked. From one angle, then, the path presupposes an antecedent aporia; from the other, aporia presupposes an antecedent passage.

This logic of mutual antecedence which attempts thereby to account for its own existence therein problematizes its own existence. For how could anything it structured even arise in the first place? It is in response to this problematic that, just prior to and in fact setting the scene for the above quotation from the *Confessions*, in the beginning of this book's genesis, Augustine raises the question of how his own text is even possible. He writes, '"Grant me Lord to know and understand" [Ps. 118:34, 73, 144] *which comes first* (emphasis added) – to call upon you or to praise you, and whether knowing you precedes calling upon you' (1992, bk.I, ch.1; p. 3) What is in the beginning? What is the condition of what? As I indicated above, if

God were not already known or present to Augustine, he would not know whom to call upon (he writes, 'the ignorant person might call upon someone else instead of the right one'). On the other hand, if God were already known and present to Augustine, he would have no need to call upon him ('But surely you may be called upon in prayer [in order] that you may be known'). So, as Augustine asks, *which comes first?* What is the origin or possibility of the other? It seems impossible to say. And yet, by this point, of course, the *Confessions* have already begun.

For Derrida, the impossibility of the origin consists in the originating event *coming to pass* within a necessarily dissymmetrical relation. According to Derrida, every event, invention or gift presupposes, axiomatically, 'that something or someone comes a *first time*, something or someone comes to someone, to someone else' (1989, p. 29).[3] As a first time, a genuine event is irreducible to and inexhaustible by the context in which it appears (this reduction would make it conventional) and therefore *must* appear to come *from somewhere else*.[4] It is in this sense that the event *phenomenologically appears* as (if) the result of a passage across a border, as (if) having come *to* this apparent place *from* some other apparent place.[5] Here, in this from–to structure, lies the dissymmetry of the event, for its trajectory goes only one way: the event comes but does not return. If it could return as it would in an economy of exchange, if the point of departure could equally and symmetrically be a point of arrival such that there was in effect no border between the two, then there would be no event, because, in that case, nothing could be said to genuinely *come* for a first time from any place else. Dissymmetry, then, instantiates a border or limit which makes the passage-ness of the event possible.

But it is this very border which also makes (possible) the event (as) impossible. For if the event were simply a transposition *from* one position *to* another, it would merely be a causal outcome, a production by something anterior. With such a logic, it would (falsely) appear possible to *know*, in the sense of empirical or cognitive knowledge, how past events arrived and, in turn, how future events will. If one could know either the point of departure (the cause) or the point of arrival (the effect) from the position of the other, there would be no point to the event: it would give one nothing one did not already know. The genuine event, then, must be a *gift* of what one cannot possibly know. '[A] gift or an event,' Derrida writes in *Given Time*, 'that would be foreseeable, necessary, conditioned, programmed, expected, counted on would not be lived as either gift or event.' As he goes on to say, the given event 'must perturb the *order of causalities*…. In any case, if the gift or the event, if the event of the gift must remain unexplainable by a system of efficient causes, [then] it is the *effect of nothing*' (1992a, pp. 122–3; emphasis added). Where above I showed how the event, as a coming to pass, appears as passage from somewhere to somewhere else, here, as the 'effect of nothing', the event comes, as it were, out of nowhere, or nothing. Here there is no passage. Hence, just after a passage I have already cited, Derrida claims that, while the aporia is a non-passage, it is also, paradoxically,

the event of a coming or of a future advent, which *no longer has the form of the movement that consists in a passing, traversing, or transiting*. It would be the 'coming to pass' of an event that would no longer have the form or the appearance of a *pas* [step]: in sum, a coming without *pas*. (1993b, p. 8; emphasis added)

Let me recast this structure in slightly different terms. In order for there to be an event, something must come here from somewhere else and so presuppose a *limit* between here and there. The identities of here and there are differentiated by the deferring and discerning limit between the two. In this first moment, the event thus presupposes a certain finitude. But because the event comes to pass 'without *pas*', that is, without traversing or trespassing a limit, there is also no limit: 'The gift,' Derrida therefore writes,

> will always be *without* border.... A gift that does not run over its borders, a gift that would let itself be contained in a determination and limited by the indivisibility of an identifiable *trait* would not be a gift. As soon as it delimits itself, a gift is prey to calculation and measure. The gift ... should overrun the border, to be sure, toward the measureless and the excessive. (1992a, p. 91)

In this second moment, on the contrary, the event, because overrunning borders, presupposes a certain infinitude. And it is the impossible combination of these two moments, of the finite and the infinite, which constitutes, for Derrida, the dissymmetry of which I spoke a moment ago. As he says in a footnote to 'Psyche: Inventions of the Other', an in-vention, which he characterizes in this text as the in-coming of the infinite Other, 'can only come about for a finite being' (1989, p. 65, n.23); it is the coming, or wel-coming, of the infinite in the finite, 'the hospitality of a finite threshold that opens itself to infinity' (1999, p. 46). It is, in classical Derridean terms, the trace of differance, which 'is finite, insofar as it is infinite' (1992b, p. 99).

How? How can the finite receive the infinite? From the other side of this encounter – in other words, from the perspective of the infinite – how can that which by definition is unlimited cross the limit and so *experience* the limit of that which is limited? That is, to ask a more Augustinian question, if the infinite is wholly everywhere because unlimited, how can something *come from* the infinite *to* the finite, from God to the human seeker, from the Other to the self? 'Can I move outside heaven and earth,' Augustine asks, 'so that my God may come to me from there?' (1992, bk.I, ch.2; p. 4).

Augustine, also preoccupied with the problematic of how things come to pass to and from God, turns in Book XI of the *Confessions* to asking how, in the beginning, heaven and earth came to pass. Previously, in Book IV, he had already discerned that all particular things within heaven and earth abide by a linearizing logic of passage, for they can exist only as parts within a chain of succession, and as such

> do not all have their being at the same moment, but by passing away and by successiveness, they all form the whole of which they are parts. That is the way [for instance, that] our speech is constructed.... What we say would not be complete if one word did not cease to exist when it had sounded its constituent parts, so that it can be succeeded by another. (1992, bk.IV, ch.10; p. 62)

What Augustine actually describes here, and characterizes just prior to this passage as 'the law limiting their being', is a version of the Aristotelian law of non-contradiction, wherein two things cannot be in the same place at the same time. Two words cannot be spoken at the same time; two words cannot be written in the same space. Existence is hereby linearized; as Augustine formulates it, 'these things pass along the path of things that move towards non-existence' (ibid.).

When Augustine goes on in Book XI to attempt to account for the very creation of this framework of the heavenly and earthly, he recognizes that he cannot do so by means of this framework. He therefore reasons,

> The way, God, in which you made heaven and earth was not that you made them either in heaven or on earth.... Nor did you make the universe within the framework of the universe. There was nowhere for it to be made before it was brought into existence. (1992, bk.XI, ch.4; p. 225)

Space did not exist before God created it, and therefore the creation of it is itself not spatial. Space was not created in space. If we position space before itself in this latter manner, then we create an infinite regress in which one space must always precede another, thereby rendering it uncreated. When Augustine turns to consider time, he proceeds similarly. Analysing the possibility of an ageless time before creation, he asks,

> How could innumerable ages *pass*, which you yourself had not made? You are the originator and creator of all ages. What times existed which were not brought into being by you? Or how could they *pass* if they never had existence?... You have made time itself. Time could not elapse before you made time. (1992, bk.XI, ch.13; p. 229)

Augustine then concludes in the next paragraph, echoing what he said about space, 'It is not in time that you [God] precede times [*sic*].' The passage into time is itself not a passage of (or within) time and thus not truly a passage. There is no border which may be crossed between non-time and time, for any crossing would already be locatable within a temporal order. Heaven and earth, then, did not *pass* into existence, and yet heaven and earth are nevertheless created. The activity of creation would thus appear to be, in Derrida's words, 'a coming without *pas*'. Augustine has dropped us and God, once again, right in the middle of an aporia.

Having ruled out both a spatial and temporal cause for the creation of space and time, Augustine considers the discursive creativity of God's Word. Congruent with his deconstruction of space and time, Augustine knows that God's Word cannot be spatial or temporal.

> You call us, therefore, to understand the Word, God, who is with you God. That word is spoken eternally, and by it all things are uttered eternally. It is not the case that what was being said comes to an end, and something else is then said, so that everything is uttered in a succession with a conclusion, but *everything is said in the simultaneity of eternity*. Otherwise time and change would already exist, and there would not be a true eternity and true immortality. (1992, bk.XI, ch.7; p. 226; emphasis added)

Now, clearly by eternal and immortal Augustine cannot mean existing forever or for all time, because, as the creator of time, God is not temporal. God's eternity, then, is not an infinitely extended or *distended* line of time but, rather – and notice that Augustine chooses the opposite and paradoxical metaphor – the *simultaneity* of eternity. This is a 'time' in which moments are not successive or reducible to one another. God's speaking takes no time at all, not because it is very fast (for that would still take a little time), but because it does not begin and then, after some time, finish. God's Word is in-finite.

Now it is important to note that this Infinite is not what the Greeks mean by *to apeiron*. In fact, what Augustine described above as the law of heaven and earth (that heavenly and earthly things 'pass along the path of things that move towards non-existence') – and which it is now clear is, in contrast to God's Infinite Word, the law of finitude – may be compared to what Aristotle means by infinite. For Aristotle, those things which are infinite, such as 'time, the generations of man, and the division of magnitudes' (*Physics*, bk.III, 206a27, 1984, p. 351), in distinction to those things which are finite, such as a *moment* of time (*nun*), a *particular* man, a *particular* magnitude, are infinite 'either by addition or by division' (ibid., 206a15, p. 351). A particular or distinct entity itself is not infinite because, as a de-limited quantity, it is necessarily finite. On the contrary, the infinite 'exists', according to Aristotle, when 'one thing is *always* being taken *after* another', that is, repetitively, 'and [when] each thing that is taken is always finite, but always different' (ibid., 206a28, p. 351). Infinitude consists, therefore, in the *continual process* of taking a finite quantity into (addition) or taking a finite quantity out from (division) a finite quantity. The infinite is therein the endless repetition of the finite. But this is not to say that the finite quantity itself is the infinite (obviously); rather, it is the endless refining or redefining of a finite quantity's limits that renders it infinite. The infinite is the endless redefinition of the finite, and therein is the de-defining, the de-delimiting, that is, the un-limiting (and therein the *infinitizing*) of the finite. The infinite, then, by definition, is the de-definition of the finite (and, if I wished to be Socratic, I would say that even this definition could not be made). For Aristotle, a definition is always of a finite entity, of a 'this', as he sometimes speaks: 'if it is possible to define … it is necessary that the things predicated in what something is', that is, those things which make it possible to say *what* and *why* a particular thing is, 'are finite' (*Posterior Analytics*, bk.I, 82b38–40, p. 135). It is, therefore, not possible to define the infinite, to mark the outlines of something that has none: 'one cannot define that of which infinitely many things are predicated' (ibid., bk.I, 83b8–9, p. 136). To *actually* define the infinite is impossible, which is why, for Aristotle, the infinite is merely *possible*.

As possible, then, Aristotle's infinite is the negation of what is actual, of what is positive, of what can be posited.[6] As such, questions of finitude and infinitude are always questions of the difference (the limit) between the positive and the negative (the same and the other), and therefore questions about division and distinction, about what can be said about the two sides of a limit. According to Aristotle, one cannot say anything about *what* is on the other or negative side of a limit – only *that* it is the other side, only *that* it is the negative. For if the positive is what the definition defines (and therefore is finite), then the negative is always the negation of the finite, the negation of the definition, and hence in-definite. I can never, then, according to this structure, say *what* the in(de)finite (the negative, the other: the negative other) is; I can only say what the finite (the positive, the same) is: 'the definition [not the infinition] makes clear *what* [a thing] is, and the demonstration', which is, therefore, the negative of definition,[7] '*that* this [thing] is …' (ibid., bk.II, 90b40–91a1, p. 149).[8] If a definition makes clear what a thing is, then the infinite makes it *un*clear, *in*definite, 'always different', as Aristotle said above; that is, always other than discourse. Discourse itself, according to this logic, is always a discourse of the same, for it can only 'define' the other *via negativa*, which thereby renders the other *in*definite. It is precisely against such an infinite, which Descartes eventually renames the *indefinite*,[9] that Augustine asserts that he is 'certain that [God is] infinite without being infinitely diffused through finite space' (1992, bk.VII, ch.20; p. 130). A God thought according to this Greek infinite would be the God of negative theology.

The creation of finitude by the Infinite, then, does not come to pass according to the finite, according to an analogy with the Greek infinite. As Augustine writes, 'everything which begins to be and ceases to be', that is, everything finite, 'begins and ends its existence at that moment when, in the eternal reason *where nothing begins or ends*, it is *known* that it is *right* for it to begin and end' (ibid., bk.XI, ch.8, p. 226; emphasis added). It is crucially important here to note three things about this passage. First, that Augustine does not say that the finite begins or ends *in* the Infinite 'where nothing begins or ends', for this would make the Infinite the limit of the finite which, in turn, would make the Infinite limited. Any supposed border between the finite and the Infinite would thus collapse into a border within the finite. All comings to pass would be from one finite entity to another. At a finite border, therefore, which as such differentiates nothing, there can be no 'coming without *pas*'; here, *pace* Derrida, events are not even impossible.

Second, by contrast, the impossible happens, finitude is Infinitely created, when, as Augustine says, it is *known* by the Infinite to be *right* for the finite to begin or end, a decision which, because logically prior to the finite, is not the logical outcome of it. 'Knowledge' of these limits, then, as not conditioned upon or derived from any premises, is not a cognitive knowledge. Knowledge here is decision and judgment.

Finally, if the finite exists as finite only when it is known or recognized (judged) as such by the Infinite, then, in itself, the finite is not finite. The creation of finite space and time, to return to our example, cannot be accounted for within space and time because any space or time designated as the origin would simply be one more space and time that themselves would need to be accounted for, thereby creating, ironically (an irony which exists only for the Infinite), an infinite regress. Within itself, then, the finite never comes to an end, it goes on *ad infinitum*, indefinitely. The indefinite, it is evident here, is merely a(n) (in)version of the finite. It is the Infinite, on the contrary, not the indefinite, which is truly other than the finite, and is so, paradoxically, precisely through having knowledge of limits. The finite, conversely, contradicting its law of non-contradiction, knows no limits. Without limits, none of its paths are blocked; the finite knows no aporias. Because the finite extends or distends indefinitely, from within the finite it is not possible to conceive of anything other than it: nothing exceeds the finite. From within the finite, therefore, it is not even possible to say, with Derrida, there is nothing outside of the text. An aporia is by de-finition Infinite: that is, an aporia presupposes the recognition of limits.

What does it mean to recognize a limit? I have suggested that the finite's limits consist essentially in pre-venting it from recognizing its limits. Paradoxically, then, to recognize a limit would have to consist, as Derrida, following Hegel, argues, in somehow being beyond the limit.[10] The Infinite, as the privileged knower of limits, would thus have to reside, *para*-doxically, on *both sides* of its border. That is,

Infinitude would demand, not that the infinite overflow the limits of the finite, as both Levinas and Derrida maintain, but that both sides of a border be Infinite. Again, one finite side would render both sides identically finite and thus without definition. Without a differing and deferring border between them – without differ*a*nce – both sides lose their difference from each other and their identities. To recognize a limit, then, would be to recognize another Infinite, the Infinite Other, an-Other Infinite Other, who also recognizes a limit. Two Infinites, then, at least. A true aporia, therefore, true difference (differ*a*nce) could only exist within the mutual, although not circular or exchangeable, recognition of two Infinites.

The structure I am developing here, through Derrida but also against Derrida, is one where reciprocity is not the annulment of the aporetic in-coming of the infinite Other but, rather, where this advent, the only true event there is, occurs according to a logic of para-dox, of side-by-side-ness and face-to-face-ness, and in this sense is reciprocal. It is not for fear of aporia or paradox that I resist configuring the relation to the Other as the relation of the finite to the infinite; it is, on the contrary, for fear that this latter configuration neutralizes the paradox inherent in the relation to the Other. It is not paradoxical that the finite cannot comprehend, in totality, the infinite – that is a geometrical axiom. What is paradoxical and aporetic is that, in order for you to be other than me without simply being another me or inversion of me, that is, in order for you to be beyond my limits and not subsumed within the indefinite replication of my finitude and myself, it is requisite that I not be finite. If I am finite, you don't stand a chance: I *will* make you an indefinite version of me; my finitude will confine you – finitude can do nothing else. The paradox is that you, the Other, are only the Infinite Other so long as I, too, am Infinite. You are beyond my limits only if I am not confined by my own. The relation with the Other, then, certainly calls me out of myself, but not because, previously, as finite, I was confined within myself: one cannot take a step (*pas*) across a finite border into the Infinite; the Infinite cannot step across a finite border to be received by the finite. On the contrary, here is the paradox: I can only be called out of myself if I am already Infinite. But again this cannot mean that I am somehow Infinite prior to your approach, for to be beyond one's limit *is* to recognize the Other beyond one's limit, which means that I cannot be Infinite without you or prior to you. Again, here is the paradox: I am not Infinite without you, and yet, unless I am Infinite, there can be no relation with you. If you are Infinite, *which you must be* if you are not simply to be another me, then I must be Infinite. Thus my Infinitude does not mean that I am the only being, the only entity (*ens*), there is; Infinitude is not ontological, as Levinas and Derrida would understand this term.[11] Rather, if I am not to be the only being, if there is to be ethics, then I must be Infinite. For if I am Infinite, then you, paradoxically, are necessarily Infinite, too. If there is to be even one Infinite, then there must be at least two Infinites.

This structure, I would now like to show, is precisely the one that Augustine uncovers in the doctrine of the Trinity. The grounding paradox of the doctrine, of course, is that one God is simultaneously three persons (the Father, the Son and the Holy Spirit), and that the three are 'of one and the same substance and essence'

(Augustine, 1991, p. 67). In *The Trinity*, attempting to make sense of this paradox, Augustine says that whatever '[God] is called with reference to itself', for instance, infinite or omnipresent, 'is said substance-wise', and that 'whatever [God] is called with reference to another [Father, Son or Holy Spirit] is said not substance-[wise] but relationship-wise'. Thus, when we talk, for instance, about God the Father in distinction to the Son of God, we are not making ontological claims about the substances or predicates of each: the Father's substance and predicates are not different from the Son's substance and predicates. For, according to the doctrine, the three persons are 'of the same substance and essence', and therefore whatever is said or predicated about the substance of each is said and predicated about the substance of all: 'Thus the Father is God and the Son is God and the Holy Spirit is God ... and yet we say that this supreme triad is not three Gods but one God' (ibid., bk.V, p. 195). As one substance, God is, therefore, not any more or less God as any one of the persons than he is as any of the other.[12] The Trinity herein maintains difference without hierarchy.

Despite insisting on the ontological identity of the three persons, however, the doctrine of the Trinity also insists on the radical relational difference between the three persons. Thus while, ontologically speaking, the Father, the Son and the Holy Spirit are all equally God, relationally speaking, it is not permissible to ascribe a single identity to each person. Augustine writes:

> If ... what is called Father were called so with reference to itself and not to the Son, and what is called Son were called so with reference to itself and not to the Father, the one would be called Father and the other Son substance-wise [that is, ontologically]. But since the Father is only called so because he has a Son, and the Son only called so because he has a Father, these things are not said substance-wise, as neither is said with reference to itself but only with reference to the other. (Ibid., bk.V, ch.1, p. 192)

Thus, even though Father and Son are not substantially different, in terms of their relation to each other, they are by no means the same. One person cannot serve the function of both; no one is superfluous.

Augustine brings to light the aporias inherent in this non-ontological difference through an analysis of the sendings (*missa*, missions) of Christ. Now Augustine knows that, where the Father and the Son are ontologically identical while *at the same time* relationally different, 'the first thing ... to ask is where the Son was sent *from* and where *to*'. Citing John 16:28, he claims that the 'being sent' of the Son is the Son's 'going forth from the Father and coming into this world'. But then, citing John 1:10, wherein 'the world was made through [the Word/Son]', Augustine concludes that 'where he was sent to is where he already was' (ibid., p. 101), which leads Augustine to ask, 'what can really be meant by this sending?' (ibid., p. 102). Would this tautological and circular exchange not simply neutralize and annul the mission? Augustine does not think so.

For Augustine, the Christ-event can only be meaningful if it maintains this aporia, that is, if the point of arrival (the Son on earth) is ontologically identical to the point of departure (the Father in heaven), while, nevertheless, maintaining that the two points are relationally different. If this difference were not maintained, if there were only a single point or person, in which case there would be no need to distinguish between substance and relation, then, as a single point, the Christ on earth (who would not now be a Son) would be, in himself and by himself, God – that is, God would then be reduced (de-limited, con-fined) to being nothing other than a single and particular person who lived at such and such a time in such and such a place. His substance, in other words, could not be separated from his particular locus. The nature of a particular person would have become the nature of God. Such a local god, clearly, could not be the atopical God who creates space and time in the beginning. To confine the Infinite God to a single position results in making God finite. It follows, therefore, that if God is to be Infinite, then Infinitude cannot be confined to a single position.

The missions of the Trinity, therefore, must maintain a double movement (moment). While relationship-wise the mission moves from Father to Son and so presupposes a deferring limit, substance-wise (ontologically) the mission is from God to God, 'from eternity to eternity' (1991, p. 172) and, therefore, without *pas*. No relation, therefore, without ontological identity; no ontology without relational difference; without their simultaneity, no aporia. It is as with *and* without limit (which is *not* the same as saying, as finite and infinite), as relational *and* ontological, respectively, that God is Infinite. As Augustine writes, 'Those three seem both to be bounded or determined by each other, and yet in themselves to be unbounded or infinite' (ibid., p. 213).

Now what about that other mission, the 'ad-mission' which is the meaning of *fateri*, the Latin root of *con-fessio*, and which is sent *from* Augustine the confessant creature *to* God the confessor–creator? Are the differences within this mission – between confessant creature and confessor–creator, between self and wholly Other – to be understood substance-wise or relationship-wise? Augustine immerses himself in this very issue in Book XII of *The City of God*, where, in one of the most stunning passages in the corpus of theology, he attempts to determine the nature of the relationship between the creator and the creature. He writes,

> as I dare not say that there ever was a time when the Lord God was not Lord, so I ought not to doubt that man had no existence before time [since God created all things].... But when I consider what God would be the Lord of, if there was not always some creature, I shrink from making any assertion. (1993, bk.XII, ch.15, p. 395)

Even though Augustine will not say everything in this passage, he has already said enough for us to conclude that it is inconceivable for there to be a creator without a creature. God cannot be God all alone. And yet, since, according to the logic of their relationship, it is the creator who creates the creature and not the other way around, the creator must exist first. Thus, as Augustine sums up the aporia (the same aporia, notice, from the opening of the *Confessions*), 'He was before [his creatures], though at no time without them.' But, as Augustine has already demonstrated in his reading of Genesis 1:1 in the *Confessions*, God's precedence is not spatial or temporal, that is, finite. '[God] preceded them,' Augustine therefore reasons, 'not by lapse of time, but by his abiding eternity' (ibid., p. 397). But if God is not before the creature in time, which would make God temporal (finite), then the creature cannot be after God in time, either, for that would also position God before the creature in time. It therefore follows that the creature who is in relation with the creator must not be conceived temporally either. Despite what Augustine says in the passages surrounding these, the creature in relation with the creator must be co-eternal with it. To appropriate the distinction from *The Trinity*, while creator and creature must be understood to be relationally different, they must be substantially the same. If they were not, then the creator would be before the creature in time, which would render the creator finite. If the creator is to be Infinite, then the creature must be Infinite, too.

As I have tried to argue, in order for God to be the Infinitely Other, God must be the *other* Infinite, not simply the other *of me*, not simply the negative in(de)finite of my finitude, but Infinitely Other to my own proper Infinitude. Infinitude is my property only because, paradoxically, impossibly, improperly, *at the same time* it is not only my property. If Infinitude were not my property, it could neither be possible nor impossible (in Derrida's sense) for it to be anyone else's, including God's. Thus, if there is to be even one Infinite, there must be more than one Infinite. '[I]t is always necessary to be more than one in order to speak,' Derrida says at the opening of '*Sauf le nom*', 'and par excellence ... when it's a matter of God' (1995, p. 35). But this plurality cannot be two things of different substance, for in that case speech or confession would not be possible – not because it is impossible, but because it is not impossible. I repeat: in order for there to be an Infinite Other, it must be the other Infinite. *Tout autre est – un autre*, I add – *tout autre*.

Notes

1. Kierkegaard (1962, p. 352).
2. 'the constancy of God in my life is called by other names, so that I quite rightly pass for an atheist' (Derrida, 1993a, p. 155).
3. See also *Given Time*: 'In order for there to be gift, gift event, some "one" has to give some "thing" to someone other' (Derrida, 1992a, p. 11)
4. See, in this regard, Derrida (1982); also *Aporias*: 'No context can determine meaning to the point of exhaustiveness' (1993b, p. 9).
5. 'Perhaps nothing ever comes to pass except on the line of a transgression' (Derrida, 1993b, p. 33).
6. Aristotle: 'a definition is a posit (for the arithmetician posits that a unit is what is quantitatively indivisible [that is, finite])' (*Posterior Analytics*, bk.I, 72a21–2, p. 116).
7. '[T]here is no demonstration of that of which there is definition' (ibid., 90b29). That is to say, definitions are *in*-demonstrable; conversely, demonstrations are, by themselves, *in*-definite, because without a definition (first principle) to put an end (*telos, fin*) to the chain of demonstration, the demonstration will, as a result, proceed *ad infinitum*. See *Posterior Analytics*, bk.I, 82b37–84b2.
8. One should also look, in this regard, at Hegel's repeated use of a that–what distinction; for instance: 'the immediate knowing of God is only supposed to extend to *that* God is, not *what* God is; for the latter would be a cognition [in distinction to the former which, therefore, is not] and would lead to mediated knowing' (*The Encyclopaedia Logic*, §73; 1991, p. 120).
9. As Descartes said, by naming things indefinite 'we merely acknowledge in a *negative way* [*via negativa*] that any limits which they may have cannot be discovered by us' (*The Principles of Philosophy*, Pt.I, 27, 1984, p. 202; emphasis added).
10. For a discussion of Hegel's and Derrida's relation on this point, see Gasché (1986), and Hobson (1998, pp. 55ff).

11. For a different reading of the history of ontology, see Brayton Polka, Chapter 1 of the present volume, as well as his *Truth and Interpretation: An Essay in Thinking* (1990).
12. Despite using what we today would refer to as ontological language, Augustine insists that, properly speaking, God is not a substance:

> The word [subsist] is rightly used for ordinary things which provide subjects for those things that are said to be in a subject [that is, predicates], like color or shape in a body. Thus body subsists, and is therefore substance; but those things are in the subsisting, in the subject or underlying body, and so they are not substances, but in substance. ... But if God subsists in such a way that he can properly be called substance, then something is in him as in its underlying subject. ... But it is impious to say that God subsists to and underlies his goodness, and that goodness is not his substance, or rather his being, nor is God his goodness, but it is in him as in an underlying subject. So it is clear that God is improperly called substance. (1991, bk.V, ch.3, pp. 226–7)

References

Aristotle (1984), *The Complete Works of Aristotle* (ed.) J. Barnes, Princeton: Princeton University Press.

Augustine (1991), *The Trinity*, trans. E. Hill, Brooklyn: New City Press.

Augustine (1992), *Confessions*, trans. H. Chadwick, New York: Oxford University Press.

Augustine (1993), *The City of God*, trans. M. Dods, New York: Random House.

Derrida, Jacques (1982), 'Signature Event Context', in *Margins of Philosophy*, trans. A. Bass, Chicago: University of Chicago Press.

Derrida, Jacques (1989), 'Psyche: Inventions of the Other', in L. Waters and W. Godzich (eds), *Reading De Man Reading*, Minneapolis: University of Minnesota Press.

Derrida, Jacques (1992a), *Given Time: I. Counterfeit Money*, trans. P. Kamuf, Chicago: University of Chicago Press.

Derrida, Jacques (1992b), 'How to Avoid Speaking: Denials', in Harold Coward and Toby Foshay (eds), *Derrida and Negative Theology*, New York: SUNY.

Derrida, Jacques (1993a), 'Circumfession', in Geoffrey Bennington and Jacques Derrida (eds), *Jacques Derrida*, Chicago: University of Chicago Press.

Derrida, Jacques (1993b), *Aporias*, trans. T. Dutoit, Stanford: Stanford University Press.

Derrida, Jacques (1995), '*Sauf le nom*', in Thomas Dutoit (ed.), *On the Name*, Stanford: Stanford University Press.

Derrida, Jacques (1999), 'A Word of Welcome', in *Adieu to Emmanuel Levinas*, trans. P.-A. Brault and M. Naas, Stanford: Stanford University Press.

Descartes, René (1984), *Principles of Philosophy*, trans. Valentine Rodger Miller and Reese P. Miller, Dordrecht: Reidel.

Descartes, René (1985), *The Philosophical Writings of Descartes*, vol. I, trans. J. Cottingham, W.A. Suchting and H.S. Harris, Cambridge: Cambridge University Press.

Gasché, Rodolphe (1986), 'Nontotalization Without Spuriousness: Hegel and Derrida on the Infinite', *The Journal of the British Society for Phenomenology*, **17** (3), October, 289–307.

Hegel, G.W.F. (1991), *The Encyclopaedia Logic*, trans. T. Geraets *et al.*, Indianapolis: Hackett Publishing Company.

Hobson, Marian (1998), *Jacques Derrida: Opening Lines*, New York: Routledge.

Kierkegaard, Søren (1962), *Works of Love*, trans. H. Hong and E. Hong, Toronto: Harper Torchbooks.

Pascal, Blaise (1965), *Selections from The Thoughts*, trans. A. Beattie, Arlington Heights: Harlan Davidson.

Polka, Brayton (1990), *Truth and Interpretation: An Essay in Thinking*, New York: St Martin's Press.

II
SEXUAL DIFFERENCE

Chapter 4

Beyond Belief: Sexual Difference and Religion after Ontotheology

Ellen T. Armour[1]

Traditionally, theology and philosophy of religion have served as guardians of belief. By subjecting particular beliefs to rational scrutiny, they provide support for those beliefs that survive the light of reason and reject those that do not. The relationship between faith and philosophy cuts differently in recent engagements between religion and continental philosophy.[2] Rather than offering the means for adjudicating and refining religion's truth, philosophy is frequently deemed the primary source of religion's infection by ontotheology. Under the guise of aiding belief, philosophy has led religion astray by providing only the false idols of ontotheological gods. Indeed, Jean-Luc Marion suggests that the so-called 'death of God' is a boon to Christianity rather than a bane. Philosophy's god has died, says Marion, making room for the (re)emergence of the true god of faith. Rather than a god whose being is in question, this god is as pure gift, as self-giving love made manifest in the Eucharist (properly administered by priests in proper relationship to the ecclesiastical hierarchy).[3]

The reading I will offer here of two essays – Irigaray's 'Belief Itself'[4] and Derrida's 'Circumfession'[5] – will call into question this tendency to limit ontotheology's reach to philosophy and to reason. I will argue that, like philosophy, belief exhibits symptoms of sexual (and racial) *in*difference, which are central to the text of metaphysics, as I have argued elsewhere.[6] Through reading these two texts together, I hope to show that sexual difference reshapes and reframes our vision of what might come after ontotheology.

Luce Irigaray on Religion and Sexual Difference

Understanding the role that religion plays in Irigaray's work requires some sense of the aim of her work as a whole. Beginning with her first book on philosophy, *Speculum of the Other Woman*, Irigaray has relentlessly exposed sexual *in*difference as the heart of our cultural economy or grammar (Irigaray, 1985). Symptoms of sexual indifference appear in our culture's primary discourse of sexual subjectivity (psychoanalysis), in the discourse that attempts to articulate what is fundamental to reality (philosophy) and in the discourse of economic liberation (Marxism). Through often dazzling readings of texts central to these traditions, Irigaray exposes the cultural economy's repeated attempts to 'fix' woman in her place: a place that denies her speech, subjectivity and rights *as* a woman even as it uses her as a resource to sustain culture.

Irigaray is not content simply to expose the inner workings of sexual indifference. She also wants to enable genuine sexual alterity to come into being. This will make possible genuine relations between women and women (mothers/daughters, friends, lovers) and women and men (mothers/sons, friends, lovers). Women must come into their own *as women*, not as men's others who reflect them back to themselves as they would like to believe they are.

Religion plays a central role in both sides of Irigaray's project. Religious sites exhibit the symptoms of the disease of sexual indifference that Irigaray diagnoses. At the same time, Irigaray often turns to religious motifs when she invokes possible passages to a future economy of sexual difference. Irigaray finds resources within the Christian tradition that contain traces of sexual difference.

Both sides of Irigaray's work with religion appear in 'Belief Itself'. Written for a colloquium at Cérisy-la-Salle on Derrida's essay, 'The Ends of Man',[7] 'Belief Itself' explores a link Irigaray sees between the presenting problem of one of her analysands and Derrida's analysis of Freud's *Beyond the Pleasure Principle* (1961) in *The Post Card* (1987). Irigaray's analysand presents her with a religious problem, reporting that, at the moment during the Eucharist when the priest intones the words of institution, she bleeds. Two additional facts heighten the strangeness of this situation. Irigaray's analysand is not present at the Mass when the bleeding occurs. Moreover, she claims not to believe in the dogmas of the Catholic church (though she 'loves the son', Irigaray writes elliptically). In a move reminiscent of Freud's *Totem and Taboo* (1962), Irigaray reads this incident as symptomatic of cultural dynamics. She suggests that her analysand's experience witnesses to a sacrifice of woman/matter/nature hidden beneath the sacrifice of the son explicitly commemorated in the Eucharist. As Irigaray's *œuvre* shows over and over again, the maternal sacrifice is enacted and re-enacted throughout the fabric of our culture (in families, in the value assigned to women in our economy, in philosophical texts, and so on). Yet complex mechanisms (psychoanalytic and otherwise) obscure its face.

Belief turns out to be one of those mechanisms. As Irigaray notes, belief by definition (and as opposed to confidence or fidelity) presupposes a denial of the real. Belief asserts an account of what is in spite of what appears to be real. In order to work, the real must remain hidden from view. In this case, the sacrifice of the maternal body (that the eucharistic sacrifice simultaneously commemorates and covers over) must be obscured in order for the sacrificial economy that it sustains to function.[8] Neither the sacrificial economy nor belief, however, resides solely within the religious realm; rather, the sacrificial economy *is* our cultural economy, which is structured and sustained by belief. For this reason, Irigaray argues, an inquiry into belief itself is crucial to any inquiry into sexual difference. Hence the link between her analysand's experience and *The Post Card*.

Among the many scenes of (mis)communication that *The Post Card* discusses is Freud's famous analysis of the *fort/da* game played by his grandson, Ernst. The game consists of physical and verbal actions. The little boy tosses a spool on a string onto a curtained bed and then pulls it out again. When the spool disappears, Ernst says 'o-o-o-o' (an approximation of 'Fort', 'away/lost/gone'). When it reappears, Ernst says, 'Da' ('there'). Freud concludes that the repetitive game is the little boy's attempt to handle his frustration at his mother's comings and goings. The game commemorates the child's 'great cultural achievement – the instinctual renunciation (that is, the renunciation of instinctual satisfaction) which he had made in allowing his mother to go away without protesting' (Freud, *Beyond the Pleasure Principle*, p. 14).

As Derrida reads this episode in *The Post Card*, the narrative and the game open onto an abyssal set of mirrors that reveal multiple *fort/da* games played by multiple subjects, including Freud himself – as founder of psychoanalysis and as a family man (father, grandfather, husband and son). These specular reflections are set in motion by the figure of the mother/daughter which occupies the (mute) centre of *Beyond the Pleasure Principle*, published in 1920, the same year in which Freud's daughter, Sophie (who is Ernst's mother) died of influenza. Sophie's death leaves a series of traces – implicit and explicit – in this text, as Derrida reads it. In a footnote added to his account of the *fort/da* game after Sophie's death, Freud connects the game to the way Sophie's son (now almost six) handled his mother's death. 'Now that she was really "gone" ("o-o-o") the little boy showed no signs of grief' (*Beyond the Pleasure Principle*, p. 16, n.7). Some of Freud's contemporaries used the connection between Sophie's death, this autobiographical episode, and the timing of *Beyond the Pleasure Principle*'s publication to challenge psychoanalysis's claim to scientific status. In *The Post Card*, Derrida returns to the question of autobiography and psychoanalysis in *Beyond the Pleasure Principle*, but in a very different vein. He, too, argues for a connection between Sophie's death and the text through a pairing of grandson and grandfather. The observing eye of Freud-the-scientist is also the specular mirror in which numerous reflections and refractions of Freud-the-family-man appear. Reflected in Freud-the-scientist's account of the son's displacement of the work of mourning his mother, Derrida finds the father's displacement of the work of mourning his daughter. Reflected in Freud-the-scientist's account of Ernst's jealousy towards his brother (Freud links Ernst's lack of grief to this additional cause) is Freud-the-family-man's jealousy of his daughter's husband. These ever-expanding circles ripple into the future, as well, towards the anticipated death of Freud's mother, towards his anticipation of his own death, towards the death of Ernst's brother (Freud's favourite grandson) and, through him, backward in time towards the death of Freud's brother, Julius.

Derrida's interest, however, does not lie in Freud's psychobiography. Rather than calling into question the text's legitimacy as a scientific contribution, the connection between Freud and little Ernst calls forth a rethinking of the relationship between autobiography and psychoanalysis; indeed, a rethinking of the auto-biographical (the links between *autos*, *bios/thanatos*, and *graphos*) itself.[9] Irigaray's reading highlights particular figures that shed important light on connections between the dynamics just described and questions of ontotheology, religion and sexual difference.

Irigaray sees significant links between this game, its place in psychoanalytic theory, and her analysand's experience. She notes a commonality between Sophie's role in the *fort/da* game (and Freud's account of it) and her analysand's relationship to the Eucharist. Like Sophie, the age of Irigaray's analysand positions her as both mother and daughter. Just as Sophie's absence is crucial to the ritual of the *fort/da* game and Freud's account of it, so the bleeding woman's absence from the scene of the actual performance of the mass is central to its success. In both cases, though, the (unremarked) presence of female figures makes the ritual possible. The elements that circulate in the Eucharistic ritual are body and blood, bread and wine – elements marked as female by our cultural grammar. Their connection to the maternal body is, then, peculiarly present and absent.

The veil or curtain around Ernst's bed through which he tosses his spool occupies a similar (non)place of presence/absence in Freud's description of the *fort/da* game. As Irigaray notes, the veil is simply background in Freud's account. He fails to take account of its texture, its colour, or the degree of its opacity. Yet without the veil/curtain, there would be no disappearance/reappearance, and no *fort/da* game. In fact, within the figure of the veil lies the key to an even more deeply hidden subtext of the *fort/da* game. The veil rises on a yet more primordial loss common to both grandson and grandfather, the loss of their original dwelling place, the maternal body. At a deeper level, Irigaray argues, it is this gift without return (uncompensated and gone forever) that the game seeks to master rather than to mourn. It is this same gift that funds the Eucharist, and to which Irigaray's analysand witnesses without knowing it.

So far, my account of Irigaray's reading of this scene has uncovered thematic similarities to her analysis of her analysand's experience: that is, both the *fort/da* game and the Eucharist cover over and commemorate the loss of female figures. However, Irigaray argues that belief *itself* – not just this particular *content* – plays a structural role in both rituals. Belief's role in the Eucharistic feast is perhaps too obvious to need comment. But Irigaray finds belief at work in little Ernst's game and in Freud's narrative of it. Ernst believes that the ritual of the *fort/da* game grants him mastery over his mother's presence and absence. And he believes it *because* it is not true. Belief plays a central role in what stands in for mourning. Ernst believes that he has mastered his mother's presence and absence, his own presence and absence, indeed, the dynamics of life and death themselves (indicated by his lack of grief at his mother's death).

Theorizing belief as a source of compensation and/or escape from the pains and sufferings of life and death is nothing new. Indeed, such views are arguably hallmarks of modernity's view of religion. Each major hermeneut of suspicion (Marx, Freud, Nietzsche) offers different versions of it. But Irigaray's account is distinctive on several fronts, especially in relationship to questions about what comes after ontotheology. Whereas Freud and Marx advocate the triumph of the secular over the religious, Irigaray challenges that very division itself. She is, of course, hardly proposing a return to a traditional sacramentalism of any sort. Rather, she exposes the presence of one of Western religion's structuring concepts, belief, in a setting that thinks it has outgrown religion. Ironically, given Freud's desire that psychoanalysis be regarded as a science, Irigaray argues that the entire account rests on belief for its validity. The boy's naïve belief serves as the guarantee of Freud's scientific account and of its appeal to Freud's readers, who must believe Freud's account of the boy's naïveté in order to find Freud's analysis persuasive. Moreover, her account suggests that psychoanalysis and Christianity share the same (effaced) object of belief, the maternal body. Irigaray's claim goes even farther. Psychoanalysis and Christianity may offer particularly clear views of the obscured female sacrifice and the unmourned maternal body, but such altars and crypts are not limited to these sites. Psychoanalysis and religion are symptomatic of a larger context, the cultural imaginary. Rather than being confined to discrete cultural arenas, Irigaray's analysis suggests that belief structures our cultural imaginary.

'Belief Itself' suggests that faith *per se* – and Christian faith, in particular – is also circumscribed by ontotheology, which challenges Marion's claims for the Eucharistic god. As I noted earlier, phallocentrism, logocentrism and ontotheology go together; thus failure to escape from one calls into question claims that one has escaped from the others. If, underneath explicit invocations of a paternal sacrifice of a son lies an unacknowledged and unmourned maternal sacrifice, phallocentrism extends to the very heart of Christian faith. The death of philosophy's god may reopen access (if it was ever really lost) to the god of Christian faith, as Marion claims, but that god as invoked by Marion is still inscribed within the circuit of phallocentrism, logocentrism and ontotheology. Access to this (masculine) god's self-giving love comes through the chain of fathers and sons that stand in for him and through whose hands circulate the (feminine) elements of the Eucharistic feast.

This is not to suggest that we are now bereft of any route beyond ontotheology. Nor does it mean that religion – Christian or otherwise – cannot survive without ontotheology. Irigaray's exposure of the truth of belief in 'Belief Itself' shifts attention away from theological or philosophical abstractions to the material realm of rituals and bodies, material practices and their symbolic meanings. If belief works only as long as the underlying dynamics that fund it remain hidden, what will happen when those dynamics are exposed and explored? What if, rather than covering up the maternal sacrifice, the pains of life and death, and one's mourning for the maternal body, one were to render these themes explicit? Could these resources traditionally mined without acknowledgment for ontotheological support actually go elsewhere? And would that 'elsewhere' be religious in any sense? When read with the texts and issues discussed so far in mind, Derrida's 'Circumfession' offers a provocative and suggestive perspective on these questions.

Circumfession

Derrida's quasi-autobiographical essay, 'Circumfession', is his contribution to a book entitled *Jacques Derrida*. 'Circumfession' serves as a countertext to the main text in this volume, an essay by Geoffrey Bennington entitled 'Derridabase' that purports to give a systematic account of Derrida's thinking. In a sense, the two texts stage a battle over the proper ownership of 'Jacques Derrida'. I describe this battle as staged for a number of reasons. First of all, as both Bennington and Derrida acknowledge, *Jacques Derrida* is as much a labour of love between friends as it is a contest. Second, the relationship between this project and its supposed subject/object, the 'real' Jacques Derrida, is problematic at best. As I will note below, 'Circumfession' seems designed to obscure as much as it reveals about its author. As Bennington notes in 'Acts of Genre', the *bio*graphical text that concludes *Jacques Derrida*, the versions of Derrida's life produced between these covers are particular to the context of this project. Other contexts would have produced other lives with their own tangled relationship to their purported subject. Similar dynamics attend Bennington's relationship to *Jacques Derrida*. As a protagonist/antagonist of this project, the author of 'Derridabase' is also a product of this collaboration. For this reason, I will follow their practice of referring to each other's textual personae by their initials (J.D. and G., respectively).

Religious figures populate the stage on which this battle takes place. In aiming to display a hidden (to the uninitiated, at least) logic within the raw material of J.D.'s thought, J.D. accuses G. of playing God. G. knows J.D.'s past, his present and – since the logic of 'Derridabase' implies a predictive power – perhaps even his future as well or better than J.D. himself. To resist G.'s ontotheological project, J.D. appropriates a religious classic, Augustine's *Confessions*, as the template for his countertext. At first glance, the two confessions – and their authors – seem polar opposites. Augustine was a devout Christian, J.D. an ostensibly secular Jew. Augustine embraced and took refuge in an ontotheological metaphysic, the very monolithic structure whose boundaries J.D. seeks to disrupt and escape. The *Confessions* mixes prayer, autobiographical narrative and philosophical analysis, all designed to lead the reader towards the one true God. 'Circumfession' seeks to mix prayers, tears and blood, J.D. writes. Rather than guiding its readers towards a singular conclusion, its stream-of-consciousness style and periphrastic organization leaves them rudderless in a relentless sea of run-on sentences and fragmentary musings.

Yet at least two important similarities bind these two texts together. Both Augustine and J.D. employ the artifice of autobiography for larger, although antithetical, purposes. Augustine tells the story of his life to illustrate divine providence, while J.D. turns to self-revelation to contest a teleological agenda. Both authors' mothers are central to their texts and to their larger purposes. Augustine's mother serves as key witness to the working out of the divine teleology. J.D.'s mother provides the means through which J.D. resists G.'s teleological agenda. J.D. surprises G. with what surprises him, what eludes his control; namely, the slow deterioration and impending death of his mother.

At about the time that J.D. begins 'Circumfession', Georgette Derrida suffers a stroke. Her debilitation and lengthy dying process plays a centrifugal role in 'Circumfession' by prompting J.D. into a chain of reflections set in motion by grief, loss and guilt. The stroke has robbed Georgette of her subjectivity and reduced her to little more than body. Most of the time, she no longer knows him, J.D. reports. But J.D.'s grief for his mother is nothing new, it turns out. He grieves as much for what never existed between them as for what used to be. Georgette may rarely recognize him now, but she seems to have hardly known him before. He searches for the letters and notes that he sent her faithfully over the years, and finds almost none of them. It is as though, like the *Envois* in *The Post Card*, they never arrived.

The link between J.D.'s grief for his mother and his writing runs even deeper, however. The loss of the maternal body leaves behind a residual longing for the (m)other within the subject that renders self-enclosure impossible. J.D. is acutely aware of this otherness within himself. Indeed, he describes it as the source of his desire and compulsion to write. All of his work is an address to his (m)other. If so, these *envois*, like his personal notes to her, have also never arrived. According to J.D., Georgette never read a word of her son's work.

Where *Beyond the Pleasure Principle* obscures the relationship to the mother, J.D.'s account of anticipatory mourning exposes the effects of the current sacrificial economy that Irigaray analyses in 'Belief Itself' on the mother/son relationship. Within that economy, no genuine relationship between mother and son – no face-to-face relationship, as Irigaray says – is possible.[10] The mother serves as the silent sacrificial ground of the son's subjectivity and the resource for his work in the world. He serves as her imaginary but altogether unreal ideal.

I have argued elsewhere that Derrida's interventions in economies of sexual indifference from the masculine side make him a useful ally for feminism (see Armour, 1999). My reading of this text so far suggests that, in exposing these effects of the current sacrificial economy, 'Circumfession' performs this service once again. In this essay, however, I aim to show that sexual difference bears on the shape religion might take on the other side of ontotheology. To make that case, I need to turn my attention to another aspect of this text.

At the heart of 'Circumfession' lie two wounded bodies. Readers familiar with John Caputo's *Prayers and Tears* will already know that the figure of circumcision, which plays a central role in Caputo's account of Derrida's religion without religion, constitutes a major (dis)organizing figure within 'Circumfession'. J.D.'s text plays on circumcision's links with familiar Derridean thematics (truth as castration, the proper name), with religion (Judaism and anti-semitic Christianity) and with autobiography (J.D. and Judaism) – all themes discussed by Caputo. *Prayers and Tears* proves that approaching 'Circumfession' through this body-wound provides provocative access to the question of religion's place in Derrida's work. I want to focus on another bleeding and perforated body that also plays a central role within 'Circumfession', that of J.D.'s dying mother whose bedsores provide a constant *leitmotif* to her son's musings. The effects of this wounded body on the text take on particular interest when read in light of 'Belief Itself'.

Georgette Derrida's stroke has reduced her to little more than a body. Bedsores have turned her body into 'an archipelago of red and blackish volcanoes, enflamed wounds, crusts and craters, signifiers like wells several centimeters deep, opening here, closing there, on her heels, her hips and sacrum'. They turn Georgette inside out, in more ways than one. They uncover what usually remains hidden, 'the very flesh exhibited in its inside, no more secret, no more skin' (Derrida, 'Circumfession', p. 82). In place of an absent internality, they also signify. Because of the mental confusion caused by the stroke, Georgette cannot serve as reliable witness to her own bodily state. Her healthcare workers read the waxing and waning of her disintegration and decay through the state of her bedsores (and other bodily signs). In this sense, then, the bedsores substitute for her (always) lacking (by Irigaray's account of femininity) subjectivity.

When read in light of 'Belief Itself', Georgette's body turns 'Circumfession' into an exposé of the sacrificial economy. The reader will recall that Irigaray uncovers a maternal body at the core of the sacrificial economy. Both the Eucharist and the *fort/da* game obscure and commemorate the loss or sacrifice of female figures (mothers, daughters, maternal bodies). Both substitute belief in the achievement of mastery over absence and death for acknowledgment of loss. 'Circumfession', on the other hand, puts loss and mourning on display. J.D.'s mother's wounded body is central to that display. In following the trail blazed by his mother's body, J.D. uncovers its place within an economy of sacrifice. Like Irigaray's analysand, Georgette bleeds without knowing why and without suffering. It is up to another

(J.D.? Us?) to read that body's messages. Insofar as Georgette's wounds fund J.D.'s writing, 'Circumfession' continues to use the maternal body as a resource. J.D.'s authorial voice feeds on Georgette's soon-to-be-perpetual silence. Yet this is the sacrificial economy with a difference. Though Georgette's access to subjectivity remains forever blocked (leaving the problem of woman's subjectivity unaddressed), the wound at the heart of normative (masculine) subjectivity is laid bare. J.D. has not mastered this resource on which he draws or the loss that provides it. It is lack of mastery, not its achievement, that J.D. puts on display. Grief and loss are not overcome, but rather give rise to a series of abyssal compensations and losses that replicate rather than staunch the original wound.

Reading 'Circumfession' through 'Belief Itself' renders visible its interventions in a sacrificial economy in which the maternal body serves as a resource. What are the implications in this reading for religion on the other side of ontotheology?

Writing the Impossible

> I gave in to the counterexemplary thing – '*only write here what is impossible, that* ought *to be the impossible-rule*' (10–11/77), of everything G. can be expecting of me ... a supposedly idiomatic, unbroachable, unreadable, uncircumcised piece of writing, held not to the assistance of his father, as Socrates would say, but to my assistance at the death of a mother about whom I ask *to ti en einai* before witnesses. (Derrida, 1993, p. 194)

> Anyone who does not go down into the abyss can only repeat and retrace the ways already opened that cover over the trace of the vanished gods ... Beyond go ... those who give up their own will ... Light shines on them once they have agreed that nothing shall ensure their protection, not even that age-old citadel of man – being (*être*) – not even that guarantor of the meaning or nonmeaning of the world – God. These prophets know that if anything divine is still to come our way it will be won by abandoning all control, all language, and all sense already produced, it is through risk, only risk, leading no one knows where, announcing who knows what future, secretly commemorating who knows what past. No project here. Only this refusal to refuse what has been perceived, whatever distress or wretchedness may come of it. (Irigaray, 1993, pp. 51–3)

Another central theme that guides Caputo's *Prayers and Tears* is 'a certain passion for the impossible' (p. 285) crucial, according to Caputo, to Derrida's religion without religion. The name of God interests Derrida in part because of its links with impossibility. And yet Caputo asks whether God is not perhaps the most dangerous name for the impossible.[11] Is it, moreover, the only name for the impossible? These questions provide an opening through which my concluding remarks will pass. Following the figure of the dying mother through this impossible confession addressed to her takes the figure of impossibility beyond the gods of logocentrism, ontotheology and belief. As I noted at the outset, accounts of deconstruction's import for religion on the other side of ontotheology have tended to view ontotheology as a philosophical problem. If Christianity, for example, can jettison philosophy, it can retrieve its kernel of truth from its ontotheological husk. The reading of 'Circumfession' and 'Belief Itself' that I offer herein challenges that narrow definition of ontotheology and its relationship to belief. It also marks out a different path for religion after ontotheology. Readers familiar with Derrida's work will recall his discussion of writing in 'Plato's Pharmacy' (in Derrida, 1981, pp. 61–171). Writing's distance from a paternal origin – from a father who guarantees truth because his word is being – renders writing suspect in the Platonic scheme. Logocentrism, then, is caught up with a desire for mastery, an assertion of its accomplishment – if not by men, then by God. 'Belief Itself', however, has shown that logocentrism is not only a philosophical construct. The *fort/da* game and the Eucharist depend upon (faith in) the union of word and being for their efficacy.

To logocentrism, J.D. opposes a writing held to the figure of a dying mother whose connection between word and being (such as it was, in this economy) has been severed. J.D. aims to escape G.'s desire for mastery, not by engaging directly in a contest for (self-)control, but by writing what lies outside his – indeed, anyone's – control, namely, the ateleological but inevitable decay, decline and death of his mother. Submitting to the gravitational pull of this loss offers J.D. particular purchase on the ontotheological system he wishes to elude because the maternal body serves as this system's resource.

What does this suggest, then, not just about where ontotheology's traps lie, but about the (im)possibility of religion after ontotheology? Religion in the modern West has been predominately a matter of a vertical relationship between a normative (masculine) subject and his perfected mirror image (God). Grounded in belief in transcendence over death, the God/man relationship has been funded by the sacrifice of sexual alterity, which in turn sustains the economy of sameness that Western religion reflects.[12] 'Belief Itself' and 'Circumfession' call attention to the price paid by women and men – believers and non-believers alike – for participation in this economy. These essays also evoke the impossible possibility of breaking through this economy and the religion that sustains and reflects it towards another sacrality. Access to sacrality on the other side of ontotheology will not come without significant risk. 'Circumfession' suggests that working from the recognition of a primordial maternal sacrifice (rather than belief in a transcendent Father God) requires confrontation with pain and loss, not compensation for them. 'Belief Itself' depicts a vertiginous path into the unknown with only fragile figures (angels and roses) for company and without the consolation of belief. As Amy Hollywood argues, Irigaray is not asking readers to *believe* in angels, but to take the risk that these figures of immanent transcendence embody and enable (Hollywood). Irigaray invites us to risk self and substance in order to encounter alterity in each other and beyond. Such an undertaking is not for the faint of heart. Yet the intertwined future of religion and sexual difference lies with the lure of the (im)possible.[13]

Notes

1. An earlier (and more extended) version of this essay appears in *The Religious* (Caputo, 2001). My gratitude to Professor Caputo and to Blackwell for permission to use this material here.

2. See, for example, Lowe (1993), Winquist (1995), Caputo (1997), Marion, (1991).

3. The Eucharist also figures centrally in *After Writing: On the Liturgical Consummation of Philosophy* (1998), by Catherine Pickstock, a proponent of so-called 'radical orthodoxy'. As the antidote to modernism's nihilism (carried to its logical conclusion,

she argues, in Derrida and Levinas), she offers transubstantiation as the true source of all meaning. I will return to Pickstock's proposal later in this essay. I did not include her in my list above of scholars working on religion and continental philosophy because continental philosophers serve only as straw enemies for her. Pickstock's readings of Derrida and Levinas, in particular, are in my view unconscionable and irresponsible.

4. Luce Irigaray, 'Belief Itself', in *Sexes and Geneologies* (1993, pp. 23–53).
5. Jacques Derrida (1993).
6. In particular, see Armour (1999).
7. Jacques Derrida, 'The Ends of Man', in *Margins of Philosophy* (1982, pp. 109–36).
8. The implications of Irigaray's reading also troubles Pickstock's confidence in transubstantation as the ground of all meaning. Loading transubstantiation (which exemplifies a belief in Irigaray's sense, a denial of *prima facie* reality) with an all-or-nothing responsibility for all meaning truly courts nihilism. Meaning would seem to be possible only so long as (and only for those in whom) that belief can be sustained – a particularly problematic position when Irigaray's account suggests that the truth of the Eucharist is not what it appears to be, at first glance.
9. There are a number of interesting links between 'Freud's Legacy' and 'Circumfession' on the question of autobiography, life and death. The present essay cannot give those links the attention they deserve, though I do want to note that a similar pattern of displacements (deliberate, in this case) marks Derrida's text. His mother's imminent demise calls to mind past losses and evokes imagined future ones, including those of J.D.'s sons and, most significantly, his own.
10. Irigaray's point provides an interesting counterpoint to Freud's claim that the relationship between mother and son was the least ambivalent of all human relationships.
11. Amy Hollywood argues that this danger motivates Derrida's desire to distance himself from negative theology. See Hollywood (n.d.).
12. See Hollywood (1998) for a particularly cogent account of this claim.
13. My thanks to Amy Hollywood, Cynthia Marshall and Dee McGraw for their assistance.

References

Armour, Ellen T. (1997), 'Questions of Proximity: "Woman's Place" in Derrida and Irigaray', *Hypatia*, **12** (1), 63–78.

Armour, Ellen T. (1999), *Deconstruction, Feminist Theology, and the Problem of Difference: Subverting the Race/Gender Divide*, Chicago: University of Chicago Press.

Caputo, John D. (1997), *Prayers and Tears of Jacques Derrida: Religion without Religion*, Bloomington: Indiana University Press.

Caputo, John D. (ed.) (2001), *The Religious*, Oxford: Blackwell.

Derrida, Jacques (1981), *Dissemination*, trans. Barbara Johnson, Chicago: University of Chicago Press.

Derrida, Jacques (1982), *Margins of Philosophy*, trans. Alan Bass, Chicago: University of Chicago Press.

Derrida, Jacques (1987), *The Post Card: From Socrates to Freud and Beyond*, trans. Alan Bass, Chicago: University of Chicago Press.

Derrida, Jacques (1993), 'Circumfession', in Geoffrey Bennington and Jacques Derrida, *Jacques Derrida*, Chicago: University of Chicago Press, pp. 3–315.

Freud, Sigmund (1961), *Beyond the Pleasure Principle*, ed. and trans. James Strachey, New York: W.W. Norton.

Freud, Sigmund (1962), *Totem and Taboo: Some Points of Agreement Between the Mental*

Lives of Savages and Neurotics, trans. James Strachey, New York: W.W. Norton.

Hollywood, Amy (1994), 'Beauvoir, Irigaray, and the Mystical', *Hypatia*, **9** (4), 158–85.

Hollywood, Amy (1998), 'Deconstructing Belief: Irigaray and the Philosophy of Religion', *Journal of Religion*, **78** (2), 230–45.

Hollywood, Amy (n.d.), 'Apophasis and Ethics in the Early Derrida', MS. provided by author.

Irigaray, Luce (1985), *Speculum of the Other Woman*, trans. Gillian C. Gill, Ithaca, NY: Cornell University Press.

Irigaray, Luce (1993), *Sexes and Genealogies*, trans. Gillian C. Gill, New York: Columbia University Press.

Lowe, Walter (1993), *Theology and Difference: The Wound of Reason*, Bloomington: Indiana University Press.

Marion, Jean-Luc (1991), *God Without Being*, trans. Thomas Carlson, Chicago: University of Chicago.

Pickstock, Catherine (1998), *After Writing: On the Liturgical Consummation of Philosophy*, Oxford: Blackwell.

Winquist, Charles E. (1995), *Desiring Theology*, Chicago: University of Chicago Press.

Chapter 5

Towards a Feminist Philosophy of Ritual and Bodily Practice

Amy M. Hollywood

The recently emerging field of feminist philosophy of religion often appeals to continental philosophy, yet perhaps without sufficiently altering philosophy of religion's stated aims and intentions. Like traditional Anglo-American philosophies of religion, Pamela Sue Anderson's *A Feminist Philosophy of Religion* (1998), for example, focuses on belief and its justification, arguing that gender must become a crucial analytic category within accounts of the process of justification and, more centrally, that philosophical arguments grounded in feminist concerns must not only justify, but also evaluate, belief and its constitution. Grace Jantzen, in *Becoming Divine: Toward a Feminist Philosophy of Religion* (1999), moves further from Anglo-American analytic philosophy of religion, claiming that feminist philosophy of religion has different aims from 'traditional' Anglo-American philosophy of religion ('becoming divine' rather than the justification of belief), yet she also focuses her attention on 'religious discourse and the symbolic of which it is a part'. Again, the goal of feminist philosophy of religion is less to justify or to argue for the truth or falsity of these beliefs than to 'restructur[e] that myth in ways that foster human dignity – perhaps in ways that oblige and enable us to become divine' (Jantzen, 1999, p. 22). Hence questions of justification give place to questions of moral or political adequacy.

Anderson and Jantzen both address the issue of the 'truth' or 'objectivity' of belief, but crucial questions about these issues remain unanswered. Although both Anderson and Jantzen challenge the split between reason and desire that would render belief solely a matter of rational and conscious cognition (with Jantzen, I think, once again going further in this direction than Anderson), they remain on the level of the discursive, the symbolic or the mythic, giving little attention to the place of ritual and practice in religion. This is related to their somewhat unsatisfactory accounts of the ontological status of the objects of belief, an issue that must be asked in new ways if we take seriously the performative nature of much religious language and practice.[1]

This feminist work offers a crucial intervention within and critique of contemporary philosophies of religion, to which I intend the following as a supplement (with all the possibilities the Derridean use of that term implies). Here I will sketch a philosophical account of religious practice and ritual that challenges the continued subordination of practice to belief within much contemporary philosophy of religion. Against those social scientists who would discount the importance of meaning and belief to ritual, however, I have attempted to articulate a theory of the relationship between belief and practice grounded in the work of Marcel Mauss, Jacques Derrida and Judith Butler. Most importantly, I think it is crucial to recognize that, just as language can be a form of action, so too can actions be forms of signification. Given the more immediately bodily nature of ritual and other forms of religious practice, any philosophy of religion attendant to them will be forced to acknowledge and to theorize those differences inscribed in and on bodies (often through ritual and bodily practices themselves). Moreover, these tools will help us analyse why religion is such an important site for the inculcation of these bodily differences (raising important questions about the relationship between religious practice, belief and sexual – as well as other – differences).

Ritual understood as a specific kind of action or as action opposed to thought is, so Talal Asad, Catherine Bell and others argue, a modern Western concept. Asad uses entries in the *Encyclopedia Britannica* to argue for a fairly recent change in the understanding of ritual. Whereas the entries from 1771 to 1852 define ritual as a book containing the script for religious ceremonies, in the new entry for 1910, ritual is universalized and attention shifts from the script to the action itself. As Asad explains,

> [a] crucial part of every religion, ritual is now regarded as a type of routine behavior that symbolizes or expresses something and, as such, relates differentially to individual consciousness and social organization. That is to say, it is no longer a *script* for regulating practice but a type of practice that is interpretable as standing for some further *verbally definable*, but tacit, event (Asad, 1993, p. 57).

Crucial to this move is the claim that rituals as expressive serve some psychological or sociological function: they symbolize meanings that have their real field of operation within the realm of the mind or the social group. For Asad, the move is one from text to 'behavior, which is itself *likened* to a text', a text to be read by the anthropologist or historian of religion (Asad, 1993, p. 58).[2]

To this conception of ritual as symbolic action, Asad opposes an understanding of 'rites as apt performances' and 'disciplinary practices', a view he argues can be seen in medieval Christian conceptions of the monastic life.[3] Through an analysis of aspects of medieval monasticism, Asad argues that injunctions for the monastic life prescribe actions and rites 'directed at forming and reforming Christian dispositions' (Asad, 1993, p. 131). Asad's understanding of ritual as 'disciplinary practice' is indebted to the work of Michel Foucault, but also to that of the sociologist Marcel Mauss. To undermine further the modern distinction between symbolic and technical actions, he makes use of Mauss's conception of bodily techniques. According to Mauss, 'The body is man's first and most natural instrument. Or more accurately, not to speak of instruments, man's first and most natural technical object, and at the same time technical means, is his body' (Mauss, 1979, p. 104).

It is through bodily practices that subjectivities are formed, virtues inculcated and beliefs embodied. Mauss first introduced the notion of the *habitus* (probably best known from the work of Pierre Bourdieu) to describe the 'techniques and work of collective and individual practical reason' that shape embodied experience (Mauss,

1979, p. 101).

Unlike Mauss, Asad wishes to assimilate ritual, at least outside of the modern Western context, with bodily practices. Mauss, on the contrary, is interested in those bodily practices that are, he argues, shaped by cultural as well as biological and psychological factors, yet do not stand clearly within the realm of formalized, ritual or ceremonial activity. His analysis begins with the problem of what to do with those miscellaneous phenomena such as gait, athletic styles, manners of sleeping and eating, clothing, birth and nursing patterns, that are marked by cultural styles yet do not seem to warrant the designation of ritual. Asad suggests that, outside of the modern Western context, these kinds of regulated bodily activities are continuous with the more constrained activities of what we would call the ritual life.[4] Thus there is no clearly marked differentiation between symbolic and technical activities, but rather the distinction is between those activities (or aspects of activities) in which bodies are the objects and means of transformation and those in which other tools are employed to other ends.

Asad's assumption of the continuity between bodily practices and ritual actions is partially congruent with Catherine Bell's argument that historians of religion and anthropologists might usefully move away from a concept of ritual to one of ritualization. Bell avoids an unreflective identification of bodily practice with ritual, while refusing to define ritual as a static entity.

> Ritualization is fundamentally a way of doing things to trigger the perception that these practices are special. A great deal of strategy is employed simply in the degree to which some activities are ritualized and therein differentiated from other acts. While formalization and periodization appear to be common techniques for ritualization, they are not intrinsic to 'ritual' per se; some ritualized practices distinguish themselves by their deliberate informality, although usually in contrast to a known tradition or style of ritualization. Hence, ritual acts must be understood within a semantic framework whereby the significance of an action is dependent upon its place and relationship within a context of all other ways of acting: what it echoes, what it inverts, what it alludes to, what it denies. (Bell, 1992, p. 220).

Although the formalization of actions – their limitation to certain times, places, contexts, ritual agents – is one of the techniques used to mark off some practices as having a special significance within the life of the community, Bell insists that the ways in which ritualization occurs are specific to individual groups and communities; in other words, ritualization works and must be understood contextually (even if the total context can never be fully determined).

Bell also argues that ritualization, in giving special significance to certain practices, does so, not because these actions refer to or symbolize meanings external to them, but rather because, through the bodily practices of ritual life, social subjects and their relations are performed and engendered. Against common functionalist theories of ritual, which understand ritual as an attempt to forge social solidarity, to resolve conflict within the community, or to transmit shared beliefs, Bell argues that it involves 'the production of ritualized agents, persons who have an instinctive knowledge of these schemes embedded in their bodies, in their sense of reality, and in their understanding of how to act in ways that both maintain and qualify the complex microrelations of power' (Bell, 1992, p. 221). To questions about the relationship between ritualization and power, then, Bell argues that power and its dispositions are generated and regulated through rituals themselves, rather than lying outside as that which constrains or otherwise marks off these activities as special.

Bell's account of ritualization is consonant with an understanding of ritual drawn from Derrida's reading of J.L. Austin on performative speech acts. For both Bell and Derrida, ritual is like language, not because it is a text whose symbolic meanings must be uncovered or deciphered, but because rituals are actions that generate meanings in the specific context of other sets of meaningful actions and discourses. Meaning is generated through the iteration and differentiation of signs. Signs refer to other signs within the signifying chain rather than to external realities. Although linguistic signs can and do refer to extralinguistic realities as well as to other signs (a question Derrida seems to be concerned with in his recent work on names), in the realm of signifying actions (such as bodily practices and rituals) the distinction between signifying chain and external reality is more difficult to maintain. In other words, ritual actions are, not surprisingly, more like performative speech acts than like constatives. Utterances and actions are constitutive of and generate that to which they refer.[5]

But what precisely empowers the performative to constitute its subject? In J.L. Austin's account of the speech act, there is a tension between the claim that it is the conventionality of the speech act, like the conventionality of ritual, that gives force to the utterance and his suggestion that the utterance-source, the speaking or signing 'I', is the locus of force.[6] In 'Signature, Event, Context', Derrida exploits this ambiguity in Austin's texts in order to argue for a 'general theory' of the mark in which its force is tied to a conventionality, not of external circumstances, but of the mark itself (Derrida, 1982, pp. 307–33). For Derrida, all language takes on the character of the performative and of ritual.[7] In making this argument, Derrida associates Austin's attempt to tie the force of the performative to the speaking subject with his interest in intentionality as a condition for the correct use of the performative.[8]

Having cited Austin's claim that the possibilities for misfiring that haunt the performative are also endemic to all 'ritual or ceremonial, all *conventional* acts' (Austin, 1962, pp. 18–19), Derrida goes on to locate the specificity of Austin's claims and make his own generalization:

> Austin seems to consider only the conventionality that forms the *circumstances* of the statement, its contextual surroundings, and not a certain intrinsic conventionality of that which constitutes locution itself, that is, everything that might quickly be summarized under the problematic heading of the 'arbitrariness of the sign'; which extends, aggravates, and radicalizes the difficult. Ritual is not eventuality, but, as iterability, is a structural character of every mark. (Derrida, 1982, pp. 323–4)

Ritual as iterability, Derrida claims, is what marks the sign as communicative and performative. Key for Derrida is the iterability or repeatability of the sign; it is this reiterative structure, the fact that the sign is the same and yet also differs and defers (both from possible referents and from other signs) that marks its force (and its power of signification).

Butler argues that Derrida is interested in ritual only insofar as it serves as a useful analogy for his account of language as iteration. I would like to develop a version of that argument here, yet ultimately I will argue that more can be derived from Derrida's deployment of ritual than he himself may have intended. Embedded within Austin's notion of ritual is the understanding of social context and external constraints as intrinsic to the felicitous operation of its performance. Derrida reads Austin as equating context with intentionality (A and B, with Gamma);[9] it is in this light that Derrida points to the impossibility of ever fully determining context: 'For a context to be exhaustively determinable, in the sense demanded by Austin, it at least would be necessary for the conscious intention to be totally present and actually transparent to itself and others, since it is a determining focal point of the context' (Derrida, 1982, p. 326). Yet, arguably, this is precisely what is not required for ritual or conventional actions. Within ritual action the intentionality of the players is often unimportant to the force of the utterance. By focusing on Austin's sovereign 'I' as the focal point for contextualization, rather than on the question of who is speaking to whom and in what circumstances, in arguing that a condition of the mark is the absence of an empirical addressee, and in emphasizing the structure of the mark over its semantic content, Derrida, as Butler argues, seems to 'evacuate the social' from the realm of language and its utterance.[10]

Yet, as Butler shows, Derrida never argues that the context is unimportant to determining the meaning and force of an utterance, only that this context can never be fully determined and thus the speaking subject cannot have full control of her meanings. Moreover, the question of force and constraint is crucial to Derrida, and is intimately related to the iterative structure of signification (which, I will argue, can occur through both linguistic marks and action). He suggests that, in providing a more general theory of language (as writing), a generalizing movement eschewed by Austin, he is able to show the way in which that which seems external to the operation of the performative is also internal to it (and, I think, constitutive of those very social institutions in which Bourdieu wants to locate the force of performatives and ritual). Derrida here points to Austin's exclusion of the citation from his account of performative and constative speech acts. For Austin, the performance of an utterance in a play or the recitation of a poem is a parasitic or abnormal use of language, dependent on the more primary 'ordinary language' he wishes to analyse. For Derrida, citation is iterability: rather than being a secondary parasite, it marks the structural conditions for signification itself. The risk of citation, that the performative cannot be tied to an intending subject, is a risk endemic to signification itself. By clinging to intentionality as a necessary condition for determining the total context in which performative and constative uses of language can be distinguished, Derrida argues, Austin misses the primacy of citation and the structural inability of any context ever to be fully determined (Derrida, 1982, p. 310).

For Derrida, the force of the utterance lies within the structure of language as iteration. This force, as I have suggested, can work in multiple (possibly endless) ways. In a concise summation of much of his early work on writing and difference, Derrida suggests the duplicity of the force of signification.

> Deconstruction does not consist in passing from one concept to another, but in overturning and displacing a conceptual order, as well as the nonconceptual order with which the

conceptual order is articulated. For example, writing, as a classical concept, carries with it predicates which have been subordinated, excluded, or held in reserve by forces and according to necessities to be analyzed. It is these predicates (I have mentioned some) whose force of generality, generalization, and generativity find themselves liberated, grafted onto a 'new' concept of writing which also corresponds to whatever always has *resisted* the former organization of forces, which always has constituted the *remainder* irreducible to the dominant force which organized the – to say it quickly – logocentric hierarchy. To leave this new concept the old name of writing is to maintain the structure of the graft, the transition and indispensable adherence to an effective *intervention* in the constituted historic field. And it is also to give their chance and their force, their power of *communication*, to everything played out in the operations of deconstruction. (Derrida, 1982, pp. 329–30)

It would be impossible to unpack these lines without an analysis of the context of its utterance, yet within it we can see that for Derrida force works in at least two ways. On the one hand, force is the result of a tethering of the mark to the same, its repetition of that which has come before; yet, on the other hand, deconstruction attempts to exploit the fact that to be repeated, the mark must always also differ and defer from that which it cites (although, as I will show, the ends towards which this break is deployed are open). Derrida's analysis of the structural conditions of the mark, and the deconstructive reversal of speech and writing, presence and absence, ordinary language and citation, mark a redeployment of the force of the mark towards new ends.[11]

Butler argues, in *Excitable Speech*, that, in evacuating the social context from the performative, Derrida denies the historicity of language. Yet for Derrida, historicity is not only the repetition of the *same*. Against hermeneutic claims, Derrida insists that history is never a fully recuperable presence or materiality, but rather is change, rupture and break (the *repetition* of the same, and hence always different). Paradoxically, the force of this rupture or of the break constitutive of history is what enables the fiction of a universal, disembodied, self-present subject. Derrida refigures or resignifies this break and its consequences, not in order to reinstall a new universalizing authority (as Bourdieu, for example, suggests) but rather to mark the alterity of history in and by writing. The universal subject is always a contextual one, regardless of whether that context is erased through a 'false break' that attempts to make generalization a total and radical decontextualization (what Butler claims Derrida himself does). The generality of the mark makes it reiterable and generative; yet this generality always requires a context. The attempt to escape contextualization in general (to claim a universality untethered to any context) is a reification of one determined context at the expense of new ones.

The invocation of ritual, as it is outlined by Austin, suggests that constraint does not come from within the sign, but is maintained by forces external to it – either convention or the conscious intention of the speaker. If, then, the apt performance of ritual, like that of speech acts, depends on who is speaking to whom and in what context, it might seem that there is something external to the ritual itself that determines this delimited context for applicability and provides the force of its action (this is what Bourdieu, in particular, will argue). Derrida claims, conversely, that Austin ultimately tries to reduce the source of performative force and the 'total context' in which performativity can be discerned to the speaking subject. We might read Austin more generously as claiming that the force of the perlocutionary utterance (which requires that the proper outcome follow from it in order to be performative) is dependent on the speaking subject and that of the illocutionary (in which the saying, in the right conditions, *is* the performance) on convention. Yet even the illocutionary always has a signatory, the one authorized to use this form of conventional speech. This leads to the question of who or what authorizes the signatory, again taking us to convention and determining contexts external to the speech act itself. Against both these moves, Derrida argues for the primacy of citation and therefore the inability ever fully to determine context. In doing so, moreover, he suggests how the process of iteration is itself constitutive of those social conventions through which performatives derive their force. For Derrida, the outside is constituted by the inside and the inside by the outside.

It is important to remember that Derrida is not interested in elaborating a theory of ritual in 'Signature, Event, Context', but rather in giving a general account of signification. Yet, if we accept the claim that ritual is signifying action, Derrida's account of the sign has implications for ritual theory. In *Excitable Speech*, Butler is primarily interested in the linguistic character of signification and so at times seems in danger of conflating signification with language and hence reading Derrida as reducing ritual to language. This runs parallel to the error made by those ritual theorists who claim that ritual is meaningless. They assume that meaning necessitates reference (of a particular sort); when attempts to understand ritual actions as referring to some other reality break down, the claim is made that rituals do not signify.[12] Derrida, in providing an account of signification not dependent on this kind of reference, offers a way to reformulate ritual as meaningful without claiming that it refers to external realities. Rather, certain social realities are constituted by ritual action. (Hence the move to say that rituals are performative – their meanings are not primarily constative but generated by the action itself.)

Rather than reducing the social complexity of ritual, then, I believe that Derrida's analysis is suggestive for understanding ritual as meaningful and productive action, particularly when brought together with Bourdieu's and Butler's attention to the body as speaker and ritual actor. For Derrida the signifying and constitutive force of the performative is a function of its reiterative structure (both as a repetition of the same and as the break) and as its effect.[13] The very contexts in which the performative operates are themselves products of performative utterances and acts, subverting the distinction between utterance and context on which Austin's analysis (at least provisionally) depends. Ritual can be understood in the same way, for just as speech acts mean as well as do, rituals are meaningful actions. For Derrida, force would lie within the reiterative structure of ritual (as repetition and break) and as an effect of ritual, rather than solely outside ritual as that which enables its performance.

Although Bell stresses the importance of the total context to understanding what counts as a ritual within a particular community, and Derrida emphasizes our inability ever fully to delimit the context and thereby to fix the meanings or ritualized nature of any activity, the basic point remains the same. Through repetition, the movement whereby actions or marks are repeated in another time and place, subjectivities and relations between them are generated. The openness of

Bell's understanding of ritualization might usefully be augmented by a crucial insight from Derrida, for repetition (at some level) is the one constraint on ritualization – the one bit of formalization that is constitutive of the process of ritualization itself.[14] This also suggests the aspect of ritualization that establishes continuity between bodily practices and more fully ritualized activities, for both depend on iteration and hence generate meanings and constitute realities. The *habitus*, in the sense used by Bourdieu and Butler, is made up of bodily practices and rituals (and the distinction between the two is itself a fluid one).

Bell's conception of ritualization and its relationship to power is directly influenced by the work of Foucault, particularly his reconceptualization of power as capillary and generative. Against those theories of ritual which see it as the field in which the power of an elite is wielded and maintained over the populace,[15] Bell argues that ritualization involves the (often very unequal) circulation of power among all the players within the ritual field.[16] (And inequalities themselves are often ritually constituted and maintained.)

> Ritual mastery, that sense of ritual which is at least a basic social mastery of the schemes and strategies of ritualization, means not only that ritualization is the appropriation of a social body but that the social body in turn is able to appropriate a field of action structured in great measure by others. The circulation of this phenomenon is intrinsic to it. (Bell, 1992, p. 215)

Like other discursive formations generative of subjectivity, ritual is productive of the subject and marks the possibility of that subject's resistance to the very norms and rituals through which it is constituted (see Butler, 1997, p. 15). Against those theorists who stress the conservative nature of ritual, Bell argues that ritual mastery 'experiences itself as relatively empowered, not as conditioned or molded' (Bell, 1992, p. 210). In a similar way, Margaret Thomson Drewal argues that ritual involves repetition, but always (as does all repetition) repetition with a difference (it has to occur in a different time and place in order for it to be repetition). The room opened for improvisation (which differs in different ritualizations) within the ritual space marks it as a site of both domination and resistance, and hence for the potential subversion of ritually and semantically sedimented structures of power and inequality (Drewal, 1992, pp. 1–11).

This account of the relationship between ritual and belief suggests that gender formation and religious belief might be even more closely linked than Jantzen, Anderson and other feminist philosophers have previously suggested. Just as ritual, bodily practices and discursive performatives construct gender, so they also construct other objects of belief that, as constituted, wield tremendous force. This suggests that gender and the objects of religious belief have a similar ontological status. According to the account I have given, they are neither natural givens nor fictions, as that term is generally used. Rather, they are constructions generated through reiteration; although subject to the changes opened by the space of temporal and spatial difference, they are in an important and inescapable way *real*. Further articulation of the ways in which performatives engender their objects and analysis of the resulting ontological structures will help elucidate the quality of this shared reality, its force and its limitations.

Notes

1. I give more detailed attention to this issue in Amy Hollywood, 'Ritual and Belief', in Pamela Sue Anderson and Beverley Clack (eds), *Feminist Philosophy of Religion: Critical Readings*.
2. For Asad this reduction of action to textuality is problematic in that it reduces action to discourse. Yet to see action as meaningful does not necessarily mean to engage in Western imperialist anthropological enterprises, as Asad seems sometimes to suggest. (See his critique of Geertz, in Asad, 1993, pp. 27–54.) On the contrary, the problem with the expressivist conception of ritual seems to me not to be the claim that actions *mean* as well as *do things*, but rather the insistence on reading the 'discourse of actions' in terms of psychology or sociology. It is the search for hidden, symbolic meanings that is the problem, for it obscures the semantics of ritual action itself. On this issue, Sperber (1975) and Lawson and McCauley (1990, pp. 37-41).
3. Asad concedes that rites as apt performances presume 'a code', but claims that is a regulatory as opposed to a semantic code. I am not clear why this is an either–or (Asad, 1993, p. 62).
4. Asad uses *The Rule of Benedict* to make this claim, which is less explicitly articulated than I have presented here. See Asad (1993, pp. 111–15).
5. I suggest here that this includes objects of belief. The question then becomes how one distinguishes fictions, objects of belief and other kinds of realities. As I suggested above, this parallels problems in feminist philosophy of religion about the status of the object of belief.

    For the claim that one can give up reference without eschewing extensionality, and thus the ability to make such judgments, Godlove (1993, pp. 118-19) says, 'The extensionalist does not require "unmediated access" to anything but merely notes that people are inclined toward "apple-talk" – when confronted with apples – the juicy little things themselves – and adds the holistic point that talk of apples makes sense only in the context of color, weight, etc.' Or rather, to color-talk, weight-talk and so on. 'For one need not defend a reference-based semantics or claim "unmediated access" to the world or even to protocol-sentences in order to feel uneasy about the meaningfulness – the cognitive content – of much religious discourse and behavior.' Donald Davidson, on whose work Godlove often relies, would no doubt put this in terms of truth (as opposed to positivist questions about meaningfulness).
6. Austin makes this even more confusing when he goes on to claim that illocutionary acts are conventional whereas perlocutionary acts are not (Austin, 1962, p. 121). This suggests that in illocutionary acts the force of the utterance derives from convention, whereas in perlocutionary acts it derives from the speaker, yet Austin never goes so far as to make this claim. Moreover, in Lecture X he raises a host of difficulties about our ability easily to distinguish illocutionary and perlocutionary acts.
7. Rather than ritual being reduced to language, as Judith Butler claims occurs in Derrida's essay (Butler, 1997, pp. 145-63).
8. Although this slide might not be entirely justified – and we might, with Shoshana Felman and Butler, more usefully tie the force of the performative to the body of the speaker, and hence to that which often escapes conscious intentionality – it is suggestive of the ways in which subsequent readings of Austin's text have attempted to delimit the performative and protect against the erosion of the constative effected within it (Felman, 1983; Butler, 1997, pp. 152–9).
9. Stanley Cavell contests this reading (Cavell, 1995, pp. 42–65).
10. This is Judith Butler's phrase. She focuses on the third of these problems, which is her reading of Bourdieu's implicit critique of Derrida. See Butler (1997, pp. 149–50).

11. Nancy Fraser argues that Butler tends to conflate the break and resignification with
     critique and positive political change. This valorization of the break is inherited, I think,
     from Derrida. My reading of Derrida suggests that he, while celebrating deconstruc-
     tion's break with previous significations, also suggests the political and ethical neutrality
     of the break as such. See Benhabib *et al.* (1995, pp. 67–8).

12. Often the fact that participants give so many divergent interpretations of the same ritual
     actions is taken to be a problem for 'symbolic' or 'expressive' accounts of ritual. Yet the
     existence of multiple meanings or interpretations of a ritual does not mean that it has
     no meaning, any more than the possibility of multiple interpretations of a text mean it
     is nonsensical. For this mistake, see Humphrey and Laidlow (1994). A similar
     problem occurs if the self-referentiality of ritual is taken as grounds for claiming it is
     without meaning. For this mistake, see Staal (1979). Lawson and McCauley offer an
     account of self-reflexive holism to counter these claims (Lawson and McCauley, 1990,
     pp. 137–69).

13. Austin begins by making a clear distinction between constative and performative
     speech, only to have the distinction blur in the course of his exposition. Finally, what he
     has described is different ways in which utterances operate, not two radically different
     forms of utterance. Similarly, ritual actions are both constative and performative – they
     both signify and do things – although as constitutive acts the performative comes to the
     fore.

14. Of course, every account of ritual I have ever read includes some discussion of
     repetition, at the very least as an identificatory criterion. Derrida's work enables us to
     see what is at stake in ritual repetition and how it is tied to ritual force and meaning. See
     Jonathan Z. Smith on the power of routinization (Smith, 1982, pp. 53–65).

15. See, for example, Bourdieu (1977) and Bloch (1989). For more nuanced historicized
     accounts, see Lincoln (1989, pp. 53–74), Lincoln (1994), and Certeau (1984).

16. Bruce Lincoln makes a useful distinction between authority, persuasion and force.
     Persuasion and force are potentialities implied by authority, 'but once actualized and
     rendered explicit they signal – indeed, they are, at least temporarily – its negation'
     (Lincoln, 1994, p. 6). If we understand authority as that which is generated through
     ritual (in keeping with Lincoln's fluid account of authority and our own of the generative
     capacities of bodily practice and ritual), then ritual actions mark the participants'
     complicity in legitimizing authority. However, as with hate speech, as analysed by
     Butler, the force of the speaker's body (or of the state or army or other body that
     legitimates this authority) always implicitly stands behind authoritative discourse.

References

Anderson, Pamela Sue (1998), *A Feminist Philosophy of Religion*, Oxford: Blackwell.

Anderson, Pamela Sue and Beverley Clack (eds) (forthcoming), *Feminist Philosophy of
     Religion: Critical Readings*, London: Routledge.

Asad, Talal (1993), *Genealogies of Religion: Discipline and Reasons of Power in Christianity
     and Islam*, Baltimore: The Johns Hopkins University Press.

Austin, J.L. (1962), *How To Do Things With Words*, ed. J.O. Urmson and Marina Sbisà,
     Cambridge, MA: Harvard University Press.

Bell, Catherine (1992), *Ritual Theory, Ritual Practice*, Oxford: Oxford University Press.

Benhabib, Seyla et al. (1995), *Feminist Contentions: A Philosophical Exchange*, New York:
     Routledge.

Bloch, Maurice (1989), *Ritual, History and Power: Selected Papers in Anthropology*,
     London: The Athlone Press.

Bourdieu, Pierre (1977), *Outline of a Theory of Practice*, trans. Richard Nice, Cambridge: Cambridge University Press.

Butler, Judith (1997), *Excitable Speech: A Politics of the Performative*, New York: Routledge.

Cavell, Stanley (1995), *Philosophical Passages: The Bucknell Lectures in Literary Theory*, Cambridge: Blackwell.

Certeau, Michel de (1984), *The Practice of Everyday Life*, trans. Steven Randall, Berkeley: University of California Press.

Derrida, Jacques (1982), *Margins of Philosophy*, trans. Alan Bass, Chicago: University of Chicago Press.

Drewal, Margaret Thomson (1992), *Yoruba Ritual: Performers, Play, Agency*, Bloomington: Indiana University Press.

Felman, Shoshana (1983), *The Literary Speech Act: Don Juan with J.L. Austin, or Seduction in Two Languages*, trans. Catherine Porter, Ithaca: Cornell University Press.

Godlove, Terry (1993), 'Review of *Rethinking Religion*', *Zygon*, **28**, 115–20.

Humphrey, Caroline and James Laidlow (1994), *The Archetypal Actions of Ritual: A Theory of Ritual Illustrated by the Jain Rite of Worship*, Oxford: Clarendon Press.

Jantzen, Grace (1999), *Becoming Divine: Toward a Feminist Philosophy of Religion*, Bloomington: Indiana University Press.

Lawson, E.Thomas and Robert McCauley (1990), *Rethinking Religion: Connecting Cognition and Culture*, Cambridge: Cambridge University Press.

Lincoln, Bruce (1989), *Discourse and the Construction of Society: Comparative Studies in Myth, Ritual and Classification*, Oxford: Oxford University Press.

Lincoln, Bruce (1994), *Authority: Construction and Corrosion*, Chicago: University of Chicago Press.

Mauss, Marcel (1979), *Sociology and Psychology: Essays*, ed. and trans. B. Brewster, London: Routledge & Kegan Paul.

Smith, Jonathan Z. (1982), *Imagining Religion: From Babylon to Jonestown*, Chicago: University of Chicago Press.

Sperber, Daniel (1975), *Rethinking Symbolism*, trans. A. Morton, Cambridge: Cambridge University Press.

Staal, Fritz (1979), 'The Meaninglessness of Ritual,' *Numen*, **26**, 2–22.

III
LOCATING DIFFERENCE IN TRADITIONS

Chapter 6

What if *Religio* Remained Untranslatable?

Arvind-Pal S. Mandair

No matter how much one wishes that imperialism had never happened, no matter how much one tries to efface its memory or to distance oneself critically from the colonial event as such, it is simply impossible to undo the consequences of the history of imperialisms (Sakai, 1997, p. 18). The event seems to be written into the very means by which post-colonials try to reconfigure their identities. Nevertheless, it may be possible to come to a recognition that imperialist discourse and its legacy today can be rethought and specific sites disclosed by forging connections that link the design of a past imperialism with its repetition in the lives of post-colonials today. In this chapter I want to explore the possibility of forging such a connection by pursuing an oblique engagement between several discourses normally considered to be at odds with each other: the discourse called philosophy of religion which claims to speak for and about religion in general and the diversity of religions, the militantly secular discourse of post-colonial theory, and, thirdly, the articulation of cultural difference by adherents of North Indian devotional traditions living in the West today. The pursuit of such an engagement will help to disclose the site of a forbidden encounter between India and Europe whose memory was soon eclipsed by what came to be called the dialogue between religions or interreligious encounter.

The aim of what follows is not simply to construct a different history of ideas but to diagnose this history in its mode of construction as the history of a repression whose effects continue to be felt today in the efforts by post-colonials to negotiate cultural difference in the academic study of religion. For reasons that will become clear, the work of thinking about religion and religions, and therefore a certain relationship to the philosophy of religion, is indissociably linked to attempts by post-colonials of North Indian origin to carve out a critical space in the Western academy.

Let me begin by juxtaposing a set of questions that are rarely asked in relation to each other. What is the philosophy of religion? To whom has the philosophy of religion spoken in the past and to whom does it speak today? Is it possible, or even desirable, for post-colonial adherents of Indian devotional traditions now living in the West to develop a suitably critical engagement with the philosophy of religion? To 'standard' practitioners of the philosophy of religion, those who relate 'naturally' to its venerable history, its definitive literature and more or less consistent readership, not to mention its very clearly defined identity, questions such as these might seem a little banal. Consider for example the following definitions by two of its leading spokesmen, John Hick and Richard Swinburne:

[W]e may reserve the name 'philosophy of religion' for what (by analogy with the philosophy of science, philosophy of art, etc) is its proper meaning, namely, philosophical thinking about religion. (Hick, 1990, p. 1)

The Philosophy of Religion is an examination of the meaning and justification of religious claims ... [that are] ... more typical of Western religions – Christianity, Judaism, Islam – than of Eastern religions such as Buddhism, Hinduism and Confucianism, which tend to concentrate much more on the practice of a way of life than on a theoretical system.... Hence Western religions proved a natural target for the philosophy of religions. The central claim of Western religions is the existence of God; and the two major problems here are: Can a coherent account be given of what it means to say that there is a God, and, if it can, are there good reasons to show that there is or that there is not such a God? (Swinburne, 1995, p. 763)

Few people would bother to question such definitions. The geoethical distinctions that comprise the self-definition of philosophy of religion, namely, the distinction between West and East[1] or between religions that think/theorize as opposed to those that do not/cannot, are regarded almost as truisms. Fewer still would dare to entertain the notion that the point at which the philosophy of religion originated as a discipline was motivated as much by an intellectual development of religion as by cultural politics and political necessity – the 'need' to save 'us', the West, from the impending dangers of encounter, contact and contamination by alien ideas from the East. The philosophy of religion as a strategy of containment? Saving the West from contamination by the East? A preposterous idea! Was it not the West that saved the East by means of its civilizing missions? Has not the West repeatedly reached out to the East, physically and intellectually, and attempted to understand it better than it had ever understood itself? And is it not the case that the East, by contrast, has never desired to respond in like manner?

With the evidence of a particular history clearly favouring the West's disavowal, what could be the purpose, then, of seeking an engagement today? Would it not be more productive for Indian devotional traditions to remain within the disciplines that have been specially demarcated for their own protection – for example, Indology, Religious Studies, Comparative Religion or even Anthropology – and which allow the proper subject matter of Indic traditions to be correctly represented as being unconcerned with the kind of problems that move Western religions or the discipline of philosophy of religion? But then, just to stretch this line of argument a little further, if these traditions are unconcerned with such questions as 'Does God exist?', does this mean that they are unconcerned with thinking itself? Or that they are simply incapable of engaging with contemporary critical thinking? To distance themselves from these debilitating questions, proponents of Indology, Religious Studies or Comparative Religion have argued that the authentic nature of Indic religious traditions can only be preserved and protected in a secular environment.

Ironically, however, and this is becoming increasingly the case in undergraduate studies throughout the UK and North America, despite their different standpoints these groups of disciplines continue to ascribe to diasporic South Asians now living in the West a static religious identity, a subject position as authentically Indian, Hindu or Sikh: that is, as someone capable of responding and taking responsibility for representing what Hindus and Sikhs ought to be. And as increasing numbers of undergraduate students of South Asian origin are now experiencing, while it is deemed necessary to accede to the particular subject position posited by the discipline within which they are studying, they are subsequently left wondering why their attempts to register any sense of difference are neatly side-stepped, deflected or absorbed by the framework of the discipline. For many of these students, what seems to be particularly difficult to get across to tutors is the idea that an authentic Indian, Hindu, Sikh standpoint is no less alien or more familiar to them than a European standpoint. My point here is how commonplace it still is not only for the predominantly Christian practitioners of Philosophy of Religion but also for the phenomenological disciplines such as Comparative Religion, Religious Studies or Indology to speak about Indic religions such as Hinduism and Sikhism in terms of clear-cut categories such as 'religion' and clearly defined cultural boundaries. Of course this is not entirely surprising, given that since the late nineteenth century neonationalist representatives speaking in the name of Indian religion(s) have continued to reciprocate these ideas in a manner that has mutually confirmed the belief in a natural relationship between religion and identity. Philosophers and phenomenologists of religion alike would probably baulk at the suggestion that the need to posit religious identities and the endorsement of these identities by Hindus and Sikhs as an acceptance of their cultural difference repeats a colonial gesture that was put into place in Anglo-vernacular mission schools during the nineteenth century, the avowed aim of which was to give back to Indians, as a gift, their original religion(s) and their mother tongues, both of which were perceived to have been lost by Indians during their fall from a Golden Age, a fall that entailed the mixing of races and religions with the resultant long history of domination by foreigners that lasted until the redeeming advent of British rule.[2]

In recent years this perspective has come to be increasingly challenged by new research on colonial and pre-colonial India conducted in the form of a series of regional micro studies.[3] These studies have convincingly shown how the indigenous cultures and psychologies of the Indian elites were transformed during the encounter with European imperialism. Space constraints prevent my mentioning in all but the most cursory fashion the central mechanisms of this transformation: (a) the imposition of English as the official language of India (King, 1994); (b) the establishment and proliferation in mid-nineteenth-century North India of a vast network of Anglo-vernacular mission schools (Oberoi, 1994; Dalmia, 1996); (c) as a result of the previous two, the emergence of boundaried vernacular languages (Urdu, Hindi, Punjabi) corresponding to and organized under strictly religious identities (Muslim, Hindu, Sikh) a religio-linguistic situation which had not existed before and which laid the epistemological foundations for the indigenous elites to enter into discursive relations ('dialogue') with European-style thinking; (d) the introduction of print capitalism which brought about the switch in cultural codes from a predominantly oral culture to print culture (Oberoi, 1994); (e) the influence, direct and indirect, of a factor which continues to be underestimated and to which I shall devote more attention shortly, namely, intellectual developments in early nineteenth-century Europe and the birth of autonomous disciplines such as Indology, the Science of Religions and Philosophy of Religion.

A major conclusion of these micro studies, a conclusion that has been endorsed elsewhere (Balagangadhara, 1994; Derrida, 1998; King; 1999) is that Indian languages do not possess a word for 'religion' as signifying something like a uniform and centralized faith community. Further, that prior to colonialism what came to be classified as 'proper' Indic religions and languages possessed fluid boundaries, with the result that most Indians participated in multiple religious and linguistic identities. In other words, the distinct entities known as Hindu-ism or Sikh-ism which philosophers and phenomenologists have long posited as the natural other of Western religions and Western thinking, are in fact recent constructions.

Although it is not immediately obvious, developments such as these are dependent on a reorientation of thinking about the translatability of the term 'religion', indeed the history of the translation of this term, or, stated differently, the intrinsic link between religion and translatability as interchangeable concepts. If translatability here implies much more than semantic exchange, referring also to the creation of an economy of colonial desire and the consequent transactions between colonizer and colonized, the question arises as to whether the work of translation as the site of this encounter is as innocent or transparent as continues to be presumed. How did the representation of Indic cultures in terms of religion come to be regarded as natural?

The connection between religion and the principle of translatability has rarely been questioned – almost not at all in the context of Indic traditions. One could even say that the genesis and continuity of Western scholarship's relation to the other via disciplines such as anthropology, Indology or Philosophy of Religion has been based in no small degree on the seemingly incontrovertible fact that non-Western cultures must, and will continue to, reciprocate terms such as 'God', 'religion', 'faith' and 'nation' from their indigenous linguistic and conceptual resources. But *what if* that which Indians have continued to reciprocate since the colonial event as God/faith/religion has been and continues to be no more and no less than a *response*, a response to the colonial *demand for* religion and, even before that, a demand for correct representation, a demand for identity? To paraphrase Derrida, *what if religion* – and along with it God, faith and theology – *remained untranslatable* (Derrida, 1998, p. 30)? What if

> religion is the response. Is it not there, perhaps, that we must seek the beginning of a response...? No response, indeed, without a principle of responsibility: one must respond to the other, before the other and for oneself. And no responsibility without a *given word*, a sworn faith without a pledge, without an oath, without some *sacrament* or *ius iurandis*. Before even envisaging the semantic history of testimony, of oaths, of the given word ... we must formally take note of the fact that we are already speaking Latin. We make a point of this in order to recall that the world today speaks Latin (most often via Anglo-American) when it authorises itself in the *name of religion*'. (Ibid., pp. 36–7)

What if religio remained untranslatable? What could this possibly mean in the context under consideration here? To pose the notion of the untranslatable is to call for the deconstruction of the history of colonial translations of Indic cultures under the category 'religion', or where such translations inaugurate the very sense of *history* for Indians as reawakening, revival, reform. It is to ask under what circumstances did the undecidability and incommensurality that are present in every encounter, as a coming-up-against-the-other for the first time, give way to the primacy of the representative function, to equivalence and total exchange, that is, to 'dialogue' as a *sponsio* by the colonizer – *we promise to save you, to give you our Word, if you confess the truth about yourself: who are you? To what religion do you belong?* – and a *re-sponsio* by the colonized – *I am a Hindu, I am a Sikh*? To invoke the untranslatable is to invoke what Derrida calls the pharmakonomy of deconstruction as a simultaneously destructive/constructive movement. To deconstruct or untranslate does not therefore mean that we forget the history of colonial translation as a mistake. Rather, the negativity inherent within the notion of untranslatable suggests twin possibilities: (a) of halting colonial translation as a return of the same, by which is meant the legacy of colonial translation as a history of *mimetologism*, the automatic and mutual conferral of recognition between West and East; and (b) the possibility of uncovering different relations, alternative sites of engagement, a 'third space', to use Homi Bhabha's term, beyond the stale oppositions of a nationalist 'third world' theology and its 'first world' others: Christian phenomenology and theology.[4]

Although one must hold out a certain optimism for such an engagement today (let us say between Philosophy of Religion and Indology) a note of caution needs to be sounded here. It is necessary to recognize that this moment of engagement is nothing new. 'We' have been here before. As the Indologist Wilhelm Halbfass reminds us, one of the most poignant contributions to the intellectual engagement between India and Europe was Hegel's reading and engagement with the emerging discipline of Indology (Halbfass, 1988, pp. 84–99). In ways that are not altogether obvious, the results of this encounter have influenced seemingly unrelated events such as, on the one hand, the religious reform movements of nineteenth-century North India, which produced the kind of constructs we know today as Hindu-*ism*, Sikh-*ism*, Buddh-*ism*, and, on the other hand, the way in which the study of Indic cultures has been neatly demarcated, distanced and ultimately confined to specialist reservations policed by 'experts' and which remain beyond the free play of critical thinking in the discourse of the humanities (Derrida, 1978, p. 278). Hegel's role in bringing this about is an important example of the continuity between the operation of imperialist discourses in the past and their effects in the present.

As a particularly good illustration of this, consider the case of what is today called Hinduism. Contrary to conventional wisdom, the ideological framework underpinning the two most important articulations of modern Hinduism, namely the monistic Advaita Vedanta (or philosophical Hinduism) and monotheistic Vaisnava bhakti (devotional or religious Hinduism) have been drawn largely from Western experience. These two articulations of modern Hindu identity should be perceived as the outcome of two very different and competing responses from Hindu colonial elites to the translatability and appropriation of the term 'religion'. For over two centuries the dominant articulation has been a representation of Hinduism centred on Advaita Vedanta as the underlying principle of indigenous Indian civilization, one that encompasses both the idea of Religion in general and the diversity of religious sects and cults of which Vaishnavism is but one. The influence of this articulation owes much to its propagation by a long line of well known Indian reformists, politicians and academics, notably Ram Mohan Roy, Vivekananda, Aurobindo Ghosh, Mohandas Gandhi, Jawaharlal Nehru and Sarvepali Radhakrishnan.

In contrast to the above, Vaishnava bhakti, the other main articulation of modern Hindu identity, had until quite recently remained politically repressed, confined to the realm of private religions, despite its vast public support base. Previously seen as little more than the driving force behind sectarian nationalism in India, Vaishnava bhakti has now come to be recognized as a legitimate expression of the shift from secularism to religion within mainstream Indian politics (Van Der Veer, 1994). An analysis of this fascinating phenomenon is beyond the scope of this chapter. However, it is safe to assume that what seems to have been consistently overlooked by conventional narratives of modern Hinduism is that the very distinction between these two movements – Advaita Vedanta as the central philosophy of Hindu civilization and therefore inclusive of all religious diversity, versus Vaishnava bhakti as the '*only real religion of India*' – could only have come about after a largely overlooked though far-reaching reversal in the nature and orientation of the Indological enterprise (Sharma, 1986).

To quickly illustrate this reversal, the early phase of Indological research (pre-1840s) which had its beginnings in the work of William Jones, Charles Wilkins and H.T. Colebrook, posited Advaita Vedanta as the central philosophy and theology of Hinduism (Halbfass, 1988; King, 1999). According to this particular representation, which continued to be propagated throughout the nineteenth century by 'Indophiles' such as Schelling, Schopenhauer and Max Müller, Hinduism could in essence be considered a philosophy but not a true religion as the term was understood in the West. The nearest thing to 'genuine religion' in India was the mélange of cults and sects based on the worship of chthonic deities. If Hindus had had a true religion, it could only have existed in the remote and ancient past, a Golden Age from which the originally Aryan race of Hindus had fallen into their present state through centuries of domination and racial mixing (Dalmia, 1996, pp. 176–210). After the 1860s, however, the work of a new generation of Indologists – amongst them H.H. Wilson, Albrecht Weber, Friedrich Lorinser, Ernest Trumpp, Monier Williams and George Grierson – began to 'discover' what soon came to be regarded as the '*only real religion of the Hindus*' or 'monotheistic' Vaishnava bhakti (Sharma, 1986; Dalmia, 1996). Not surprisingly, this view received intellectual support from orthodox Hindu scholars and publicists, which led during the last two decades of the nineteenth century to the integration of the mélange of *sampradayas* (sects) under the all-encompassing political leadership of the Vaisnava sampradaya (Dalmia, 1996, p. 396). As a result, Vaisnava bhakti, often solely identified with Hindu sectarianism or religious nationalism, has constantly vied for political representation, resulting in the late 1990s in the transformation of the previously secular Indian state into an overtly self-conscious Hindu state (Pandey, 1989; Jaffrelot, 1996; Singh, 2000).

Redefining Cultural Boundaries: Hegel, Indology and the Science of Religion(s)

The important question here is what brought about this virtually ignored reversal in the nature and orientation of Indology? This reversal occurs at the intersection of a whole series of intellectual debates that were going on simultaneously during the early nineteenth century, including the theorization of religion, aesthetics and the history of philosophy. Much of this activity was centred particularly in Germany during the 1790s upon two parallel movements: first, what Bernard Reardon describes as the 'intellectual rekindling of Christianity both Protestant and Catholic without parallel since high middle ages' (cited in Perkins, 2000, p. 357); secondly, the growth of national consciousness motivated in particular by a need felt by leading European intellectuals to respond to a proliferating knowledge of Oriental religions and cultures, particularly as this was presented through its most effective vehicle, the new discipline of Indology (Bernal, 1987; Perkins, 2000).

Yet, despite its common concern for rethinking Christianity, responses to the 'Oriental Enlightenment' was motivated by opposing desires: on the one hand, exemplified by the responses of Schelling and Schopenhauer, a desire to present a cultural difference or foreignness that is already at the heart of Christian European traditions, a difference that precedes anxieties relating to perceptions of native and foreign, inside and outside;[5] on the other hand, exemplified by the dominant tradition of modern Western philosophy and illustrated most powerfully by Hegel, there is the response according to which Oriental knowledge needed to be systematically ordered and controlled. The most effective way to do this was to suture any gaps present in the growing databank of knowledge about Oriental cultures, thereby keeping the possibility of any harmful influence at a safe distance. The problem was how this was to be done intellectually and in a way that removed the threat of Oriental religions and at the same time the threat of those like Schelling who colluded with such ideas.

Perhaps the best example of this process in Hegel's *œuvre* is his posthumously published *Lectures on the Philosophy of Religion* (hereafter *LPR*), which present his most sustained encounter with Hindu thinking. Most treatments of the *LPR* focus on Part I of this lecture course, the 'Concept of Religion', which has remained of continuing interest to philosophers and theologians. However, the more voluminous Part II, on the 'Determinate Religion', rarely tends to be discussed, being regarded as little more than a bulky supplement to the theoretical first part or, as has been the trend in recent decades, to be dismissed as a prejudiced account of non-Christian cultures which was quickly superseded by more informed and 'disinterested' works. From a post-colonial perspective, starting with Part II provides an important insight into present dilemmas as well as a 'natural' point of departure. A close reading of Hegel's key moves in this lecture course reveals three main concerns in the Part II texts: the 'need', first, to establish a firm theoretical standard for thinking about religion in general; second, to use this standard as the basis for bringing the growing diversity of Oriental religions into some kind of manageable order; third, by ordering them, to counter the influence of Indophiles such as Schelling in whose philosophy the prevailing definition of God/religion brought the origins of Oriental and Occidental civilizations unbearably close, so that the dominant vantage point of Euro-Christian identity based on its exclusionary claims to history, reason and metaphysics, not to mention the colonial enterprise itself, would be threatened. Even to suggest the possibility of coevality between true metaphysical thinking and the type of thinking possessed by Orientals would be to render the very source of Western thinking impure.[6]

The clearest articulation of Hegel's concern can be seen in the transition from the 1824 to 1827 lecture course and most noticeably in the long discussions about the proper constitution of the first two stages of the dialectic: the stage of primal unity associated with religions of nature exemplified by Oriental religions, and the stage of artistic religion exemplified by Graeco-Roman religions (Hegel, 1987, pp. 144–8). For Hegel, the need to account rationally for a qualitative difference between these two stages was crucial both in order to justify a cultural boundary between India and Europe and for any systematic classification of the religions of other nations or races. The entire argument in this section revolves around the problem of beginning – more specifically, the problem of identifying the nature of this beginning which is also the 'original condition of mankind' (ibid., p. 147).

The dilemma for Hegel was how to classify Indic culture *as* religion and yet keep it outside of history which, properly speaking, belonged to the West. There were two obstacles here. First, there was an abundance of seemingly compelling evidence relating to the antiquity of Sanskrit as the source of Indo-Aryan languages and race. This evidence, which was backed by the philological authority of Sir William Jones and the philosophical arguments of Schlegel and Schelling, amongst others, tended to suggest that Orient and Occident had the same origin, given which there could then be no moral justification either for the colonization of India or for placing Indian religions outside the pale of history. Secondly – and what in fact stemmed from the purely metaphysical/conceptual definition of religion, which, being grounded on the notion of *pure* movement or *aufhebung* as the principle not only of historical motion and therefore histori*cism*, but also of the very first impulse whereby spirit definitively extricates itself from nature, the negation of negation, this *pure* movement being at the same time the very definition of religion as such – this moment of emergence must account for history and religion simultaneously: the co-origination of history and religion.

Hegel's resolution to this problem was to implement a move originally formulated in his 1812 *Science of Logic* where the ontological proof for God's existence, with its implicit assumption of the identity of being and thinking, is made the central criterion for thinking about religion as such and the phenomenal appearance of determinate religions during the course of human history. This move allowed Hegel to think *philosophically* about religion in general and *historically* (which means *phenomenologically*) about other religions and thus to classify them according to the degree to which a particular culture was capable of thinking God's existence, its remove from the ontological proof as the ultimate standard for measuring the progress of religion(s). As a result it was now possible to classify Hinduism under the category 'religion' (the idea of divinity was clearly there) but still outside history. The Hindu idea of divinity was as yet 'confused', 'monstrous', 'terrifying', 'idolatrous', 'absurd', 'erroneous', clear evidence for Hegel that Hindu thinking was limited to thinking nothingness. To think nothingness was to think improperly about God's existence. History could *begin* only when a culture became capable of thinking properly about God.

What emerges in the transition to the 1827 lectures is not simply an improved system for describing other religions and therefore a precursor to the phenomenological method, but a specific device which prefigures the very possibility of phenomenology, namely an ontotheological schema – indeed, Hegel's own reworking of ontotheology – which ensures the production of stereotypical versions of Hinduism. With the ontological proof providing the law for thinking about religion (*God cannot* not *be thought, therefore God cannot be nothing or thought as nothing*) schematization consists in a prior operation of marking out a visual time chart upon which any culture encountered by the ontological proof is automatically compared and fixed in its proper place. This time chart is of course the history or phenomenology of religions whose primary axis is drawn automatically by the Hegelian narrative itself. As Gayatri Spivak points out in her perceptive readings of Hegel on the *Srimadbhagavadgita*, 'Hegel places all of history and reality on a diagram. By reading off the diagram the law of motion of history is made visible as the Hegelian morphology is fleshed out' (Spivak, 1999, p. 39). As Spivak rightly suggests, what we have in Hegel's narrative is not an epistemo*logy* that is, an account of how individual subjects produce religion, but an epistemo*graphy*, a graduated diagram showing how knowledge comes into being. Whereas in the West the proof of God's existence provides the ontological law for thinking about God's existence as an exclusion of the nihil, Oriental religions, by comparison, by automatically reading off the epistemograph, have not sufficiently evolved to this stage of thinking. By this consigning of the essence of Oriental cultures to a past moment, to pre-history, currently lived experience as Hindus is consigned to a non-utile state which must be repressed to the realm of privacy in the real world.

Although it is often overlooked, the ontotheological nature of the Hegelian epistemograph, mediated through the two new of disciplines of Philosophy of Religion and the History of Religions, whose essential form Hegel had outlined in the *LPR*, exerted a theoretical and practical influence with important consequences for the colonial and current post-colonial encounters between India and Europe. For our purposes, brief mention will only be made of the two most relevant ones: the reconstitution of Indology and the increasing dependence of the academic study of religion(s) on the phenomenological operation.

The second phase of Indological research after the 1860s focused mainly on the translation and exegesis of North Indian *bhakti* or devotional texts and traditions by a new generation of Indologists trained at institutions such as Tübingen, Göttingen and Berlin, where Hegel's ideas continued to set the tone for thinking about religion long after his death. In contradistinction to the previous phase dominated by British Indologists which had found philosophy but no true religion in Hinduism, this 'post-Hegelian' generation of Indologists were now able to identify *bhakti* as the 'only true religion of the Hindus' (Sharma, 1986, p. 83; Dalmia, 1996, pp. 396–9). This important shift in perception was made possible by a new framework for thinking about religions that was at the same time *ontotheological*, which allowed the Indologist access to Hindu thinking about God's existence, and *phenomenological*, which allowed them to introduce classificatory distinctions, that is, the correct degree of historical spacing between different phenomena. An important consequence of this new standpoint was that it allowed Indologists to remain committed to a Euro-Christian standpoint, given that many of them were also active missionaries, and yet claim scientific status for their work. Consequently, for the first time in Western intellectual history, terms such as theism, monotheism and pantheism became standardized world-historical categories for classifying non-Western cultures. They became formulaic concepts imposing a logic of the stereotype onto the activity of thinking about religion and religions. This had particularly important consequences for the various responses to Indology by indigenous scholars and for the subsequent 'dialogues' that ensued between them, resulting in a one-way traffic of leading ideas into the ideology of the religious reform movements of the nineteenth century.

Although the distinction between pantheism and monotheism overtakes and replaces earlier traditions of distinguishing pagan from Christian religions, a more important issue arises here than a mere improvement in classifying procedure. If, as already alluded to, this world-historical thinking is a peculiarly modern and imperialistic way of thinking that finds its most comprehensive expression in Hegel's various lecture courses and will only be *refined* in Husserl's later version of phenomenology, does it not become entirely questionable to speak of pre-colonial cultures in terms of pantheism and monotheism? If these categories are not natural but part and parcel of the evolution of metaphysical thinking *per se*, does this not bring into visibility the very basis of the modern study of religions, namely the historico-comparative or phenomenological enterprise, as an apparatus which continues to protect the various centres of Western intellectual tradition (of which theology and philosophy of religion are two of the most conservative examples) either from a cross-fertilization of ideas or from a radical questioning of grounds?

It may be pertinent here to invoke an argument in Eric Alliez's important work, *Capital Times*. Alliez qualifies the idea that the use of phenomenology as a tool for encountering non-Western cultures is a modern development reflecting the separation between religion and secularism. Instead, for Alliez, phenomenology since Hegel and Husserl must be seen as a continuation of the tradition of distancing non-Christian otherness inaugurated by Augustine's treatment of time and consciousness in Book IX of the *Confessions*. As a result, our modern sense of the 'phenomenological positioning', as elaborated in the tradition running from Augustine, through Hegel and Husserl, to Eliade and Ricoeur, 'in its most dynamic effects must be considered the ultimate *process of covering over* the Christian conception of the world' (Alliez, 1996, p. 134). If Alliez is right, then relatively modern disciplines such as the philosophy of religion, which has its roots in Augustinian theology, will always have deployed a 'phenomenological positioning' in order to distance and install its non-Christian interlocutors – an operation not dissimilar in its effects to what Derrida calls 'auto-immunity', that is, the consigning of cultures that are distanced and installed (by the philosophy of religion) to the task of confirming and policing the West's own boundaries in the very act of invoking, on behalf of its interlocutors, the promise of a 'global translation of *religio*' or, to use Derrida's neologism, 'globalatinization' (Derrida, 1998, pp. 29–30). Through this process of globalatinization – where the word '"religion" circulates in the world, one might say, like an English word that has been to Rome and taken a detour to the United States' – non-Christian interlocutors will have been seduced into acknowledging the 'disinterested' standpoint of secular phenomenology not only as a safety zone providing protection from the missionary impulse of a Christian philosophy of religion (could there be any other philosophy of religion that would not from the outset be a mimetic cofiguration of its exemplar?) but as the very condition for the appearance of an 'authentic' enunciation and/or objectivity of the other in a global-Latinate discourse.

Studying Religion(s) and the Negotiation of Cultural Difference: are they Incompatible Tasks?

If the above conflation between 'authentic' enunciation and objectivity seems problematical it may be instructive to view this issue in relation to the pedagogical experience of those post-colonial (multilingual diasporic) subjects whose identity is best conceived as a chiasmic hybridity: specifically, in the context of this essay, British Sikhs/Sikh Britons, Hindu Britons/British Hindus, Sikh Americans/American Sikhs, Hindu Americans/American Hindus – the permutations are almost endless. The increasing numbers of students of South Asian origin who, today, first learn to think or theorize about their 'own' religion through an encounter with the academic study of religion(s) in the Anglo-American academy provides a peculiar insight into the nature and dilemmas facing post-colonials. The central issue for these chiasmatic subjects is the articulation of cultural difference, more specifically, the negotiation of cultural difference within a pedagogical context that from the outset will, on the one hand, favour the assumption of a universal definition of what constitutes religion that then becomes naturally applicable for thinking about other religions, and on the other, even in its benign 'pluralistic' versions, will have accommodated all interlocution on this matter under a framework governed by the opposition between host and foreigner. Yet, prior to any interlocution, the cultural difference proper to the post-colonial subject must be *experienced* as a resistance to stable religious and cultural identities and even before that as a resistance to the phenomenological positioning which demands the mutual exclusion of incompatible identities as an epistemological requirement for there to be objectness or objectivity. Grounded in an experience that is essentially aporetic, the articulation of cultural difference is potentially a caesural practice that dislocates and releases the kind of identities that coexist only through the double repression (Sikh/Hindu at home in private, British/American outside in public) that is constitutive of post-colonial subjectivity.

   To acknowledge cultural difference as a dislocatory practice is to be in a position to remove both the mirror and the mimetologism that has enabled disciplines such as philosophy of religion to relate to non-Christian others through the all too familiar 'dialogue' between religions in which cultural difference is reciprocated by each party as the difference of identities: that is, the assumption that, for there to be dialogue at all, identity must be the condition for difference. And this is by no means an imaginary scenario. Indeed, as I recall from my own experience, the visible presence of a representative of an 'Eastern religion' always provided an occasion during class discussion for testing some of the foundational premises of the course: the universal validity of arguments for God's existence, whether God is good, or, even better, the reconcilability of science and religion. From my ascribed position as a 'true' Sikh or Hindu, I was supposed to be able to respond. Yet in responding one inevitably ran the risk of re-enacting the colonial mirroring that was first played out in the Anglo-vernacular mission schools in mid-nineteenth-century India. In other words, one would, in responding to the modern debates in philosophy of religion, simply reproduce oneself as a native-informant answering to the master's voice. And yet, as Derrida incessantly reminds us, *one must still respond. And without waiting too long*. But *how* to respond? How to respond *critically* to a discipline that takes the translatabilty of 'God'/'religion'/'faith' as a premise? Clearly, this is the central issue for post-colonial scholars and students who will continue to engage with the philosophy of religion.

Although the trend in post-colonial theory and modern area studies disciplines such as Asian Studies, South Asian Studies and so on has been generally hostile towards thinking centred upon religious or theological concerns, it should be clear from the foregoing that I do not share this attitude. In fact the hostility towards theology and philosophy of religion reveals not simply a disengagement but rather a *denegation* of something which avowedly secular disciplines try to reject, yet in the very act of rejecting must ultimately affirm, namely, the influence of Western theology and philosophy on the re-formation of modern Indian identities by Indian elites. Rather, the strategy of articulating cultural difference that I have advocated above – the ultimately temporal strategy of dislocating (oneself from) the dialogical mirror – can only begin by historicizing disciplines such as the philosophy of religion, thereby revealing them not only as concerned with 'sources of the [Western] self',[7] but, in the moment of their self-constitution as disciplines, to be founded on a fundamental repression of otherness: that is, as practices created from the outset in response to and in relation to knowledge of the other – in this case, as I have shown, knowledge of Indic cultures.

In excavating the history of ideas that has been repressed by a particular discipline, what comes to light is not merely repressed ideas but alternative ways of relating and engaging in the present. For many people any attempt to discard or tamper with the safety mechanism intrinsic to the working of the dialogical mirror would be seen as a dangerous and irresponsible act resulting in the infection and destabilization of healthy identities and the relativization of all cultural values; or, what most traditional theologians and philosophers of religion dread most of all, the return of a viral nihilism against which they had thought themselves to be immunized long since. But before 'we' fall prey to such fears of religious and intellectual anarchism, or of being contaminated by the varieties of Eastern nihilisms now on the market, it needs to be remembered that such fears may be no more than the projection of a particular cultural imaginary. To quote Eric Alliez once again, perhaps 'we' ought not to look to the East as the source of a contamination which the West has always feared. Perhaps the disease is not nihilism but the will to capture time itself in the objectivization-subjectivization of being. Perhaps 'Western Europe is where that "very pestilineal disease" germinates, mentioned right from the beginning of the Statute, lodged in the cloister of the theological age, which turned countless masters away from the "texts of Aristotle, of other masters and exegetes of old texts" to plunge them into those "philosophical questions and other strange disputations, opinions and suspicious alien doctrines" that are useful "neither for the home, nor in the fields, nor elsewhere"' (Alliez, 1996, p. 238). Yet the 'trick of this history, which is still our own, was in its wanting the university authorities to perceive in those reticular subtleties the prodrome of a black plague about to ravage Europe' (ibid.).

Acknowledgements

Arvind Singh Mandair wishes to thank the Guru Nanak Educational Trust for funding his position as Research Fellow in Sikh Studies at the University of London, S.O.A.S.

Notes

1. Although part of the purpose of this essay is to problematize the East/West opposition, one cannot simply deny that they do not correspond to a certain 'reality'. As a result, I continue to use them, mainly to draw attention to the privileged status of the West in giving reality to the distinction itself.
2. For a detailed treatment of this topic, see my *Religion, Language and Subjectivity: Translating Cultures Between East and West.*
3. Particularly important are the following works: Kenneth Jones' *Arya Dharm*, Vasudha Dalmia's *The Nationalisation of Hindu Traditions*, Harjot Oberoi's *The Construction of Religious Boundaries,* Peter Van Der Veer's *Religious Nationalism* and David Lilyveld's *Aligarh's First Generation.*
4. As Eric Alliez argues in his *Capital Times: Tales From the Conquest of Time* (Alliez, 1996*)*, the opposition between theology and phenomenology has been overplayed, perhaps to stress that theology had been overtaken by the secular project, thereby covering over the intrinsic link between them and their rootedness in a Christian (Augustinian) experience of time and world.
5. It is now increasingly recognized that this kind of response, which has since been caricatured as Indomania or as a perversion of Christian thinking, anticipates important aspects of the post-structuralist movement which opens up new avenues of contact between Western and Eastern traditions. See, for example, Graham Parkes' *Heidegger and Asian Thought* or *Nietzsche and Asian Thought.*
6. For a more detailed argument, see my *Religion, Language and Subjectivity: Translating Cultures Between East and West.*
7. I refer of course to Charles Taylor's influential *Sources of the Self: The Making of the Modern Identity* (1989), which never once acknowledges that the event of imperialism might have contributed to the making of the Western self.

References

Alliez, Eric (1996), *Capital Times: Tales From the Conquest of Time*, trans. G. Van Den Abbeele, Minneapolis: University of Minnesota Press.

Balagangadara, S.N. (1994), *The Heathen in His Blindness: Asia, the West and the Dynamic of Religion*, Leiden: Brill.

Bernal, Martin (1987), *Black Athena: The Afroasiatic Roots of Western Civilisation*, London: Vintage Books.

Dalmia, Vasudha (1995), *Representing Hinduism: The Construction of Religious Traditions and National Identity*, New Delhi: Sage Publications.

Dalmia, Vasudha (1996), *The Nationalisation of Hindu Traditions*, New Delhi: Oxford University Press.

Derrida, Jacques (1978), *Writing and Difference*, trans. A. Bass, London and New York: Routledge.

Derrida, Jacques (1998), 'Faith and Knowledge: The Two Sources of "Religion" at the Limits of Reason Alone', in J. Derrida and G. Vattimo, (eds), *Religion*, Cambridge: Polity Press.

Halbfass, Wilhelm (1988), *India and Europe: An Essay in Understanding*, Albany: SUNY Press

Hegel, G.W.F. (1987), *Lectures on the Philosophy of Religion*, ed. P. Hodgson, Berkeley: University of California Press.

Hick, John (1990), *The Philosophy of Religion*, London: Prentice-Hall International.

Jaffrelot, Christophe (1996), *The Hindu Nationalist Movement and Indian Politics*, London: Hurst and Co.

Jones, Kenneth (1989), *Arya Dharm*, New Delhi: Manohar.

King, Christopher (1994), *One Language, Two Scripts: The Hindi Movement in 19th Century North India*, New Delhi: Oxford University Press.

King, Richard (1999), *Orientalism and Religion: Post Colonial Theory, India and the Mystic East*, London and New York: Routledge.

Lilyveld, David (1978), *Aligarh's First Generation: Muslim Solidarity in British India*, Princeton: Princeton University Press.

Mandair, Arvind-Pal S. (forthcoming), *Religion, Language and Subjectivity: Translating Cultures Between East and West*, Manchester: Manchester University Press.

Oberoi, Harjot (1994), *The Construction of Religious Boundaries*, New Delhi: Oxford University Press.

Pandey, Gyan (1989), *The Construction of Communalism in Colonial North India*, New Delhi: Oxford University Press.

Parkes, Graham (ed.) (1987), *Heidegger and Asian Thought*, Honolulu: University of Hawaii Press.

Parkes, Graham (ed.) (1991), *Nietzsche and Asian Thought*, Honolulu: University of Hawaii Press.

Perkins, Anne (2000), *Nation and Word: Religious and Metaphysical Language in European National Consciousness*, Aldershot: Ashgate Publishing.

Sakai, Naoki (1997), *Translation and Subjectivity: On 'Japan' and Cultural Nationalism*, Minneapolis: University of Minnesota Press.

Sharma, Arvind (1986), *The Hindu Gītā: Ancient and Classical Interpretations of the Bhagavadgītā*, London: Duckworth.

Singh, Gurharpal (2000), *Ethnic Conflict in India*, London: Macmillan.

Smith, Jonathan Z. (1999), 'Religion, Religions, Religious', in Mark C. Taylor, (ed.), *Critical Terms For Religious Studies*, Chicago: University of Chicago Press.

Spivak, Gayatri Chakravorty (1999), *A Critique of Postcolonial Reason: Toward a History of the Vanishing Present*, London: Harvard UP.

Swinburne, Richard (1995), 'Philosophy of Religion', in Ted Honderich (ed.), *The Oxford Companion to Philosophy*, Oxford: Oxford University Press.

Taylor, Charles (1989), *Sources of the Self: The Making of the Modern Identity*, Cambridge: Cambridge University Press.

Van der Veer, Peter (1994), *Religious Nationalism: Hindus and Muslims in India*, New Delhi: Oxford University Press.

Chapter 7

Virtual Corpus: Solicitous Mutilation and the Body of Tradition

Navdeep Singh Mandair

Introduction

> But of course, come in, sir, there is no colour prejudice among us … Quite the Negro is a man, like ourselves …' My body was given back to me sprawled out, distorted, recoloured, clad in mourning in that white winter day. (Fanon, 1986, p. 113)

In this passage it is possible to detect in Fanon's voice a note of despair, a sense of emotional nullity which wells up, filling to repletion that void left over after the dissipation of rage, a gesture of resignation before some oppressive fate, faceless and ineluctable, which closes upon him with the air of a massive finality. This sense of abjection is precipitated by the crushing recognition that cultural oppression is a phenomenon that inhabits every space and is always ahead of every encounter with it, a huge presence that obliterates brightness for a ubiquitous funereal pallor, an insuperable subjection to tyranny and this precisely because the white Frenchman concedes equality to the subaltern. This apparent paradox constitutes what will be termed in this chapter the problem of virtual alterity.

The primary concern of this chapter is to interrogate the representation of cultural alterity in the contemporary discourse of the humanities and, in particular, to problematize the idea that this alterity is such that it enables a transparent dialogical engagement between different religious traditions. Although the philosophy of religion[1] as the intellectual space within which this putatively univocal encounter occurs has recently become considerably more attentive to the question of religious alterity, it seems almost inconceivable that a discourse inaugurated as a critical appraisal of Christian belief, and which remains intimately concerned with the anxieties of the Christian subject, could do justice to the strange ontologies of the other. Its advocacy of a conception of religion which privileges universality over specificity – ostensibly a gesture receptive of cultural difference – is informed by a criteriology deriving ultimately from the conceptual perspective of Christian theology; dissimulated as the ground(s) of religion *in se*, it exerts an invisible, though nonetheless inexorably coercive, effect on other religious traditions to conform in order to speak legitimately, thus reducing religious encounter to a mimetic event, an echolalia, which serves merely to confirm the Christian *weltanschauung*.

The other in question in this inquiry is the Sikh who professes a Khalsa[2] identity. Given the other's installation within the fideiographic imaginary of the philosophy of religion, it follows that its ontological status must be conceived in terms of a *relation* to the Christian subject, that is as the dependent term in a binary opposition; yet, paradoxically, in view of this ontology of dependence, the other continues to be (mis)construed as expressing its alterity in a completely authentic manner. Thus, if the identity of the other is always subverted in its relation to the self, and if this distortion remains unrecognized, does this not render the authenticity of the other merely specious?

The other's failure to recognize that its identity has undergone a revisionary act during cultural encounter facilitates the dissembling of its ontological dependency on the Christian self in terms of a relation between two culturally specific subjects who are properly differentiated by a deficiency in power. Thus what is in effect an ethnocidal event enacted via the fideiographic scrutiny of religious pluralism is dissimulated as a transparently discrepant situation for which the facile intervention of increased cultural empowerment exists as a remedy. This act of self–miscognition amounts to the same thing as a substitution of the other's desire – a desire which only finds itself at the moment of redemption – for an indigent phenomenon, one conditioned by the lack of an object. This indigent desire, which demands a levelling of the disparity in power between self and other, would seem to constitute the obvious point of departure for any sympathetic readdressing of the question of the subaltern; certainly, even Fanon, despite his deep suspicion of liberal society's concessionary gestures, is seduced by this desire when he situates his critique on the question, 'What does the black man want?' (Fanon, 1986, p. 10) – what else but to have his cultural existence regarded by the self as the self regards its own.

Sikhs also have asked and continue to ask this question, ironically however, for like all other marginalized groups seeking admittance to the centre of the fideiographic imaginary, it is in the completion of the lack implied in the question, which appears to open up a space for an authentic intersubjective relation, that the ontological dependence of the other unfolds.

Ultimately, what this radical subjugation of the other inscribes is the (im)possibility of its speaking at all. The other's rhetoric of appeal, always already inhabited by the voice of the Christian subject, communicates nothing (of its alterity), this mute condition testifying rather to the self's desire, an engine of pure narcissism, which wants only its own presence or, amounting to the same thing, a vista of ashes and human wreckage. It is the case, then, that any attempt to find the Sikh other in his difference cannot be inaugurated by first asking, 'what does a Sikh want?' This question must be absolutely resisted.

Incorporating the Foreign: the Enigma of Stereotyping as Alteriophagy

Perhaps the fundamental error concerning the representation of the other in the philosophy of religion, an opinion which permeates the discourse of all the human sciences, is the unproblematic manner in which the other is determined as being synonymous with the not-self. What the acceptance of this synonymity involves is an *invisible* slippage in the ontological status of the other *qua* other to a position where the other exists pseudonymously. This slippage becomes apparent when we consider that, in being designated not-self, the other is established as the self's signifying not, therefore as in a negative dialogical alignment with it. Thus the other speaks and acts in opposition to the self and, crucially, though its negations signify, they are meaningful to the self. However, given that the other is *other*, that is, radically incommensurable with the self, its ontological juxtapositioning with the self signified in the not-self indicates the effacement of a 'proper' other, and therefore he who speaks for the other is an impostor, but one for whom this imposture is indiscernible as such.

The dissimulation of the other's identity following its construal as not-self is clearly encoded in the semantic structure of the latter term, where being not-self represents the other as constituting a privative mode of the self. Its meaning is therefore subsumed in the significations of the self; it functions simply as a sign for the distance remaining to the achievement of selfhood; it is in effect a proto-self. It will be suggested that the slippage of the other to an ontological position which is a modification of the self's existence is effected via the dynamics of cultural stereotyping, but that the way in which this process is usually conceived as operating by social theory is unsatisfactory.

Stereotyping is usually conceived of as a process which installs an irreducible 'difference' between a subject and its other; the self decontextualizes the other and simultaneously exaggerates its alien topographic[3] features into the other's 'proper' context. Thus reified in its foreignness, it is rendered (apparently) incommensurable with and therefore perpetually excluded from the domain of the self. Gilman summarizes this perspective on stereotyping in his assertion that 'stereotypes are a crude set of mental representations of the world ... [that] perpetuate a needed sense of difference between the self and the object which becomes the "Other"' (Gilman, 1985, p. 18).

It may, however, be more consistent to interpret the 'differentiating' event enacted in the installation of stereotyped images as actually constituting an erasure of difference. What is in dispute, then, is not the dynamics of stereotyping (which proceeds by perpetuating a zone of exclusion from the self), but rather the vector of this process which is actually incorporative, enacting the assimilation of the other into the body of the self.

As was indicated above, stereotyping proceeds initially through a decontextualization of the other. This involves a suppression (or forgetting) of the other's cultural background, its 'proper' context or *alterionomy*, and a simultaneous foregrounding (or remembering) of its salient features or *alteriography*. The crucial move in the stereotyping process is the *appropriation* of this alteriography, that is, the confusion or (erroneous) identification of the topographical aspects of alterity abstracted from its 'proper' context with the 'proper' context itself. The other's unproblematic acceptance of this appropriative event, where its alteriography is installed as alterionomy, entails the erasure of this alterionomy without this ever appearing to have occurred. Thus the other who stands in relation to the self is nothing but a specious edition, it has been displaced from its deviant corporeality and returned to a body which perfectly replicates its deformations, a virtual embodiment that speaks exactly like, but never *as*, the other.

It is evident, then, that the mnemonic operation informing the stereotyping process (the decontextualization or forgetting of the other's 'proper' context and the remembering of its topographical features) essentially constitutes a re-membering (that is, a restructuring) of the other as a virtual entity. Irigaray registers a similar concern about the speciousness of woman's identity in its relation to the patriarchal economy of truth; since she is regarded as an inferior version of the standard operating in this system, her accession to this truth requires that 'she can only be known and recognized under disguises that denature her; she borrows forms that are never her own and that she must yet mimic if she is to enter even a little way into knowledge' (Irigaray, 1985, p. 344).

Crucially, the other continues to be represented as *other* to, as incommensurable with, the self, given which, the other is never able to perceive itself as virtually embodied, this virtual difference *is* its proper difference, that which situates it outside the self. The problem that obtrudes, then, is that if the other could only have access to its otherness *qua* virtuality, how could it possibly ever come to know that which is absurdly outside the outside, its 'proper' difference?

The function of the stereotyping process as conceived in social theory is posited erroneously as perpetuating difference because it fails to register that the stereotyped other is a virtual entity, that is, one subjected to the erasure of its difference and which, because it continues to be represented as a 'proper' other (that is, incommensurable with the self), has its virtual status entirely occluded, thus maintaining the illusion of difference between self and other. This stereotyping theory, then, by ascribing propriety to the other invokes a paradigm of intersubjective difference which does not in fact exist.

Religious pluralism, as a position which is informed by this alteriophagic mode of stereotyping, dissimulates a repudiation of the discriminatory perspective expressed in the inscription of stereotypes of the other, a dissimulation which *de facto* locates the enunciation by the philosophy of religion of its contempt for alterity. Pluralism ostensibly constitutes an affirmation of religious alterity, yet the invocation of this receptive gesture is contingent upon the possibility of transcending this difference, an expectation reflected in the insistence on interreligious dialogue. It is this paradox, rendered anonymous by its attentiveness to the question of difference, which provokes that dreadful sense of vacuity informing the being of the virtual other, an identity which exists within a twilight world, a gloomy in-between interrupted by the vicious turbulence of a burgeoning anxiety, where every step towards the affirmation of itself enacts a retreat, an ineluctable slide into self-rejection.

On the one hand, the self baulks before the mute violence of the glyphs inscribing the other's body, they remain absolutely unfathomable, a vast semantic lacuna; nevertheless, a sense of signification is retrieved by conceiving this hiatus as *encrypting* a common cultural grammar or, at the very least, a cultural dissonance which is recognizable as such. Thus, beyond the dark and impossibly opaque phenomenological ground of alterity, the possibility exists of (de)scribing the other through the fideiographic cipher of the philosophy of religion. This cipher represents concerns which are proper to a Christian affirmation of faith as natural to all cultures or, to none in particular, an imposition which simultaneously precipitates an occlusion of the act of deciphering, and posits an other whose religious concerns appear to reflect transparently the phenomenological or corporeal ground of its cultural difference. In this manner the alien topography of the other undergoes exposure, an act which, ostensibly, constitutes a recognition of the irreducible distance between religious traditions but *de facto* serves to erase the ontological autonomy of the other. The other, then, is seen to be (in)commensurable with the self, and the very moment in which it asserts the semantic opacity of its identity locates the disclosure of an ontological transparency. This nakedness, however, does not amount to the same thing as the stark presence of a nude body, reflecting rather a divestiture, a scraping clean, a mutilation, which has shaped flesh to the contours of the fideiographic cipher. Yet the other remains insensible to the savage agonies of its slaughtered body, deaf to the appeals for mercy, since it perceives the concerns informing the fideiographic imaginary as properly its own. Therefore the impropriety of its assimilation is never recognized as such and what comes to view is a cultural alterity which retains a sense of incommensurable difference.

In short, then, the deciphering of difference by the philosophy of religion is an act which remains indiscernible since it is perceived by the other as a proper expression of its own ontology. This concealment of the act of deciphering constitutes the same thing as the reproduction of the other as a virtual object, its virtual ontology signalling the (im)possibility of decrypting difference, for it discloses an other who is at once taciturn and loquacious. However, since this resistance to dialogue only emerges to view in respect of this loquacity, its futility stands as a sign for the complete transcendence, or expropriation, of the semantic inertia of radical alterity.

It will tentatively be suggested that the deep, indeed, almost crippling, sense of anxiety often experienced by individuals from non-European diaspora communities located in a Christocentric Western milieu, a condition which is all the more distressing since it has no readily discernible cause, arises in the wake of this virtual refiguration of the other's ontological status. This anxiety points to the existence of a vast and imperceptible lacuna at the heart of the other's being which reflects the burgeoning discrepancy between what the other *qua* virtuality believes itself to be, following the affirmation of its cultural identity and what it is in fact becoming so that every (apparently) positive enunciation of its identity by the other is always already a crypto-identification with the Christian subject. To put it another way, the sense of foreboding inaugurated following the surreptitious dislocation of the other's cultural propriety signals the proximity of an imminent, but amorphous, danger which always remains beyond thematization, since this threat is immanent within the other itself conditioned as a virtual entity, and every effort made to dissipate this disquiet is in vain since it serves merely to bring this lurking horror ever closer.

Violent Religion: Returning Sikhism to Itself

Prevailing opinion concerning the notion of a ground for religion insists that the coherency of this abstraction can only be posited insofar as it embraces a politics of pacifism, this commitment to (world) peace, ostensibly inscribing a tolerance of cultural difference or, amounting to the same thing, a solicitude towards the other. However, a tension becomes apparent in this proposition given the problematic status of certain religious traditions, pre-eminently Sikhism, *vis-à-vis* their ontological entanglement with the question of conflict. Given that being a Sikh consists in accession to an ontology of violence, then, to posit Sikhism as commensurable with the contours of a transcendental conception of religion, one which privileges a pacific engagement with the world, seems unjustifiable.

It is the case, however, that Sikhism is perceived as conforming, quite unproblematically, to the criteriological ground constituting this putatively proper notion of religion. What is disclosed in this identification of Sikhism as a world religion, as a tradition whose word inspires universal consent, is the specious nature of its religious alterity, and every announcement of its militant ontology is always already informed by a whisper of regret, an inscrutable rhetoric of apology, instantly enacting the renunciation of an encounter with the world which is violent all the way down.

Paradoxically, then, it becomes necessary to put into question the extent to which an ethics of consensus, as a corollary of a pluralist hermeneutics of religion, can be justified as the possible grounds for solicitude towards the other. Given that the legitimacy of religious alterity is contingent upon accession to this consensual perspective, an affirmation which locates the indiscernible alienation of the other from his otherness, then what comes to view in this act of dislocation is the destructive face of pluralism or, what amounts to the same thing, the inscription of Christianity as mega-machine, its obliteration of the other's presence marking the point at which the anxiety of the Christian subject concerning his self-identity is overcome.

A particularly distinctive feature of the religious compositions of Guru Gobind Singh[4] is the consistent representation of the 'divine' using the rhetoric of conflict; thus this 'divinity' is disclosed as 'all-steel' *(sarbloh)* or as the 'revered sword' *(sri bhagauti)*, a mode of expression that reveals a dark and turbulent presence which is only ever encountered through the convulsive events of battle and love, birth and death. One of the texts in which this thematization of the 'divine' as violent presence is conspicuous is *Jap Sahib*.[5] In couplet 52 of this work, Guru Gobind Singh articulates the fierce nature of this 'divinity' through expressions of obeisance: *'namo sastarpaneh, namo astarmaneh, namo param geeata, namo lok mata'* (I bow before the wielder of the sword, I bow before the sender of arrows, I bow before the knower of the unknowable, I bow before the mother of the world). (Singh and Singh, 1999, p. 11)

In this verse it is clear that approaching the Other always entails risk, indeed, it is to invite disaster, since every such encounter unfolds violently; yet, intriguingly, it may also be conceived as locating an act of love, since this event unfolds in the nurturing presence of the mother. In other words, because a confrontation with the belligerent nature of the Other is an expression of a maternal concern with the world, a relatedness, therefore, conditioned by (a nurturing) love, then what this encounter inscribes is an act of despoliation, a prostration before a m(Other) who loves us violently.

Surely, however, the claim that a seamless conjunction obtains between love and violence entails contradiction, since these two terms putatively inscribe conditions which are mutually exclusive, a semantic tension which invests in Guru Gobind Singh's conception of the 'divine' a contrary nature, one who one comes to view as a god at war with himself. This view is prompted by the acceptance of the idea that acts such as violence and love must ultimately conform, at which point even repudiations of this notion inscribe detours, to a utilitarian schema; however, if, as

Bataille maintains, 'Beyond (the assignation of) immediate ends, man's activity in fact pursues the useless and infinite fulfilment of the universe' (Bataille, 1988, p. 21) then the possibility arises of the contradiction posited between violence and love overcoming itself.

The ostensibly contradictory relation between the conditions of violence and love seems to belie the coherency of that experience of pure intensity inscribed by the violating encounter with the m(Other), yet because this contradiction itself locates a tension it participates in the very *intensity* which it proscribes. The tension present in contradiction is never disclosed as intensity because, in the wake of its decryption through the utilitarian cipher of modernity, it is conceived as a condition obtaining between, and therefore contingent upon, identifiable terms. However, given that the ascription of a strictly utile function to human activity represents a valuation which is culturally perspectival, thus foregrounding modernity's erroneous generalization of the isolated situation (Bataille, 1988, p. 23), the tension which is bound or relative to the contradictory terms, now substantively empty, is liberated as pure intensity. In other words, the utilitarian conception of human acts such as violence and love, which posits them as differentiated totalities marked by a tension *qua* contradiction, actually constitutes the dissembling of an endless act of differentiation, an act which renders all identities immanent to the operation of tension or, amounting to the same thing, which locates the presence of 'gradients' of tension, and thus circumscribes a general field of intensity.

The fissured narrative of *Jap Sahib,* then, foregrounds a notion of violence and love that is radically different from the way in which it is usually conceived. This radical sense of violence is irredeemably excessive, incommensurable with any aim whatever, except, perhaps, that which signals the absence of aim. As such this violence resists every act of identification, is always ahead of, and, elsewhere to, identity, and therefore constitutes the horizon for the unfolding of a radical Otherness. The Sikh's experience of this Otherness, mediated through the act of remembrance *(jap)*, does not reflect an encountering of God, but rather locates the moment of becoming other (to himself); this Otherness, then, is the condition for the possibility of enunciating (a proper) Sikh identity, it testifies to the fact that being Sikh cannot be thought apart from an ontology of self-violation. It is evident, then, that the violent nature of Sikh identity, far from expressing an aggressive disposition towards alterity, in fact constitutes the very condition necessary for a solicitude towards the other. Given that the ontological signature of Sikhism inscribes an endless act of resistance to the hegemony of self–identity, what comes to view is an Otherness which remains irretrievably alien, inapproachable, out of reach; thus, because Sikhism is ontologically constituted by this Otherness, it follows that its every encounter with other cultures must posit a repudiation of the possibility that this alterity could be identified as such; that is, concedes the absolute incommensurability of others.

This interpretation of Sikh interior experience, mediated through the quietism of devotional practices such as the act of remembrance *(jap)* as, primordially, an expression of violence, problematizes that prevalent idea in Sikh historiography which posits a radical divergence between early *(Nanakpanthi)* Sikhism and the later Khalsa tradition. This opinion has been most notably expounded by the historian of Sikh religion W.H. McLeod, who implicitly asserts that a deviation in the nature of

Sikh identity has been enacted, when he asks 'why a tradition built on Nanak's *interior* practice of *nam simran* (or meditation on the Divine Name) should have become a militant community and proclaimed its identity by means of prominently displayed *exterior* symbols' (McLeod, 1997, p. 111, original emphasis). However, given that the practice of remembrance properly locates an act of self-violation, it is disclosed as inscribed by the signature of militancy, a violent act of resistance to a hegemonic authority. This conflation of quietism and militancy signals the inadequacy, indeed, the spuriousness, of conceiving (Sikh) religious identity in terms of a dichotomy between interiority and exteriority, but also puts into question the idea, written into this dichotomy, that the interior religious experience constitutes religion's proper mode of expression. It is tempting to suggest that McLeod's espousal of this dichotomy in Sikhism amounts to the imposition of a Christian view of religion, one that privileges the spirit over the body, an interpolation which remains indiscernible since it is represented as a precise historiographic reproduction of the Sikh religion.

It would also be a mistake to conceive the militant nature of Sikhism as, simply, a transcription into the political domain of that violent ontology which, mediated through the contemplative act of remembrance, unfolds as something proper to the individual. Such an interpretation, in effect, retrieves the dichotomy between interior religion and exterior identity. If, however, militancy situates the sense of the religious as surely as the meditative event, what comes to view is the simultaneous penetration, by this violent ontology, of the political and private dimensions.

This conception of militancy, inevitably, provokes a question concerning its semantic propriety. Because thinking is conditioned by a subscription to a hermeneutics of utility, that is, where nothing can be thought which is not ultimately decipherable by a utilitarian key, then the militant signature of Sikhism, as the trace of a violating ontology, a becoming other, an endless tension, simultaneously stands outside and transcends this mode of conceptualization. Thus conceived, militancy appears as something uncanny, the location of a threat, since it signals an absolute resistance to appropriation, to the idea that a proper meaning, informed by the question of purpose, can be ascribed to it. In other words, the violence inscribed in acts such as the conspicuous bearing of weapons and the eulogizing of the virtues of battle play engenders anxiety in the modern subject because, at bottom, it is gratuitous. The corollary of this proposition is the highly counterintuitive idea that the entire history of Sikh militant action, regarded as *dharma yudh* ('war in the cause of righteousness'), is accidental to the expression of a (gratuitously) violent ontology.

It cannot be denied, however, that this reading of Sikh militancy runs counter to the way in which it is conceived by most Sikhs. Sikh tradition advocates the view that, confronted by the oppressive religious bigotry of the Mughal empire, and, following the empire's disintegration, aggression during the Afghan invasions of India, militancy became exigent in order to prevent Sikh identity from being obliterated – an act which, because it registers resistance to hegemonic rule, strikes a blow in the defence of righteousness.[6] A classic statement of this viewpoint is found in Harbans Singh, who declares that the purpose 'of the sword was to secure fulfilment of God's justice … It stood for righteous and brave action for the protection of truth and virtue. It was the emblem of manliness and self-respect and was to be used only in self-defence, as a last resort' (Singh, 1994, p. 83). However, it may be argued that this view constitutes an inheritance from the Sikh encounter with (British) colonialism; this encounter precipitated an indiscernible revision of the properly gratuitous nature of Sikh violence, that is, where its inscription in the acts of resistance to a hegemonic authority was speciously represented as a defence of identity or righteousness.

Sikh resistance to a tyrannical authority, then, does not constitute a repudiation of this hegemonic Self, a gesture which enacts conformity even as the Sikh retreats into his 'own' identity, but, rather, expresses the affirmation of an ontological incommensurability; thus the seeping fissures and wounds marking the progress of the sword across the body of the self gape, revealing nothing beyond the fact of trauma itself, the trace of an absolute rupture between the Sikh and an authoritarian identity. This ontological disjunction, reflected in the violating encounter with the Self, situates the liberation of a radical heteronomy, a total affirmation of otherness, since its subversion of authority exposes the incommensurability of all identities, or the possibility of an infinite number of conflicting, yet proper, truth claims. It is not a little ironic, then, that it is only through violence that an authentic sense of love for the other unfolds, a love which, in turn, is the condition for the possibility of violence. For the Sikh, then, the assertion of cultural incommensurability, as an inscription of the transcendence of the other, signals accession to an identity informed by the absence of ontological plenitude. Thus, in perpetrating violence against the Self, the Sikh enacts his own self-violation, and, paradoxically, the real target of Sikhism's belligerency is the Sikh himself.

To the colonial imagination, there was a sense in which the aggressive pursuit of a politico-economic hegemony over non-European peoples, mediated via the enactment of expansionist programmes of territorial annexation and cultural expropriation, could not possibly be conceived as inscribing a violent event. This was because the subjugation of a backward people was regarded as accidental to the proper function of colonialism as the means by which they could be civilized. Thus, for instance, the British were able to justify the authoritarian nature of their presence in India since this was merely a 'symptom' of that underlying process which sought the inculcation of 'Public Virtue' (Metcalfe, 1997, p. 8) in their subjects. Colonialism, then, was primordially, a process of *pacification*, at once a gesture of subjugation and, as the imposition of a civilizing regime, the condition for the possibility of peace. This representation of colonialism, as a phenomenon which is absolutely determined by a pacific orientation, entirely occludes its expropriative function; given that colonialism's aggressive desire for hegemony can only signify *vis-à-vis* a pacific ideal, it is never disclosed as a substantive phenomenon, as aggression *in se*, but, rather, comes to view as a privative modification of a pacific act. Paradoxically, then, the aggression of colonialism is never violent, for it simply locates the unfolding of a phenomenon which is not-pacific. Ultimately, the appropriation of violence, mediated through its construal as the not-pacific, signals the ascription of a purpose to it, specifically, as the force necessary to defend and propagate the pacific ideal; as such, its assimilation to the pacific is a reflection of its absolute conformation to the utilitarian perspective of colonialism.

This representation of violence as not-pacific did not, of course, render violence illegitimate, as something outside the purview of civilized existence; on the contrary, it was simply one of the modes of expression of the pacific ideal itself. Thus the British, in India, came to regard the possession of a militant nature as one of the cultural signifiers which marked the contours of a properly civilized condition. By this means the British were able to distinguish themselves from those of their subjects whose lack of martial vigour indicated their cultural degeneracy. This deviation from the normative standard imposed by colonialism was regarded as most pronounced in the '"extraordinary effeminacy" of the Bengali, whom "no necessity would induce to fight"' (Metcalfe, 1997, p. 127). By contrast, the British asserted the existence of an affinity between themselves and those Indian peoples, pre-eminently the Sikhs, who readily affirmed a militant ontology; thus, because these '"martial races" were those who most closely resembled what the British imagined themselves to be' (ibid.), their cultural propriety was never in question.

It was actually the case, however, that this gesture of affinity surreptitiously imputed to the Sikhs the very same cultural degeneracy which was transparently predicated of the Bengali Babu. This proposition appears highly counterintuitive; surely the positing of a cultural affinity between colonizer and colonized, what amounts to an expression of ontological parity, renders impossible its instantiation as an act of cultural discrimination. However, this objection can be rejected because it fails to recognize that this gesture of affinity is not as transparent as it appears. It will be argued below that, in the wake of colonial encounter, the Sikhs willingly acceded to the view that a (martial) affinity existed between themselves and the British; this affinity, as a concept determined by colonial ideology, necessarily encrypted a colonial notion of militancy, one which conceived violence as subject to a purpose. However, since Sikh militancy properly inscribes a gratuitous phenomenon, the affirmation by Sikhism of this affinity signals its displacement from its cultural alterionomy, an event which remains indiscernible since propriety is ascribed to this specious edition of militancy. Thus the (martial) affinity putatively obtaining between the Sikhs and the British does not, contrary to the opinion of most commentators, constitute a recognition of an ontological parity, but, rather, as a relation posited between a virtual reproduction of Sikhism and a colonial identity, reflects an acknowledgment of this religion's degeneracy.

The transition from Sikh alterionomy to alteriography, following colonial encounter, was coterminous with the recognition of fundamental cultural affinities between Sikhism and the Christocentric identity of British colonialism. In other words, both cultures were regarded as expressing similar notions of religious faith. This expression of affinity reflected the introduction of cultures, properly incommensurable with the conceptual ground of Christocentric colonialism, into its teleocentric (utilitarian) register, an act of fideiographic scrutiny that posited a specious account of the Sikh religion, but which was never discerned as such, since it involved the willing participation of Sikh interlocutors in the event of virtualization. What this means, then, is that what is ostensibly a transparent disclosure of Sikh cultural topography *vis-à-vis* its utilitarian value, to a fideiographer, actually reflects Sikhism's affirmation *qua* purpose(s) of the cultural propriety of colonialism. Thus the dialogical encounter between fideiographer and Sikh interlocutor situates the expropriation of Sikhism by the colonial identity, where the Sikh 'recognizes' his religious identity as degenerate, prompting a desire for development.

Crucially, however, this remedial intervention did not necessarily mean the explicit adoption of the topographic features of colonial identity, Christian belief and the 'Hellenic' facial appearance; it could also refer to the modernization or reform of the native culture where it was purged of retrograde practices and ideas believed to have been acquired over time. An episode of reformation (re)presented the divine 'presence', invoked in Sikhism as the m(Other), in monotheistic terms. It (re)presented Sikh militancy, properly a gratuitous phenomenon, as not-pacific, a defence of the pacific ideal and, in so doing, indiscernibly enacted the substitution of an ontology of violence, by a mode of existence assimilated to the thinking of purpose(s). In other words, the dissembling of Sikh tradition was conditioned by the perception of its adherents that reformation inscribed a revisionary exercise, a return to an original religious practice, indicating that its votaries did not develop into anything other than that which they already always were. Modernization, then, was never disclosed as a developmental phenomenon, and the event precipitating this revisionary intervention, the native's 'recognition' of his culture's degeneracy, went unrecognized.

Thus the affinity posited between Khalsa Sikhism and the British did not inscribe an authentic sense of kinship but constituted, rather, the adoption of an alternative strategy by the incorporative drive of colonial desire to that used to expropriate Bengali culture. This desire was effected through an erasure of difference and its specious perpetuation, (re)producing Sikh identity in a virtual form, which, *vis-à-vis* its militant signature, is transcribed as an ontology ultimately oriented towards the pacific, a virtualization which always remains encrypted by its conflation with the act of reform or, amounting to the same thing, is deciphered through the key of the fideiographic imaginary.

Conclusion

In conclusion I would like to highlight the following points. It is generally acknowledged that, in the cultural encounter between colonizer and colonized, the native is compelled to conform to the politico-economic perspective of the dominant colonial identity and, as such, it inscribes an act of subjugation. The recognition of, and the expression of resistance to, this subjugation is reflected in the advocacy of pluralist interpretations in the philosophy of religion, a view which, in some measure, grounds the discourse of post-colonial and post-modernist theory.

However, the politico-economic hegemony imposed on native cultures by colonialism also effects a fundamental refiguration of the other's ontological status, an event which is insidious since this specious or virtual alterity – regarded by the other as autogenous – is miscognized as such. Thus the sympathetic reception of the other's position ostensibly informing religious pluralism merely dissembles a liberation of heteronomy, since by uncritically accepting the *post*-colonial relation between the virtual other and the Western–Christian self as a properly intersubjective event (the fideiographic relation), it surreptitiously perpetuates the act of subjugation. Indeed, it might not be unreasonable to suggest that pluralism is simply the solicitous face of a colonial–modern identity absolutely intent on maintaining its own authority. Thus, if it is the case that the cultural narcissism of

Western subjectivity dissimulates what amounts to an ethnocidal act, via the detours of a pluralist solicitude, then the question before interreligious dialogue is not what the other has to say, but, rather, whether the other can be spoken of.

By problematizing the transparency of interreligious dialogue, a notion of religious alterity is signalled which is utterly incommensurable with the received understanding of religion which assimilates it to an ontotheological ground. Ultimately, the existence of competing interpretations of the religious puts into question the very tenability of the category *world religion*. The principal objection to this nihilistic proposition concerns the disastrous consequences putatively precipitated by spurning consensus as the ground of ethics for one constituted by provocation, violence and difference. However, as this chapter has attempted to show, it is *de facto* an ethics of consensus which inscribes contempt for the other, a disdain which is simply a modification of that explicit debilitation of conscience which facilitates the rationalization of cruelty.

Notes

1. What is being problematized here is that 'liberal' school of thought in the philosophy of religion which advocates a pluralist interpretation of the religious, and particularly as represented in the *œuvre* of John Hick. Hick has proposed a neo-Kantian hermeneutics of religions pluralism in which the Real as manifested within the intellectual and experiential purview of different religious traditions is a culturally perspectival understanding of 'the Real *an sich*' (Hick, 1989, p. 236). Thus the cultic phenomenologies of different religious traditions are merely culturally specific modalities through which a single noumenal essence makes its presence known.

2. Strictly, the Khalsa Sikh is one who has undergone the initiation ceremony known as *Khalsa ki pahul* (the 'tempering by the sword') and which commits the initiate to the way of life inscribed in the *Rehat maryada* (the Sikh code of conduct). Khalsa Sikhs must maintain a distinct bodily form determined by the adoption of five articles of which visually the most significant are the *kes* (unshorn bodily hair – in the case of male Sikhs the hair of the head is covered by the turban), *kirpan* (a steel broadsword) and the *kara* (a steel bracelet worn on the right wrist).

3. The term 'topography' here does not simply denote those disfigurements of the other's body which render it deviant *vis-à-vis* an idealized Christian–modern corporeality; it also refers to the pathological signature inscribed in the corpus of the other's textual and customary tradition. The topographic representation of the Sikh 'body', then, entails exposing both, the strange corporeal signifiers of the dark face and untamed beard, the turban and steel broadsword, as well as those conceptual (dis)figurations amongst the most conspicuous of which is the *sant-sipahi* or militant religiosity. Thus the mutilations of the other, inscribed in the act of stereotyping, are performed on a 'body' which exists simultaneously in a deviant corporeal and conceptual space, this intersection locating the other's identity as such. In short, then, it is necessary to avoid thinking of the terms 'body', 'identity', image as used in this discussion in a literalist manner, and to keep in mind that they express multiple meanings coterminously.

4. Gobind Singh (1666–1708) was the tenth, and last, of the human Sikh Gurus. During his incumbency as Guru, Gobind Singh was responsible for reinterpreting the ontological signature of Sikhism in terms of Khalsa identity. A highly capable military leader, Guru Gobind Singh was also a prolific author. His compositions, written in a dense poetical style, included both theological and mythological tractates, and were brought together

in a volume known as the *Dasam Granth Sahib* (The Book of the Tenth Guru).

5. *Jap Sahib*, the first composition in the *Dasam Granth*, is one of Guru Gobind Singh's most important works. It is ostensibly concerned with 'describ(ing) the nature and qualities of God' (Cole and Sambhi, 1997, p. 88); however, the conflicting representations of this 'divinity' which occur throughout the text belie this interpretation. It may be more consistent to read this work as a disclosure that the 'divine' constitutes an irretrievably fissured presence, one which is ontologically mediated by the act of fissuring itself, and thus the inadequacy of any attempt to describe something which is never *there* to be described.

6. In the work of W.H. McLeod, a somewhat different interpretation is advanced for the rise of Sikh militancy, which concedes its role as a phenomenon intended as a defence of righteousness, but qualifies the nature of this intent as something subject to 'the influence of the social, economic and historical environment' (McLeod, 1997, p. 116). The polarization of opinion between the advocates of the historicist and traditional approaches to the question of militancy in Sikhism continues to be one of the key, and, indeed, most vituperative, debates within Sikh scholarship. This is, however, largely an artificial dispute, since the question of violence needs to be thought of in terms of purposes or the absence of them, given which the 'differences' between the historicist and traditional interpretations are disclosed as merely modifications of the idea that a purpose needs to be ascribed to militancy; and, if, as suggested, the sign of militancy inscribes a violence which is gratuitous, an entire tradition of thinking concerning this problem needs to be repudiated.

References

Bataille, George (1988), *The Accursed Share: Volume 1*, trans. Robert Hurley, New York: Zone Books.

Cole, Owen and Piara Sambhi (1997), *A Popular Dictionary of Sikhism*, Richmond: Curzon Press.

Fanon, Frantz (1986), *Black Skin, White Masks*, trans. C. Markmann, London: Pluto Press.

Gilman, Sander (1985), *Difference and Pathology: Stereotypes of Sexuality, Race and Madness*, Ithaca: Cornell University Press.

Hick, John (1989), *An Interpretation of Religion: Human Responses to the Transcendent*, Basingstoke: Macmillan.

Irigaray, Luce (1985), *Speculum of the Other Woman*, trans. G. Gill, Ithaca: Cornell University Press.

McLeod, W.H. (1997), *Sikhism*, Harmondsworth: Penguin.

Metcalfe, Thomas (1997), *Ideologies of the Raj*, Cambridge: Cambridge University Press.

Singh, Harbans (1994), *The Heritage of the Sikhs*, New Delhi: Manohar.

Singh, Jodh and Dharam Singh (1999), *Sri Dasam Granth Sahib Text and Translation: Volume 1*, Patiala: Heritage Publications.

Chapter 8

Religious 'Worlds' and their Alien Invaders

Paulo Gonçalves

Disenchantment of the concept is the antidote of philosophy. It keeps it from growing rampant and becoming an absolute to itself. (Adorno, 1973, p. 13)

Introduction

This chapter will seek to address certain current trends in the theorization and representation of religious identity in the study of religions. The use of the concept of 'worlds' to represent the conglomerates which we speak of as 'religions' will act as a focus and paradigm of the range of approaches I will seek to critique. I will suggest that some current tendencies to represent religions as autonomous worlds of praxis and discourse exemplify an unjustified reification of identity – a reification which is not only ahistorical and inadequate to the phenomena being theorized, but which both implicitly and explicitly serves to further the interests of those committed to essentialist interpretations of their own traditions in the pursuit of allegedly orthodox authenticity. Such reification allows the theorization of hybridity and transformation only in terms of heterodox deviation or alien contamination. I will first set the scene with a brief overview of the recent trends I will be engaging with. This will be followed by a critique of some exemplars of these trends, principally of the representation of Christianity by 'Radical Orthodoxy' and of the notion of 'worlds' as employed by Hans Frei and the so-called 'Yale School'. I will then attempt to analyse this drive to reification and authenticity using Jacques Derrida's reflection on these processes in the history of Western philosophy. The final section of the chapter will consider alternative ways of theorizing religious identity and make several proposals which seek to maintain the tension between abstraction and specificity which arises during the course of such theorizing.

   One of the principal objections to perennialist and pluralist theories of religion, particularly John Hick's pluralist hypothesis (Hick, 1989), has been that, in their very project of harmonizing different religions, they actually betray the particularity of each religious tradition and replace this with a levelling generalization which continues the universalizing and imperialist tendencies of the Enlightenment. Kenneth Surin has most notably developed this critique in his equation of Hick's pluralist hypothesis with the universal spread of the McDonald's hamburger as the common meal in a neo-imperialist age. In such a situation, where 'All adherents of the major traditions are treated democratically in the pluralist monologue about difference' (Surin, 1990, p. 200) the difference of the other is inadvertently glossed over and betrayed by the misplaced charity of liberalism.

This type of objection has been accompanied by calls for a focus on specific religious traditions as integral, autonomous systems of organizing the world and experience, each composed of its own particular forms of life – rules, rituals and narratives – and thus not necessarily commensurable with each other. This focus on *difference* and particularity, in various guises, characterizes certain Wittgensteinian, postliberal, postfoundationalist, postmodern and communitarian approaches to religions. It is also present to a certain extent, and with specific reference to Christianity, in the 'Radical Orthodoxy' proposed by John Milbank and his colleagues.

A significant achievement of this trend, as evinced by the response to Hick's pluralist hypothesis, has been the problematizing of universalist, positivist and allegedly neutral presuppositions – the nefarious offspring of the Enlightenment – which underlie methodologies employed in much contemporary theology and religious studies. However, I am concerned that, precisely in their attempts to affirm the particularity, alterity and difference of various traditions, such approaches are not, as they claim, so much *describing*, but rather *generating, promoting and perpetuating* idealized or romanticized fantasms of quasi-autonomous and homogeneous religious traditions – fantasms which are possibly far removed from their actual and historical forms, and which ignore the agonistic history of their constitution as 'traditions' or 'religions'. In this manner, approaches which rightfully criticize the universalist notions of mysticism and essential religiosity which have dominated the discourse on religions are now seduced by what I will suggest is another chimera of strongly differentiated religious identities.

I perceive here three interrelated problems. First, there is a problem relating to the model of identity which is presupposed in these approaches, and the way in which this can easily function in scholarly discourse to filter and arrange historical, theoretical, sociological and empirical data according to allegedly clear boundaries or religious 'worlds'. Second, and inseparably, there is a problem relating to the self-conception of religious traditions when such a model is adopted or internalized by particular parties within these traditions. This can be seen as a potential continuation (though now in a postmodern mode) of the historical process of the translation (and internalization) of Asian traditions into homogeneous 'religions' with their respective 'faith' and 'doctrines' under colonialism. This has been traced by, amongst others, Richard King (King, 1999) and Arvind Mandair (in this volume). Third, I perceive a problem relating to the way in which these self-conceptions, once deployed, affect the relations of traditions to various forms of alterity – variations of internal interpretation, traditions which border it and variations which do not fit either category but which render problematic the distinction between the inner and the outer. These are not only problems in relation to the constitution of Asian traditions as homogeneous 'religions' through colonialism. What I would like to suggest is that *the very same forms* of homogenization, and thus the very same problems, occur in the representation of Christian identity, theology and history, and that consequently these representations can and should be challenged by the same sort of critique.

Narrative Identity and Totalization

An example of the trend I have been describing can be found in the work of Gavin D'Costa, arguably John Hick's most competent critic. In his programmatic article on 'The End of "Theology" and "Religious Studies"', he draws heavily on Hans Frei's *The Eclipse of Biblical Narrative* and echoes many of John Milbank's arguments in *Theology and Social Theory* in providing an account of theology's fall from grace from the medieval to the post-Enlightenment era (D'Costa, 1996; Frei, 1974; Milbank, 1990). D'Costa thus tells the story of a proper, pre-Enlightenment Christian theology, undertaken by a believing community, whose 'appropriate' methods 'were dictated by the subject matter, and not by criteria *alien* to it' (D'Costa, 1996, p. 341, emphasis added). This eirenic picture of a proper medieval theology is, however, spoilt by the improper and unruly invasion of alien Enlightenment and post-Enlightenment presuppositions. This invasion, says D'Costa, stands 'theology on its head' and, quoting Frei, 'Rather than "incorporating *the* world into *the* biblical story", theology becomes more and more a "matter of fitting *the* biblical story into *another* world" (which was constructed by *secularity and policed by its rules and methodology*).' (ibid., emphasis added). This invasion alters theology's '*fundamental nature*' and is considered to be a 'non-Christian tradition' which prizes theology 'apart from its *original form* of life and praxis' (ibid., pp. 341–2, emphasis added).

We are thus presented by D'Costa and certain 'Radical Orthodox' thinkers (Blond, 1998, pp. 6ff; Pickstock, 1998, pp. 121ff) with the picture of an allegedly unified and good practice, theology, corrupted by another, external and nefarious tradition labelled the 'Enlightenment', 'secularity' or 'secular reason'. The terminology used is noteworthy: '*the* world'; '*the* biblical story'; the use of 'theology' without qualifiers, presenting it as a clear univocal practice, and the ascription to it of a '*fundamental nature*' and '*original form*'; the similar strategy adopted with reference to something called 'secularity' or 'secularism'; the use of the terms 'corruptions' (Pickstock), 'alien' (D'Costa) and 'surrender' (Blond). All of these promote a view of 'theology' and 'secularity' as discrete worlds whose interrelation can only be theorized as a combative one involving invasion and corruption. Important questions can be raised in relation to this strategy. Does theology have a 'fundamental nature' and 'original form'? Who decides what this 'fundamental nature' is, and what interests does this serve? Is there a uniform and homogeneous pre-modern Christian theology? Can we speak of 'theology' in this abstract manner? Is it accurate to depict the Enlightenment as an alien invasion of theology, and to what extent can we reify and speak of such a thing as 'secularity', and identify 'its rules and methodology'? I will keep returning to these questions in what follows.

As an alternative to this alleged kidnapping of the Queen of the sciences and her transformation (both in status and sex!) into 'a graceless, stumbling knave' (D'Costa, 1996, p. 341), D'Costa proposes the model of sectarian religious departments run by the various theological traditions. He proposes that these, if dominated by what he qualifies as a 'good' sectarianism, will lead to a 'richer pluralism and a deeper engagement between different traditions (of course in proportion to those willing to engage in debate)' (ibid., p. 348). What makes 'bad sectarianism' *bad* in D'Costa's proposal is that it is characterized by 'closed forms of enquiry', and 'would refuse intellectual engagement with currents and traditions with which it disagreed' (ibid.). But to what standards can he appeal in this judgment? Given that he has moved from intersystematic to intrasystematic forms of legitimation, this evaluation surely cannot hold since it makes a trans-systemic evaluation which looks very much like a liberal valuation of the notion of dialogue, and seems to suggest a *remainder* of modernity in D'Costa's proposal. As a consequence, those who take D'Costa's suggestion of sectarian departments to heart, but whose sectarianism is precisely characterized by 'closed forms of enquiry', can rightfully dismiss his evaluation as an illegitimate move.

While D'Costa decries the 'stifling homogeny' of 'the logic of secular modernist institutions' (ibid.), it is unclear how his own proposal can avoid leading to what is possibly an even more vicious homogeny. It also ignores the fact that it is not only members of religious traditions who consider these traditions to be interesting, important and worthy of study. The following spectral question thus arises: if one is to move away from *external*, universal criteria and theories of religious interaction like pluralism, and focus on the alleged *internal* criteria of specific traditions, might this not signal a return to forms of antagonistic exclusivism unable to deal with otherness and difference except through suppression (who gets to decide what is 'traditional' in a 'tradition-specific' department?), caricature and demonization in the form of 'heresy', 'nihilism' and 'idolatry'?

That this poses a serious problem is evident not only from the totalizing and often pejorative blanket labels, such as 'paganism', 'idolatry' and 'nihilism' applied by certain 'Radically Orthodox' thinkers to all which falls beyond the limits of their particular vision of theology (for example, Blond, 1998, pp. 27–30, 48–9, 55–6) but also in several other contexts which appeal to community-based narrative legitimation. It can be seen, for instance, in the problematic question of whether there are any mechanisms for self-critique or, aside from suppression or exclusion, for dealing with views which deviate from the norm in communitarian theories such as that of MacIntyre (Welch, 1990, pp. 124–6). It is also evident in an analogous manner in the upsurge in conservative postfoundationalist philosophy of religion as championed by Alvin Plantinga (although here the question is one of epistemological foundation rather than narrative legitimation). Here the validity of Christianity is based on its holding what is referred to as a 'properly basic' belief concerning the existence of God. However, 'proper basicality', which is supposed to be a *general* epistemic category, is withheld from any alternative claims on the basis of a *particular* fideistic judgment concerning the falsity of other religions *vis-à-vis* the Christian god's revelation. Rose Ann Christian has rightly pointed out the 'epistemic permissiveness' which such a stance can lead to (Christian, 1992, pp. 553–73). In such a situation, where, to quote one of Plantinga's colleagues, it is 'all a matter of epistemic priorities' (Morris, 1986, p. 64), the real risk exists that, far from an eirenic 'good sectarianism', the relations between reified traditions can only be conceptualized in terms of a conflict of relative powers where force is the sole arbiter.

Steven Shakespeare, in a highly perceptive study, has consequently, and rightly, highlighted the *tone* of 'Radical Orthodoxy', as being one of its major problems: the fact that many of its texts are marked by forms of rhetorical violence and caricature (Shakespeare, 2000, p. 165). What is highly ironic is that John Milbank, Radical

Orthodoxy's most eloquent proponent, considers his proposed neo-Augustinian vision of theology to be precisely a move *away* from violence and towards a 'counter-ethics' of peace (Milbank, 1990, pp. 389–434). Indeed, violence is identified rather with pagan Roman antiquity which, according to an Augustinian reading, embodies political and social structures of domination and power which prevent true justice and virtue. Drawing on the work of René Girard, Milbank presents Roman paganism as being primarily devoted to the appeasement of the 'lust, greed and power' of the diverse gods through sacrifice (ibid., p. 392). By contrast, Christianity offers a new beginning with a vision of a 'heavenly city', a 'vision of peace' characterized by a fellowship not of domination, but of selfless forgiveness in a world which exists as 'an act of peaceful donation' from God (ibid., p. 391). In this 'city of God', differentiation is a result of God's 'gratuitous creative giving of existence', and thus not something to be condemned, but rather held in harmony through relation (ibid., p. 423). Milbank even parts company with Augustine here by rejecting punishment and judgment within the Church, and indeed, within God. Sin carries its own punishment, since it is a rupture of the relation to God, and thus an ontological self-nihilation (ibid., pp. 421, 432).

Milbank thus presents a radical vision of Christianity, seeing it as offering the *sole* possibility for the absence of violence and the overcoming of nihilism (ibid., pp. 432, 434). He acknowledges, however, that the Christian interruption of history has failed and that Christianity has 'unleashed a more "naked" violence' on the world, promoting 'a hellish society beyond any terrors known to antiquity' (ibid., pp. 432f, 417–22). However, while acknowledging that the Church has not lived up to the ideal he has sketched (which, though masked in the language of abstraction, remains *his* interpretation of what is and is not essentially Christian), we need to consider carefully *why* Milbank considers it to have 'failed'. Two reasons are presented. Firstly, the Church has 'compromised' with the forms of dominion of late antiquity by adopting coercion. 'The Church' (whose church?) is presented as being on one side of a dividing line of the use of power, while pagan political dominion is on the other. One is non-coercive, the other is coercive: 'For Augustine, as we have seen, as for the early church in general, the division coercion/non-coercion was the important criterion in separating the political from the ecclesial' (ibid., p. 418). Their interaction is thus necessarily one of 'compromise'. The second reason for the failure is a direct result of this 'compromise': 'The Church did not succeed in displacing politics, and as a result, politics returned, yet in a virulent form unknown to antiquity' (ibid., pp. 432–3). This is said to occur in the early medieval period in a process through which the Church, through its failure, is argued to be responsible for the creation of secular reason from the eleventh century onwards.

Certain questions need to be raised in relation to this picture. While claiming that he is not seeking a restoration of a 'pre-modern Christian position' or a 'past epoch of Christian dominance' (ibid., pp. 2, 432), it seems evident that Milbank is in certain clear ways referring *back*, not only to Augustine, but also to an image of 'the early church in general' which in his view identified itself with 'non-coercion' as opposed to the political realm of the coercive. Indeed, this *harking back*, which one might characterize as a form of ambivalent nostalgia, is characteristic of Radical Orthodoxy in general, particularly insofar as it considers the late medieval and early modern periods as having been periods of falling away and corruption (Milbank,

Pickstock and Ward, 1999, pp. 1–2). But where can we find this non-coercive church? And whose church is it? Is it the church of the party that eventually dominated (through coercion) as 'orthodox' in the early church, or is it Milbank's idealized church projected backwards? In a study of Christian relations to paganism, the eminent scholar of the early church, R.P.C. Hanson, in fact presents a view of Christianity and paganism which is diametrically opposed to Milbank's: 'when all allowance has been made, it must not be denied that one of the great reasons Christianity prevailed over its rivals was its intolerance … whereas paganism was for the most part almost endlessly tolerant' (Hanson, 1985, p. 211). As Milbank's own reading of Augustine reveals, there are various conceptions of 'the Church' in early Christianity, many of which, in both idealized textual interpretation as well as social reality, actively promoted and exploited forms of dominion not as a 'compromise' with an alien dominion, but rather as a direct outworking of their theology.

This has been amply chronicled by such scholars as Elaine Pagels in her study of the relations between theology (particularly monotheism) and forms of authority and coercion in the struggles between various Christian groups in the second and third centuries (Pagels, 1982) and by Bart Ehrman in his study of the role of textual emendation of authoritative scriptures in the Christological controversies of the same period (Ehrman, 1993, pp. xi–xii, 3–46). The status and treatment of women throughout Christian history likewise involves a direct outworking of theological ideas in forms of domination and coercion which Radical Orthodoxy on the whole remains uncomfortably silent about. The studies of MacMullen (1984, 1997), Brown (1995) and Cameron (1991) explore the relations between ideology and power in Christianity's conflict with, and violent suppression of, paganism. Given this highly differentiated view of early Christianity, one is justified in asking why, and with what textual, historical and even *theological* legitimacy, Milbank chooses to present a certain reified and idealized view of a non-coercive Christianity as being essentially and truly Christian, while rejecting what does not fit this essence as an external form of political and pagan dominion? Whose essence and which orthodoxy? Rowan Williams has thus rightly questioned Milbank's utopic ecclesiology and refers to 'the trap of fusing historical narrative with "essentialist", diagrammatic accounts of ideological options' (R. Williams, 1996, p. 436). One might even ask whether Milbank's ideal of peace and the non-coercive, relational coexistence of differences does not reveal a strikingly *modern* set of commitments, though these are worked out in the categories of Augustine's Trinitarian theology?

As pointed out earlier, what remains strikingly incongruous in the work of many Radical Orthodox theologians is that, despite Milbank's extremely eloquent and in some ways moving appeal for a Christianity of peace, non-coercion and absence of judgment in a differential harmony, this very discourse is accompanied by another whose tone is combative, rhetorically coercive and highly judgmental – projecting apocalyptic caricatures of 'paganism' and 'nihilism' onto the broad swathe of whatever is not 'Radically Orthodox'. Steven Shakespeare's analysis of this characteristic is worth quoting:

> The irony is that the picture of the world that is created is one of incompatible, competing

discourses, locked in a war to the death – precisely the kind of agonistic account of reality for which secularism is condemned. … Outside the Christian language and field of vision, there is only war and death. (Shakespeare, 2000, p. 167)

Shakespeare rightly points out that, in such a scenario, 'It is presumed that narratives are seamless wholes, with no room for connection or conversation between them' (ibid.). Milbank thus holds that the persuasiveness of his position is not due to an appeal to a chimeric universal human reason, but rather 'this should be a persuasion intrinsic to the Christian *logos* itself' (Milbank, 1990, p. 1). However, if the *form* of this persuasion is that of rhetorical violence and caricature, I would propose that this constitutes a striking example of my contention that the shift from universal modes of discourse to a focus on the integrity and reified identity of particular narratives carries with it the very real risk of a return of violence, or of what D'Costa unsuccessfully attempts to exclude from such a shift through the label of 'bad sectarianism'.

The range of problems, highlighted above, that face approaches which understand the identity of Christianity to be a function of homogeneous narrative integrity is faced also by approaches which apply such a theory of identity to the study of religious traditions in general. This is perhaps most evident with reference to the work of George Lindbeck (like Hans Frei, a representative of the 'Yale School'), particularly in his influential *The Nature of Doctrine: Religion and Theology in a Postliberal Age* (1984). Lindbeck's study moves away from universalist interpretations of religions. Drawing largely on the work of, amongst others, Wittgenstein and Clifford Geertz, as well as of another of his Yale colleagues, William Christian, Lindbeck offers a 'cultural–linguistic' theory of religion. Reinterpreting doctrines as functioning less like propositions and rather more like the grammatical rules which govern the specific language games of varying religions, he proposes that religions be seen as 'comprehensive interpretive schemes, usually embodied in myths or narratives and heavily ritualized, which structure human experience and understanding of self and world' (ibid., p. 32). Lindbeck both is aware of, and seeks to provide a response to, the problems of incommensurability which such a model raises (ibid., pp. 46-72).

However, the question must again be asked as to whether such an approach does not promote the creation of ahistorical, narratively enclosed, religious 'worlds'? Indeed, such a model might lead to the institution or reinforcement of the drive to essentialist descriptions of religious traditions. Thus, in discussing interreligious dialogue, Lindbeck suggests that 'one of the ways in which Christians can serve their neighbours may be through helping adherents of other religions to purify and enrich their heritages, to make them better speakers of the languages they have' (ibid., pp. 61–2). But what exactly is being gained and what is being lost through such 'purification' and 'enrichment'? This would seem to lead to a repetition of the dialectical and mimetic constitution of alterity which has characterized the construction of 'the world religions' along Western and Christian notions of what constitutes a 'religion'. There is thus a clear bias towards religions that have developed formal canonical writings since these allow for easy structural and semiotic analysis, and form a standard according to which differing expressions of that religion can be assessed for 'faithfulness'. Indeed, having canonical writings is seen by Lindbeck as the 'condition, not only for the survival of a religion, but for the very possibility of normative theological description' (ibid., p. 116). What is important to note here is that systematicity, canonicity and normative description are valued since they sustain a particular notion of authenticity whose cultural and historical situatedness is insufficiently explored or even acknowledged. Thus, while Lindbeck's cultural–linguistic proposal attempts to respond to the possibility of difference in a way which earlier universalist approaches ignored, both the model suggested and the concept of 'purity' referred to, mediate certain ideals of structural homogeneity and autonomy which recent studies of both Asian religions as well as of Christianity have shown to be rather dubious historically. Indeed, such ideals suit the agendas of power of those who choose to see themselves as the authentic purifiers and representatives of religious traditions, both in terms of self-definition and in the formal contexts of so-called 'inter-faith' dialogue.

Hans Frei and the Lure of the Premodern

I have attempted to indicate some of the problems which arise in terms not only of Christianity, but also of other religious traditions, when models of identity which presume structural homogeneity are employed in their representation. The thought of Hans Frei has been a near constant (either explicitly or thematically) in most of the thinkers discussed, in terms of his account of a shift in theology from a pre-critical biblical purity to a post-critical fall from grace under the impact of the Enlightenment and secularity, as well as in his use of the terminology of 'worlds' to represent this shift. Given the important role which these two themes play in the approaches being discussed, I propose in what follows to examine more closely the legitimacy of the arguments which Frei puts forward in their development in *The Eclipse of Biblical Narrative* (1974).

The earlier discussion of D'Costa's views has already introduced us to the historical narrative which Frei has proposed. For Frei, Enlightenment secularity, and particularly the historical critical approach to the Bible, led to an alien 'postcritical' transformation of what he identifies as a proper 'precritical' approach to biblical narrative. This is spoken of as a 'breaking down' and a process of 'disintegration' (Frei, 1974, p. 4) whereby 'interpretation was a matter of fitting the biblical story into another world with another story' (ibid., p. 130) rather than seeking to incorporate 'extrabiblical thought, experience, and reality into the one real world detailed and made accessible by the biblical story' (ibid., p. 3). According to Frei, the distinguishing characteristic of the pre-critical approach is that it employs a combination of figurative (or typological) and literal reading in order to unify the canon and provide one continuous story or narrative – the biblical 'world' (ibid., p. 2). Figurative reading is thus an 'instrument for unifying the canon' and 'an instrument for uniting the Bible' (ibid., pp. 2, 6–7, 13).

There are, however, two problems which face this particular account of a lost holism. The first relates to the origin and status of the valued concept of canonical unity, whose loss is lamented. On a formal level, in which 'world' is the concept to be found? It would seem that, far from being the product of the biblical 'world' or 'story', it is something that needs to be presupposed in the construction of this 'story' and this 'world'. Inquiring into the historical provenance of this concept immediately complicates not only the concept itself, but also the holism suggested for the pre-critical approach by both Frei and D'Costa. The process of canonical formation in the early church was largely characterized, and motivated, by conflict between various Christian groups concerning the nature and interpretation of Christianity, as well as the varying forms of revelatory authority and their limits. Indeed, the first such list was produced by Marcion of Pontus circa 140CE – a list which excluded the Hebrew scriptures entirely and whose author was condemned by an emerging 'orthodoxy'. Montanism in the second century, with its powerful charismatic emphasis on revelation through prophecy, similarly raised questions about the limits of revelation and authority. Conflicts raged between different Christian groupings, each claiming the orthodox label, on which texts should be considered authoritative – most notably the conflict involving what are currently referred to as 'Gnostic' forms of Christianity, admirably charted by Elaine Pagels (1982). There are significant variations in lists of authoritative books between so-called 'orthodox' Christian thinkers until late in the fourth century. These conflicts not only reveal the significant variety of 'pre-critical' Christianity, but lead us to ask of Frei's position, 'Whose canon? Whose story? And whose world?' Frei's representation of 'the' biblical story as a neutral, monolithic and trans-historical 'it', with 'its world' and 'its structure' (Frei, 1974, pp. 3, 6) obscures the polemical history of canonical development and the questions of power raised by this history. The questions become even more insistent in light of recent studies, particularly that of Bart Ehrman (1993), of the textual emendations made to canonical scriptures by 'orthodox' writers in the Christological conflicts of the second and third centuries. Appeals to canonical unity, and the affirmation of one biblical story and world, therefore, are neither transparent nor innocent, but are implicated in agendas of power and legitimacy with a dramatic genealogy.

The second problem faced by Frei's account is that, in its description of a uniform pre-critical mode of reading, it misrepresents the significant complexity of pre-enlightenment modes of interpretation. This is particularly evident in his description of allegory as a successor to pre-critical figurative reading: 'figuration found successors in such mirror-image categories of interpretation as allegory and somewhat later, myth' (Frei, 1974, p. 6) Given the long history of allegorical modes of interpretation in Christianity, this seems somewhat disingenuous (Pepin, 1958; Hanson, 1959). One should not exaggerate the extent of disagreement in interpretative principles in early Christian writers: there is a general favouring of literal, or historico-grammatical exegesis (Ehrman, 1993, pp. 20–2) combined with typology (Kelley, 1977, pp. 71–2). However, there were differences of emphasis which led to polemics, particularly in relation to 'gnostic' Christian interpretations (Ehrman, 1993, p. 21), but also between 'orthodox' traditions – the latter usually associated with doctrinal disagreements, particularly in terms of Christology. This is most evident in the well-known doctrinal and exegetical tensions between the Alexandrian and Antiochene 'schools' (Kelley, 1977, pp. 69–79). These differences and tensions call for a more nuanced account of 'pre-critical' forms of reading than that suggested by Frei.

A consideration of the process of canonical formation as well as of early Christian modes of interpretation thus suggests that Frei's projection of a lost holism, as well as his identification of a biblical 'world' in the singular, cannot be sustained. On closer analysis it also startlingly emerges that, far from describing modes of reading in the early and medieval church, Frei is in fact speaking of the hermeneutical principles of the Protestant reformers in his description of the 'pre-critical' approach. Frei's second chapter, entitled 'Precritical Interpretation of Biblical Narrative', thus surprisingly does not contain any discussion of early and medieval forms of interpretation, but is an exposition and discussion of Luther's and Calvin's hermeneutics.

Ironically, whereas in his first chapter Frei refers to analogy as a 'mirroring strategy' which is a modern or post-critical successor to typological interpretation, in his second chapter he speaks of Luther's typological approach as representing

> his drastic alternative to the complex and long development of traditional theory of scriptural interpretation which had come to distinguish among literal, allegorical, anagogical, and tropical senses of the text. Against that multiplex view Luther's simplification meant drastic relief. (Frei, 1974, p. 19)

This not only contradicts his earlier assessment of analogy, and constitutes an acknowledgment of the complexity of early Christian and medieval forms of interpretation, it also clearly demonstrates that, for Frei, the *'pre-critical' is not equivalent to the 'traditional'*, which predates it. He subsequently also approvingly describes Calvin's rejection of allegory (ibid., pp. 24–5). Thus the 'pre-critical' holism whose loss Frei laments is in fact located at the dawn of modernity in the seventeenth century and stands in contrast to the preceding tradition. While these are by no means absent from earlier interpreters, it is in Luther and Calvin that Frei locates the various dimensions of his 'pre-critical' approach – figurative or typological reading employed as a means of unifying the canon, and leading to the generation of 'the' biblical world (ibid., pp. 19–20).

From the preceding critical discussion of Frei's project and the resultant exploration of the diversity of early Christianity, certain conclusions can be drawn concerning the two themes which we have seen that thinkers such as D'Costa and Lindbeck draw from him. Firstly, while it initially appears that Frei is describing a simple fall from a pre-critical form of reading which would embrace the medieval and early Christian periods, in fact the 'precritical' holistic interpretation is identified with the reformers, and *stands in contrast and provides an alternative to* medieval and early Christian approaches, as well as later 'post-critical' secular approaches. The term is thus somewhat misleading and its appropriateness can be queried. This renders highly problematic, and also ironic, the use made of Frei by D'Costa to defend and lament a lost medieval holism, given that D'Costa is a Roman Catholic theologian. Secondly, the notion of a biblical 'world' is rendered highly problematic when the differentiated status of early Christianity, and the complex history of canonical development, authority and interpretation are taken into account. Thus the description of modern forms of reading as a simple reversal, by which a felicitous pre-critical 'biblical world' is absorbed by 'another world', is shown to be not only naively simplistic, but also rather misleading: 'Whose canon? And whose world?' become pertinent questions, with widespread implications in terms of authority, representation and legitimation.

Identity and Transformation Between Structuralism and Deconstruction

The above conclusions thus reinforce the questioning of idealized and essentialized descriptions of a unified and allegedly 'proper' Christian theology which I initiated earlier. They also call into doubt the appropriateness of using homogeneous categories such as 'worlds' to represent religious traditions and their transformations. There are strong parallels between such approaches and the presuppositions operative in structural approaches to language. In Lindbeck, the lines of structuralist influence are quite explicit, particularly through the work of Clifford Geertz and of Lindbeck's Yale colleague William Christian, leading to a focus on 'the internal logic or grammar of religions' (Lindbeck, 1984, pp. 16, 27–8, n.16, 114–15). I believe one can legitimately speak of the terminology of 'religious worlds' as employed in these approaches and in introductory works such as Paden's *Religious Worlds* (1994) as representing a 'structuralist' moment in the study of religions. As in structural linguistics, we have seen that such approaches, despite important qualifications, tend to value the description of abstract synchronous structures or systems over diachronous development (Ricoeur, 1974, p. 81). In Derrida's words, 'the internal originality of the structure compels a neutralization of time and history' (Derrida, 1978, p. 291). As in structural linguistics, where 'The collection of signs must be maintained as a closed system in order to submit it to analysis' (ibid., p. 82), religions are also interpreted as self-contained, autonomous systems of discourse. Finally, and particularly with reference to the structuralist anthropology of Lévi-Strauss, Derrida has pointed out the 'ethic of presence, an ethic of nostalgia for origins, an ethic of archaic and natural innocence' which characterizes what he calls 'the structuralist thematic of broken immediacy' (Derrida, 1978, p. 292).

The implications of this are far-reaching. Firstly, given this static, synchronous interpretation, 'change, considered as such, is unintelligible' for linguistic systems (Ricoeur, 1974, p. 81). To quote Derrida, 'the appearance of a new structure, of an original system, always comes about – and this is the very condition of its structural specificity – by a rupture with the past, its origin, and its cause'. The genesis of a new structure has to be conceived 'on the model of catastrophe' (Derrida, 1978, p. 291). Similarly, religious transformations can only be interpreted agonistically in terms of calamitous invasion, corruption or compromise, a process of fundamental *alteration and loss*. Secondly, and related to this, innovation, described as 'free combination', and the 'producing of new utterances', is excluded, as is time and history (Ricoeur, 1974, pp. 83–4): a synchronous, closed structure can only repeat itself. Whether these parallels constitute explicit lines of influence in the theorizing of religions or are simply analogous, I would suggest that, given the preceding analyses, this form of modelling and of understanding religious traditions, transformation and identity is not only inadequate to describe the range of phenomena being investigated, but also misleading and irresponsible. This calls, then, for the exploration of alternative modes of theorizing religious identity and its representation which are sensitive to blurred boundaries, variations of interpretation, marginalization by influential elites and the dynamics of innovation and transformation.

Derrida has been one of the thinkers who has most rigorously analysed the drive for propriety and the reappropriation of difference by normative accounts in the history of Western philosophy, particularly in relation to the metaphysical concepts of unity, autonomy and presence which have dominated conceptions of identity and relations to alterity. Engaging with structuralism, but extending his analysis chronologically, he has thus spoken of the history of metaphysics as the various determinations of a controlling centre which would delimit, orient, found and ensure the coherence of a structure (of both knowledge and of being) (Derrida, 1978, pp. 278–9). Derrida understands 'metaphysics', therefore, primarily as what he calls the 'metaphysics of the proper' animated by a desire for 'self-presence, unity, self-identity, the proper' (Derrida, 1974, p. 26; 1978, p. 194). It is clear that Derrida considers the 'history of metaphysics', not as a homogeneous 'tradition', but rather as the attempts by certain discourses within this history to achieve normative force in pursuit of this desire for propriety, stability and closure, whereby 'anxiety can be mastered' (Derrida, 1978, p. 279). He consequently argues, 'There is no metaphysical concept in and of itself. There is a work – metaphysical or not – on conceptual systems' (Derrida, 1982, p. 329; 1981b, p. 6). What this implies is that, for Derrida, such systems are not univocal, so that one might make a facile distinction between a metaphysical and a post-metaphysical epoch:

> The closure of metaphysics, above all, is not a circle surrounding a homogeneous field, a field homogeneous with itself on its inside, whose outside then would be homogeneous also. The limit has the form of always different faults, of fissures whose mark or scar is borne by all the texts of philosophy. (Derrida, 1981a, p. 57)

In Derrida's view, therefore, normative accounts, while potentially justified, simultaneously engage in a process of abstraction which has a levelling effect on the system or text under consideration. A clearer indication of what this means can be had from his discussion of the relation between 'Platonism' and the Platonic corpus:

> Platonism would mean, in these conditions, a thesis or the theme which one has extracted by artifice, misprision, and abstraction from the text, torn out of the written fiction of 'Plato.' Once this abstraction has been supercharged and deployed, it will be extended over all the folds of the text, of its ruses, overdeterminations, and reserves, which the abstraction will come to cover up and dissimulate. This will be called Platonism, or the philosophy of Plato, which is neither arbitrary nor illegitimate, since a certain force of thetic abstraction at work in the heterogeneous text of Plato can recommend one to do so. [...] 'Platonism' is thus certainly one of the effects of the text signed by Plato, for a long time, and for necessary reasons, the dominant effect, but this effect always turned back against the text. (Derrida, 1995, pp. 119–20)

Consequently, according to Derrida, normative and abstract interpretations can be considered to be legitimate, but simultaneously occlusive. With reference to early Christianity, for instance, there is a similar 'force of thetic abstraction' at work in the heterogeneous writers of this period. Reading ecclesiastical historians of the third and fourth centuries, such as Eusebius of Caesarea, and his translator into Latin, Rufinus of Aquileia, one is faced with a representation of a difficult but relatively rapid triumph of an orthodox Christian monotheism over a declining paganism. In Peter Brown's words 'By means of this representation, Christian writers imposed (with seemingly irrevocable success, to judge by most modern accounts of the period) a firm narrative closure on what had been, in reality, in the well chosen words of Pierre Chuvin, a "Wavering Century"' (Brown, 1995, pp. 4, 6). As indicated by him, this 'abstraction' both informs and legitimizes the 'narrative closure' which we have seen in current accounts of a lost Christian 'world'. Such readings, however, need to contend with the important resistances, folds, fissures and faults which characterize both the periods and the texts under discussion.

Derrida attributes the resistance to normative accounts to several factors. Firstly, as we have seen, this might be a function of the heterogeneity of the written corpus of a certain writer. This is particularly evident in the case of a writer such as Plato, who, if we are to grant the authenticity of his seventh letter, deliberately eschews the writing of a systematic treatise on his views (341b–d; see also Friedländer, 1969, pp. 113–15). Secondly, Derrida traces such heterogeneity to the transmission of Greek philosophy, whereby it is affected and fissured by 'heterogeneous elements of Judaism and Christianity', and by the translation of Greek concepts into other languages and, similarly, by the 'translation of Hebraic or Arabic ideas and structures into metaphysical terms' (Derrida, in Kearney, 1984, pp. 116–17). Finally, Derrida sees this heterogeneity not only as the function of a process of interaction and translation with an external 'other':

> this 'otherness' is not necessarily something which comes to Greek philosophy from the 'outside', that is, from the non-Hellenic world. From the very beginnings of Greek philosophy the self-identity of the *Logos* is already fissured and divided. I think one can discern signs of such fissures of 'differance' in every great philosopher. (Ibid.)

This final point relates to the particular deconstructive readings which Derrida has engaged in where he has sought to demonstrate the *structural* failure of attempts to assert the autonomy and self-identity of founding concepts by tracing their differential relations to the alterity and mutability they seek to exclude. These readings challenge not only notions of identity based on autonomy, but also the structural closure which such notions seek to ensure, thus challenging the totalization which, for instance, is aimed for in structuralist accounts (Derrida, 1978, p. 289). It is impossible to provide a more detailed account of these in the scope of this chapter but I would refer the reader to three classic exemplars of Derrida's readings: his essays, 'Signature Event Context' (Derrida, 1982, pp. 307–30) and 'Plato's Pharmacy' (Derrida, 1981b, pp. 61–172), and his introduction to Husserl's *Origin of Geometry* (1989).

It is because of these various forms of difference and heterogeneity in the history of philosophy that Derrida refers to philosophical texts as possessing a 'future' of meaning: 'all the great philosophical texts – of Plato, Parmenides, Hegel or Heidegger, for example – are still *before* us' (in Kearney, 1984, pp. 110, 113–14). And it is for this reason that he considers 'deconstruction' to be a 'positive response' to this alterity (ibid., p. 118), since it seeks to bring this alterity into play against totalizing or levelling readings. He consequently makes an appeal for 'the rigorous reading of metaphysics, wherever metaphysics normalizes Western discourse, and not only in the texts of the "history of philosophy"' (Derrida, 1982, pp. 22–3).

Deconstruction and the Theorizing of Religious Identity

I would like to suggest that such deconstructive readings are equally necessary in both the study and representation of religious traditions wherever forces of 'thetic abstraction' attempt to 'normalize' the agonistic history of the genesis, transformation and constitution of those things we call 'religions'. Such readings and analyses should be, and indeed have been, directed against the thetic abstraction and assumed propriety inherent in the concept of 'religion' itself, with its structural, systematic, textual and doctrinal filters (McCutcheon, 1997). Picking up Derrida's description of the manner in which an abstraction can be extracted from a heterogeneous text or system and then deployed over all its irregularities, I would argue that this is precisely the mechanism which is operating in the creation of idealized and romanticized notions of religious 'worlds' or golden eras of unsullied or 'proper' theology. These can be seen as a succession of layerings of abstraction onto the past, giving it an artificial unity in the arena of current academic, religious and political debate. This problem seems particularly acute in relation to the Orientalist construction of a series of '-isms' in the image of European modes of representation during the colonial period (King, 1999) but it is also a widespread problem in the study of religions in general. Thus, in his recent landmark work, *Rethinking 'Gnosticism': An Argument for Dismantling a Dubious Category* (1996), Michael Williams has shown how the term 'Gnosticism' is an eighteenth century invention for which there is no equivalent in antiquity.

> This is not to deny the existence of the persons or writings themselves that are usually treated under this modern category. They did exist, and their story constitutes one of the most intriguing chapters in the history of ancient religion. But in actuality we should speak of their 'stories,' for a recurring argument in this study will be that interesting and important things about these people have been consistently obscured by the very decision to reduce their stories to the story of a single movement or religion, or '-ism.' (M. Williams, 1996, p. 7)

I have attempted to demonstrate that very similar things could be said about Christianity and constructions and representations of Christian history and identity. Robert Doran has written of this process of abstraction in the representation of Christian history as 'the mustard-seed fallacy', where

> the development of early Christian doctrine is imagined in almost evolutionary terms, as providentially leading to what is best in an almost inevitable, inexorable movement, with the rest imaged as nonadaptable organisms, as relics to be discarded, as wrongheaded heretics. (Doran, 1995, p. 6)

He makes three important points in relation to this 'imaginary'. Firstly, it reflects the idealized representation of a certain male elite which, as we saw earlier, puts a 'narrative closure' on the triumph of its particular brand of Christianity by interpreting it as a providential necessity. Secondly, 'It also gives the impression that the root stock of the tree is pure and unsullied', that is, it occludes the heterogeneity which an ascendant form of Christianity attempted to obliterate (often successfully) both rhetorically and physically. Thirdly, such an impression leads to a '"golden age" view of history: Heresies were a later infection brought into the church, usually by the alien virus of Greek philosophy' (ibid., p. 4) Beginning with the ground-breaking work of Walter Bauer (1972), such a view has long been untenable. We have, however, seen ample evidence of the persistence of such a nostalgic 'golden age' view in influential current representations of Christianity.

In a perceptive analysis of the way in which religious innovations are represented, Michael Williams (whose study was referred to above) has considered precisely the use of metaphors such as 'virus', 'parasite' and 'nonadaptable organism' to describe such innovations, particularly in relation to 'Gnosticism'. He provides a trenchant critique of such metaphors, many aspects of which speak to our analysis of certain current representations of early Christian identity. Such metaphors are not only suspiciously pejorative, they also imply the existence of a pure 'host tradition', in relation to which differences and innovations are considered to be either invasive viruses or parasitical appendages. However, given that the origins of the alleged 'host' traditions can themselves be described in terms of adoption and adaptation through a web of relations and a process of transformative inheritance, he observes that 'In this sense, every new religion has begun as a "parasite."' He continues by suggesting that, 'we might ask, for example, what a "pure" or "nonparasitical" Christianity would look like' – a pertinent question to pose to those who appeal to a lost Christian holism (M. Williams, 1996, p. 83). Williams argues, not only that these metaphors are problematic when applied to an abstraction such as 'Gnosticism', but that they are highly problematic when used in the history of religions in general: 'the phenomena being described as a "parasite" religion do not actually constitute some special species or type of religious movement, but rather "less successful" innovations' (ibid.). This then begs the question as to *why* these innovations have been 'less successful' and marginalized, demonized or obliterated. Such a question moves us out of the rarefied world of idealized 'religions' and abstract narrative constructs such as religious 'worlds' and into a consideration of issues of power, gender, political manoeuvring and oppression within these narrative constructs.

There are several important and related ways in which the strategies of deconstructive reading, and Derrida's analyses of the processes of totalization in the history of Western philosophy, can assist us in providing more nuanced and responsible accounts of religious identity, representation and transformation. His analyses encourage us to challenge and look beyond the homogeneity suggested by ahistorical and reified structuralist or idealized accounts and to consider the differences, resistances, folds and fissures, in both textual representation and social and historical reality, of what is 'normalized' and occluded by such accounts. *In this sense*, many of the works which have been referred to above, not many of which necessarily make any explicit reference to deconstruction, could be considered 'deconstructive'. This holds for readings which challenge the construction of abstract and reified '-isms', such as Gnosticism (M. Williams, 1996) or Hinduism and Buddhism (King, 1999), but also for those which challenge general abstractions that function in scholarly discourse about religious traditions, such as 'mysticism' and the notion of 'religious texts' (Jantzen, 1995; King, 1999). It holds also for approaches which challenge the hegemonic descriptions of particular traditions by revealing the rich complexity of their constitution; in the context of this study, I refer particularly to the representation of early Christian history, and the important but often overlooked point that 'at no point in its history has the religion constituted a monolith. But the diverse manifestations of its first three hundred years – whether in terms of social structures, religious practices, or ideologies – have never been replicated' (Ehrman, 1993, p. 3).

Beyond this generalized understanding of 'deconstructive' reading, there is also scope for drawing more directly or explicitly on the strategies of deconstructive reading in order to challenge established hegemonies, interpretations or hierarchies. For example, Grace Jantzen draws on Derrida's strategy of 'double reading' to displace a masculinist symbolic in the philosophy of religion: 'a sort of reading which on the one hand pays close attention to a text, but which, in that very attention, discloses a rupture in that text which requires a radically different reading of it, thus destabilizing it and in the undecidability thereby created opens the possibility of thinking otherwise' (Jantzen, 1998, p. 61). I similarly draw on a Derridean strategy of inversion and displacement in order to critique and destabilize both the idea of radical divine transcendence and the border between Christian purity and Pagan 'idolatry' which early Christian apologists attempted to establish (Gonçalves, 1998). In both cases, a dominant and exclusive tradition is differentiated and rendered strange to itself by a reading which demonstrates how its apparent borders are fissured or fold back into itself, thus revealing the fluidity and permeability of an identity which represented itself as hegemonic and impermeable.

Deconstructive approaches, insofar as they challenge hegemonic accounts of identity, would thus encourage a sensitivity to difference and particularity which goes well beyond the simple acknowledgment of differences between 'religions' which characterizes contemporary challenges to universalist views, derived from the Enlightenment, that consider religions to be varying paths to one ultimate reality or varying expressions of a common human religiosity. Through a careful attentiveness to location, and to the plurivocity and resistances of texts and contexts, deconstructive approaches likewise allow a greater sensitivity, and ability to articulate the agendas of power operative in these. They encourage more 'textured' representations of religious traditions and their histories which are not shackled to the needs of either structural neatness or the normativity desired by powerful elites. It is evident that this attentiveness to detail and particularity might generate considerable methodological inconvenience for academic approaches which prefer to paint theories with broad brushstrokes, and which would rather examine, arrange and bounce a neat set of 'religions' off each other as one might a bag of marbles. However, the loss of such abstractions is hardly something to be lamented. The temptation to abstraction, while a general one for scholars of religion, is particularly acute for philosophers of religion and philosophical theologians by the very nature of the abstractive dimension of their discipline.

What I have attempted to demonstrate is the importance of a detailed knowledge of, and historical sensitivity to, the constitution of the traditions upon which philosophers of religion base their general theories. This, I suggest, would lead to more delimited and focused, but far more productive and responsible, scholarship than has resulted from what has often been an ahistorical and uncontextual plundering of past authors for 'proof-texts' in the service of modern homogeneous constructs of religious traditions, with little sensitivity to questions of conflict, hybridity, power, gender and colonialism.

Conclusion

In this chapter I have attempted to provide a survey and critique of certain modern trends in religious studies and the philosophy of religions which represent religious traditions as homogeneous narrative 'worlds'. While detailed critiques of such approaches in relation to the construction of Asian 'religions' during the colonial encounter have been produced, I focused particularly on similar trends in certain influential modern representations of Christian history and identity, particularly 'Radical Orthodoxy' and the 'Yale School'. I attempted to demonstrate that these employ historical narratives and idealized views of a 'lost' age of Christian propriety and identity which are historically and theoretically unsustainable given the incredible diversity of early Christianity.

Primarily, I hope that the highly problematic nature of abstract and totalizing models such as 'religious worlds' to represent the identity of religious traditions has been demonstrated. Such models suffer from several important weaknesses. They are first of all ahistorical. Secondly, their representation as hegemonous narrative wholes occludes their continuity and relations with surrounding movements, ideologies and trends. Thirdly, they serve the interests of specific elites and 'orthodoxies' within traditions, to the detriment of less influential, though potentially more widespread, variations. Fourthly, in so doing they occlude and misrepresent the inner heterogeneity of these traditions (and in some cases the heterogeneity is of such an extent that it challenges the concept of an easily identifiable 'tradition'). Finally, they are committed to viewing innovation, change and variation as forms of corruption, alteration or invasion of an original purity, whereas such a 'purity' is not historically forthcoming. They thus misrepresent the dynamics of continuity and change, of inheritance and transformation, which characterize the genesis and transformation of traditions.

Drawing on Jacques Derrida's analysis and critique of similar hegemonic trends in structuralism and the history of Western philosophy, I subsequently explored the ways in which deconstructive reading, with its attention to difference, offers useful resources not only for a more nuanced, textured and differentiated theorization and representation of religious identity, but also methodologically for the identification, analysis and challenging of totalizing or hegemonic approaches. The following would constitute some of the central features of such an approach: by being attentive to differences, resistances and tensions within texts and contexts, deconstructive readings challenge the abstractive force of totalizing descriptions – descriptions which are often, though not always, rooted in the texts and contexts being investigated and which seek to dominate their heterogeneity. They thus allow for a more detailed articulation of identity which recognizes normative trends and their interests, but is able to situate these, and is thereby able to take account of variation, relationality and hybridity. This would lead to more nuanced and precise ways of speaking which eschew levelling abstractions and which recognize that the identity of 'the same' and its 'other' might not be as clear-cut as such abstractions might suggest. Unlike structuralist approaches, the admission of diachrony into the theorizing of religious identity involves a rooting and delimitation of theoretical reflection, making it attentive to historical and physical situatedness and to questions of power in the negotiation and mediation of identity. Such delimitation also leads to a more informative and responsible tension between particularity and abstraction which, with reference to the opening quotation from Adorno, would prevent an abstraction or a concept 'from growing rampant and becoming an absolute to itself'.

While remaining appreciative of the great importance of the emphasis on difference, discontinuity and traditional particularity which has been promoted with reference to religious traditions, particularly in response to universalist trends stemming from the Enlightenment, I believe that the ahistorical abstractions to which such emphases often lead ought to be mitigated through a questioning of the narrative closure and totalization which is taken to characterize their identity. By means of deconstructive strategies of reading and inquiry, I suggest that their 'borders' can be demonstrated to be far more ambiguous and fluid than is suggested by these representations, and similarly that these occlude both 'internal' variations and differences as well as continuities and constitutive relations with their alleged 'outsides'. These forms of occlusion, in representing certain hegemonic interests, have often had, and continue to have, disastrous consequences for those who represent both internal and external alterity. This implies that philosophers of religion, and scholars of religion in general, need to maintain a critical awareness of, and assume responsibility for, the sociopolitical impact and influence of their representations on current polemics over the nature and identity of religious traditions.

A deconstructive focus on the differential and hybrid nature of religious identities also provides a potential alternative in current debates over the nature and future of theology and religious studies. By recognizing that theology and, more recently, religious studies have always been characterized by, and occurred within, situations of hybridity and change, we are to some extent liberated from the 'either/or' bind of either 'tradition-specific' departments dominated by idealized spectres of homogeneous traditions or secular departments dominated by the equally idealized spectre of a homogeneous and absolute secularity. These spectres are reifications which simply are not historically forthcoming. Given the hybrid polyphony which I have suggested characterizes forms of religious identity, I would like to endorse Daan Goosen's proposal (drawing on the work of Mikhail Bakhtin on the polyphonic novel) that the study of religion and theology can be recognized, understood and appreciated as a 'polyphonic event' (Goosen, 1992, pp. 25–9). Given the rootedness of the polyphonic novel in the tradition of the carnival, with its subversion and displacement of univocity, identity and established hierarchies, I would suggest, again with Goosen, that the hybrid polyphony of religious identity implies the continuation of both 'religious studies' and 'theology' as carnivalesque, messy, agonistic, creative, critical, multiple, transformative and unpredictable areas of study (ibid., p. 29).

References

Adorno, Theodor W. (1973), *Negative Dialectics*, trans. E.B. Ashton, London: Routledge & Kegan Paul.
Bauer, Walter (1972), *Orthodoxy and Heresy in Earliest Christianity*, London: SCM Press.

Blond, Phillip (ed.) (1998), *Post-Secular Philosophy: Between Philosophy and Theology*, London: Routledge.

Brown, Peter (1995), *Authority and the Sacred: Aspects of the Christianisation of the Roman World*, Cambridge: Cambridge University Press.

Cameron, Averil (1991), *Christianity and the Rhetoric of Empire: The Development of Christian Discourse*, Berkeley: University of California Press.

Christian, Rose Ann (1992), 'Plantinga, Epistemic Permissiveness, and Metaphysical Pluralism', *Religious Studies*, **28** (4), December, 553–73.

D'Costa, Gavin (1996), 'The End of "Theology" and "Religious Studies"', *Theology*, **99** (791), September/October, 338–51.

Derrida, Jacques (1974), *Of Grammatology*, trans. G.C. Spivak, Baltimore: The Johns Hopkins University Press.

Derrida, Jacques (1978), *Writing and Difference*, trans. A. Bass, London: Routledge & Kegan Paul.

Derrida, Jacques (1981a), *Positions*, trans. A. Bass, Chicago: University of Chicago Press.

Derrida, Jacques (1981b), *Dissemination*, trans. B.Johnson, London: Athlone.

Derrida, Jacques (1982), *Margins of Philosophy*, trans. A. Bass, London: Harvester Wheatsheaf.

Derrida, Jacques (1989), *Edmund Husserl's* Origin of Geometry: *An Introduction*, trans. J.P. Leavey Jr, Lincoln: University of Nebraska Press.

Derrida, Jacques (1995), *On the Name*, ed. T. DuToit, trans. D. Wood, J.P. Leavey and I. McLeod, Stanford: Stanford University Press.

Doran, Robert (1995), *Birth of a Worldview: Early Christianity in its Jewish and Pagan Context*, Boulder: Westview Press.

Ehrman, Bart D. (1993), *The Orthodox Corruption of Scripture: The Effect of Early Christological Controversies on the Text of the New Testament*, Oxford: Oxford University Press.

Frei, Hans W. (1974), *The Eclipse of Biblical Narrative: A Study in Eighteenth and Nineteenth Century Hermeneutics*, New Haven: Yale University Press.

Friedländer, Paul (1969), *Plato: An Introduction*, trans. H. Meyerhoff, Princeton: Princeton University Press.

Gonçalves, Paulo F.M. (1998), 'Vital Necrographies: Deconstruction, God and Arche-Idolatry,' *The Scottish Journal of Religious Studies*, **19** (1), Spring, 83–100.

Goosen, Daan (1992), 'Die Teologiese Onderwys as Dialogiese Gebeure – 'n Perspektief', *Theologia Evangelica*, **25** (1), March, 24–34.

Hanson, Richard P.C. (1959), *Allegory and Event: A Study of the Sources and Significance of Origen's Interpretation of Scripture*, Richmond: John Knox Press.

Hanson, Richard P.C. (1985), 'The Christian Attitude to Pagan Religions', *Studies in Christian Antiquity*, Edinburgh: T. & T. Clark, pp. 144–229.

Hick, John (1989), *An Interpretation of Religion: Human Responses to the Transcendent*, Basingstoke: Macmillan.

Jantzen, Grace (1995), *Power, Gender and Christian Mysticism*, Cambridge: Cambridge University Press.

Jantzen, Grace (1998), *Becoming Divine: Towards a Feminist Philosophy of Religion*, Manchester: Manchester University Press.

Kearney, Richard (1984), *Dialogues with Contemporary Continental Thinkers: Paul Ricoeur, Emmanuel Levinas, Herbert Marcuse, Stanislas Breton, Jacques Derrida: The Phenomenological Heritage*, Manchester: Manchester University Press.

Kelley, J.N.D. (1977), *Early Christian Doctrines*, London: A & C Black.

King, Richard (1999), *Orientalism and Religion: Postcolonial Theory, India and 'The Mystic East'*, London: Routledge.

Lindbeck, George A. (1984), *The Nature of Doctrine: Religion and Theology in a Postliberal Age*, London: SPCK.

MacMullen, Ramsay (1984), *Christianizing the Roman Empire (A.D. 100–400)*, New Haven: Yale University Press.

MacMullen, Ramsay (1997), *Christianity and Paganism in the Fourth to Eighth Centuries*, New Haven: Yale University Press.

McCutcheon, Russell T. (1997), *Manufacturing Religion: The Discourse on Sui Generis Religion and the Politics of Nostalgia*, Oxford: Oxford University Press.

Milbank, John (1990), *Theology and Social Theory: Beyond Secular Reason*, Oxford: Blackwell.

Milbank, John, Catherine Pickstock and Graham Ward (eds) (1999), *Radical Orthodoxy: A New Theology*, London: Routledge.

Morris, Thomas V. (1986), *The Logic of God Incarnate*, Ithaca: Cornell University Press.

Paden, William (1994), *Religious Worlds: The Comparative Study of Religion*, Boston: Beacon Press.

Pagels, Elaine (1982), *The Gnostic Gospels*, Harmondsworth: Penguin.

Pepin, Jean (1958), *Myth et allégorie: Les origines grecques et les contestations Judéo-Chrétiennes*, Aubier: Montaigne.

Pickstock, Catherine (1998), *After Writing: On the Liturgical Consummation of Philosophy*, Oxford: Blackwell.

Ricoeur, Paul (1974), *The Conflict of Interpretations: Essays in Hermeneutics*, Evanston: Northwestern University Press.

Shakespeare, Steven (2000), 'The New Romantics: A Critique of Radical Orthodoxy', *Theology*, **103** (813), May/June, 163–77.

Surin, Kenneth (1990), 'A Politics of Speech: Religious Pluralism in the Age of the McDonald's Hamburger', in Gavin D'Costa (ed.), *Christian Uniqueness Reconsidered*, New York: Maryknoll, pp. 192–212.

Welch, Sharon (1990), *A Feminist Ethic of Risk*, Minneapolis: Fortress.

Williams, Michael Allen (1996), *Rethinking 'Gnosticism': An Argument for Dismantling a Dubious Category*, Princeton: Princeton University Press.

Williams, Rowan (1996), 'A Theological Critique of Milbank', in Robin Gill (ed.), *Theology and Sociology: A Reader*, London: Cassell, pp. 435-43.

Chapter 9

Thinking a Critical Theory of Postcolonial Islam

Youssef Yacoubi

Tout comme le discours littéraire, le discours logocentriste opère donc un travestissement: au lieu de rechercher une réconciliation avec l'inéluctable dans la condition humaine, il cherche à compenser les faiblesses de cette condition par la promesse d'une Félicité future. (Arkoun, 1984, p. 231)

The discourse of logocentrism operates in the same way as the discourse of literature, in accordance with a disguise: instead of exploring a reconciliation with the ineluctable in the human condition, it strives to compensate for its weaknesses with the promise of a future felicity.

Introduction

My aim in this chapter is to problematize two issues pertaining to a conceptualization of a critical theory of Islam. First, I shall engage with Said's influential book, *Orientalism*, and its instrumental blind spots, so as to remap a dialogue with a theoretical space for Islam, especially in its textual tradition. This is not a critique of Said's thesis on colonial discourse, but an attempt to negotiate those moments in the book that have been relegated to the periphery to maintain procedures of coherence and political commitment. Second, I shall attempt to locate this space of Islamic textual practice within a poststructuralist expression of difference and heterodoxy. Heterodoxy is the space passed over by interpreters of orthodox affiliation. It is here in the margins of official consensus that a critical theory of Islam finds its interruptive and unsettling energies. I am thinking particularly here of Mohammed Arkoun, who synthesized and urged the cross-fertilization between new approaches in linguistics, semiotics, sociology, ethnography, anthropology, history, literary criticism, philosophy and Islamic thought. Arkoun's methodology of 'applied Islamology', rejected by confessional Muslim scholars as foreign, destructive and irredeemably dehistoricizing, concentrates on the suppressed debates of peripheral thinkers of Islam – heterodox schools, popular attitudes and sensibilities of magic and myth – and the interiority of these elements to Islam's psyche and sense of self-definition. He sums up the broader parameters of his project:

enrichir l'histoire de la pensée en mettant en évidence les enjeux cognitifs, intellectuels, idéologiques des tensions entre les multiples écoles de pensée; dynamiser la pensée islamique contemporaine en fixant l'attention sur les problèmes qu'elle a refoulés, les taboos qu'elle a érigés, les frontières qu'elle a tracées, les horizons qu'elle a cessé ou interdit de regarder: tout cela au nom de ce qu'elle a progressivement imposé comme l'unique vérité. (Arkoun, 1982, p. xii)

to enrich the history of thought by investigating the cognitive interplays, intellectual and ideological tensions between multiple schools of thought; to dynamize contemporary Islamic thought by paying attention to the problems that it has rejected, the taboos that it has erected, the borders that it has drawn, the horizons that it has interdicted seeing: all in the name of what it has progressively imposed as the unique truth.

In this spirit, I shall attempt to read *Orientalism* as a book that has left out an indispensable debate about the limits of Islamic reason that Arkoun and a few others have started to theorize since the late 1960s.[1] I shall attempt to highlight Arkoun's usually overlooked contribution to a construction of a critical reflection on Islamic studies. On this account, I shall discuss poetics and mysticism as two possible dimensions of the aporia embedded in Islam's official inquisition. To achieve this aim I shall discuss Taha Hussein's most persuasive and controversial analysis of the history of Arabo-Islamic poetics and its role in shaping the textual practice of the sacred. Then I shall consider alternative readings to *Orientalism*'s discussion of mysticism in orientalist thought. My choice of Said and Arkoun, who come from differing intellectual formations, but nevertheless belong to the same generation of post-colonial thinkers, is to emphasize one important point: that the overdetermined construct 'Islam' has been, more often than not, substantially eclipsed by an Anglo-American 'intercolonial diction'. By this I mean that the proliferation of scholarship on Islam since the publication of Said's book has invigorated a number of academic Islams: the Islam of theology, sociology, history, political science, anthropology, linguistics, history, and even an interdisciplinary Islam. However, a theoretical, post-theological, intellectually rigorous and self-reflexive Islam (as Arkoun would like to see it) is not comprehensively conceived. Furthermore, the term has not only been infected by the great violences of globalization, colonial and neocolonial histories and imageries, as Said and others have convincingly demonstrated, but it has been consistently mobilized by theological, quasi-theological and so-called 'liberal' voices to enforce innumerable falsehoods, to persuade Muslims that the idea of Submission is an eternal truth.

It is important to move away from Said's legacy of interrogating the structure of colonial knowledge into another relevant inquiry, that of 'intercolonialism', the interrogation of the ethnocentrism that has dominated Islamic political, economic, pedagogical and intellectual practices for many centuries. Within such critical practice, it is important to speak about '*le fait Islamique*' (Islam as an event), which decentres the ideology of abstraction. A final qualification, and this is where I think the marginalized contribution of Arkoun and many others has to be taken seriously, is that the archaeology of the idea of Submission cannot be circumspectly theorized or perceived in relationship to its others without its interior metaphysical configurations of myth and imagination. This is Arkoun's exigency of 'radical beginning' (*La table rasée*) in order to reconstruct the fragments of history and epistemology from inside Islam's immediate others. Arkoun's deconstructive gesture thus dares to interrogate Islam's logocentrism and recasts its philosophical 'overassemblage of meanings'. For neither the well-rehearsed clichés of polygamy, polygyny, oppression of women, holy war, zealotry, sloth, fatalism and an unfair system of inheritance, each constructed as eternal, essential to the Book, nor the inexhaustibility of post-colonial 'political' alternatives, have addressed the archaeology of historio-epistemological conditions and the fundamental relationship between ideology, history and epistemology. To move beyond the politics of blame, injury, victimhood, charity and ideological commitment, I shall concentrate on what may be called 'the intercolonial flow'. This concept assumes the complexity and ambivalence of the colonial encounter, but sees the apparent irredeemability of the East–West chasm as a positive energy for meditation over the limits of religious reason.

Orientalism as a Point of Departure

Why start with a book whose major purpose is not a discussion of the textual anxiety of Islamic thought, but the representation by the West of the *phenomena islamica*? The reason is twofold. First, *Orientalism* has become almost the most influential book in the development of an emerging field of inquiry called post-colonial theory, whose aim is to question Western monolithic constructions of the other, as discussed in some chapters in this volume. Homi Bhabha and Gayatri Spivak, for example, have reformulated Said's thesis and shaped the political commitments of many young scholars, rejecting the West's neocolonial and globalizing mischaracterizations of Islam. For Said, orientalists constructed Islam since the medieval period as an unchanging essence. The guild of orientalists has built a systematic secular theology of the Orient, and has demonstrated a self-evident complicity with structures of imperial power. Furthermore, since the late 1980s more sympathetic readings of Islam in the West have been advanced by some *new* Islamologists and many Muslim scholars based in the West. They have continued to refute current purgative projections of Islamic realities, and to confer the same values of complexity, ambivalence, inconsistency and nuance on Islam.

Secondly, the book's major limits have heightened one major discussion about voice and the possibilities for the oppressed to speak from inside their own transcolonial experience. The lead in this has come from the ensemble of Muslim scholars and some orientalists who questioned Said's humanist methodology. Said's exclusion of Islam's theological voice, as we detect from his introduction, was necessary and useful for his political project to gain credibility. As many opponents, especially the practitioners of orientalism, have protested (see, for example, Bernard Lewis, in his *Islam and the West*, 1993), Said has neglected a rigorous analysis of the heterogeneity of the corpus of Islam's texts and has hardly quoted an Arab or Muslim scholar, or critically considered at length any substantial Islamic text of influential thinkers such as Ibn Rushd (Averroës), Ibn Khaldun, Ibn Sina (Avicenna), Taha Hussein, Najib Mahfouz (one of Said's favourite Arab contemporary writers), or even a critical analysis of the Qur'an and the *Hadith*, except through the predatory interpretive eye of the orientalist. I use the term 'exclusion' because I am not interested in reproaching Said for the exigent blindness that was necessary for his project, for indeed, this aporia is necessary for any act of writing – this is the space, the boundary, the edge and periphery where many insights have emerged to enrich the debate. Without attempting to correct Said, or expect too much from his 'deconstructive' gesture of the orientalist libidinal repository, I shall attempt to focus on the space and anxiety of Islamic textuality that has remained hidden in Said's own textual devices.

Islamic consciousness has always *thought* itself *inside* the morass of colonial history and has produced its own representations, imaginings and frustrations that reflected not only its capacity to speak back, but also the anxiety of its own incapacity to respond properly. The intercolonial play, as I will show in my discussion of Islamic poetics, on a conceptual level, should shuttle between the different ideologies, the traces that inhabit all cultures as they interlap. When Said left out the semiotic and epistemological relevance of religion and its languages in the interplay of colonial experience of oppression and textual production of knowledge, it was because he was conceiving religion within the limits of humanist thinking. Said was trained in a particular intellectual tradition that has prioritized the 'worldly' experience in the production of the text. Therefore the structure of the *mythos* that informs religious sensibility was perceived to be a construction of human imagination in secular history. However, as Said now admits, there is no way of understanding Zionism without a critical reference to biblical studies and the theology of the Promised Land (Pasto, 1998).

Zionism, in spite of its secularization, derives its ontological force from its theological determinations by the mythical demands of the sacred. Concentrating entirely just on what the orientalists thought, wrote and imagined reduces the complex construction called Islamic Orient into a silent recipient without a system of producing its own knowledge. The Muslim is a waif, or, as Tharand puts it, he is 'imprévoyant, poétique. Dans un siècle comme le nôtre, ils [Muslims] sont nécessairement sacrifiés' (*Fête Arabe*, 1912, p. 56). The Muslim, the proper sacrifice for reason's latent impulse of construction and destruction – the Muslim being outside the critical project of enlightened subjectivity – is brought to notice by the orientalist's superior expertise of analysis and historiography. The Muslim of philology operates according to pre-modern limits of the exotic distant logos, and has now been rescued to materialize his potential 'intersubjectivity' through the orientalist's subjugation to the truth claims of modern reason. In each case it was one absolutist reason attempting to conquer and invalidate another more unfathomable reason, whose codes, systems and organization somehow always escaped the procedures of the orientalist. Said's book shows little indication that dismantling orientalism's fundamental aporias may have demanded another necessary dismantling of religious reason and, more importantly, an exploration of the intercolonial play of reasons.

What do we make, then, of numerous illuminating statements that invite necessary elaboration? 'Take the Abbasid period from the eighth to the eleventh century as an instance. Anyone who has the slightest acquaintance with Arab or Islamic history will know that it was a high point of Islamic civilisation, as brilliant a period of cultural history as the High Renaissance in Italy' (Said, 1995, p. 303). Or Said, speaking about Massignon's obsession with Islam's heterodox traces: 'The principal feature of mysticism was of course its subjective character, whose nonrational and even inexplicable tendencies were towards the singular, the individual, the momentary experience of participation in the Divine' (ibid., p. 268).

Sylvestre de Sacy, Volney, Ernest Renan, *Description de l'Egypte*, texts by Flaubert, Marx, H.A.R. Gibb, Louis Massignon, reports of army officers and journalists in *La Revue Africaine* (1880–1950), the linguistic 'Colonial Science' of William Marçais, René and André Basset may be open again, not as a coherent ensemble, but as mutated and intertextual, inhabited by an axiomatic cataloguing of myth making, illusions and lies, the *stuff* that gives their texts force and durability. *Orientalism* is saturated by silent pregnant statements that allude to Islam's elements of 'disrupting influence' within official transcolonial theology.

It is in this sense that one may argue that many images and realities that orientalists uncritically constructed were appropriated and imagined from a monolithic tradition that has viewed Islam as a consistent, inimitable reality in history, a result of systematic methodology. The orientalist was constructing an Islam in a state of decline with oppressive political regimes that derived their legitimacy from the institution of official orthodoxy. The philologist did not derive his consistency from the consistency of orthodox official documents, the Qur'an and the *Hadith* that have been appropriated to legitimize the power of the king, the khalif and the Nawab. The orientalist was himself operating according to the institution of colonial knowledge that demanded the formation of a secular theology of alterity. The philologist who was close to Islamic texts had to investigate and read them according to his logocentric rationality that was suspicious about figural conditions of textuality. On a textual level, the consistency that Said emphasizes relates to the scholar's logocentrism. With varying degrees of engagement and disengagement, the orientalist has remained imprisoned by the superiority of his culture and secularized religious methodology. Philological criticism, for example, managed to locate with precision stylistic weaknesses of Islamic scripture, establishing reasons of difference between Mecca's moments of revelation and those of Medina, the former being poetic, and the latter being prosaic.

This criticism has also re-ordered the historical and narrative chronology of the Qur'an according to modern procedures of biblical criticism. Orientalists, especially those dealing with religious psychology, or what they called 'magic', 'superstition' and 'witchcraft', reported and catalogued events and instances which were, ironically enough, not fundamental to the theological construction of Islam. There was no interest in moments of ritualistic citation, liturgical repetition, the symbolic order of iconoclastic forms and the semiotic structures of magic, belief in the supernatural and myth that represented the underlying mechanics of exegesis. The orientalists' methods of philology, drawn from those applied to the Hebrew Bible and New Testament, hardly deviated from historicism; they adhered to the regulations of empirical evidence for oral transmissions, textual accuracy, syntactic certitude and so on. It is not surprising, then, that when Said talks about Sacy, the father of modern orientalism, he italicizes such terms as Sacy 'having *uncovered*, *brought to light*, *rescued* a vast amount of obscure matter', 'the *making visible*', and 'to *present* the Orient' to demonstrate the authority that legitimizes reason.

Confessional Critiques

Many readings of *Orientalism* by confessional Muslim scholars rightly speak about an urgent need for post-Saidian reconceptualizations of the relationship between the West and Islam, with an urgent attention to the intrinsic claims of Islam's theology and ethics. In the light of populist so-called returns to the theological *ancien régime*, as valorized by Western media and Islamizers of knowledge, there has been a frustrated Muslim international *corps d'élite*, primarily based in the UK, devoted to anthologizing and theorizing Muslim animus. Having been immediately affected by the 'Rushdie Affair', Ahmad Akbar's *Postmodernism and Islam: Predicament and Promise* (1992) argues that Western culture has been exclusionist, elitist, sexist and inhumane because of the Greek ethos. The Greeks still influence Western culture and shape it in almost every domain, from politics and philosophy to musicology. Akbar situates Islam outside the Hellenic conceptual framework because Islam, in spite of its rigorous engagement and translation of Greek sciences, has retained the concepts of God, piety, wisdom, sacrifice, obedience and moderation as central precepts to its epistemology. He critiques the violences of the Greek legacy starting from Plato and Aristotle, and its subsequent modern exclusions of women, the impoverished and the aged. Most of postmodernism for Akbar excels at the politics of pleasure and self-indulgence, the cult of Superman and Rambo, the essentialism of masculinity and prestige. In spite of the ambivalence of the divide, there is a fundamental disjunction between the two worldviews: 'One civilisation views the world as linear progression … By contrast, in the Semitic tradition humanity began, literally, at the very top: the eponymous ancestors, Adam and Eve, started life in heaven. Their "fall" also symbolises mankind's fall from grace' (Akbar, 1992, p. 90). In a gesture of inter-religious dialogue and 'intimacy', Akbar quotes Massignon's phrase, '*Nous sommes tous des Sémites*', to articulate that monotheism is what separates secular humanist thought from Semitic tradition.

In the same breath of missionary zeal, Ziauddin Sardar's *Orientalism* (1999) insists that the voice and theological credibility of Islam must be articulated outside the Western paradigms of secularism and liberalism. For him, Said's defence of Islam is deeply inadequate because in Said's vision there is no place for Islam or Muslims to exist by their own 'theocratic' definition. 'While all Islam, for Said, is a figment of someone's imagination, "acts of will and interpretation", secular humanism emerges in his thought as something real and concrete that he employs with all the force of neo-colonialism' (Sardar, 1999, p. 74). Sardar's reading is typical of many Muslim scholars, trying to theorize an alternative vision of an Islam capable of reforming itself from inside its own language. Sardar wants Muslims to reclaim their own Islamic spaces by questioning the absolutist and exclusionist agendas of secularism, and by articulating the Islamic experience based on some transcendental impregnable essence. He rejects all orientalizations of Islam, including Said's 'worldly' or Rushdie's, Hanif Kureishi's and Tariq Ali's 'post-modern' reformulations of Islam's histories and canonical texts.

Sardar considers *The Satanic Verses*, for example, to be atrabilious, 'the post-modern genre of magical realism' which 'aims at turning history into amnesia' by blurring 'the boundaries of fact and fiction. This is done with the aim of proving and showing that reality is often imagined and imagination often becomes real. In a reductionist sense, the novel can be seen as a fictional form of Marxist theorist Jean Baudrillard's theory of simulacrum' (Sardar, 1993, p. 278). For him, all of Rushdie's work is postmodern; *Harun and the Sea of Stories* 'divides the world into two blocks: the light of secularism and the darkness of religion.... In this children's story we see the ideology of postmodernism spelled out clearly; but like all ideologies, *Harun and the Sea of Stories* presents an inversion of reality: it is not religion that spells Khattam-Shud but the grand narrative of secularism' (Sardar, 1991, p. 87). Sardar's mediation of an alternative space imagines a definition of Islam that prioritizes knowledge inside a faith-consciousness founded on the Book. It is not enough for Sardar that Said's *Covering Islam* (1981) is passionately relentless in its dissection of prejudiced depictions of Islamic realities in Western media, because Said fails to recognize other indomitable 'epistemologies of liberation' inspired by revelation. Sardar rejects Said's humanist reading because it does not recognize revelation as the inaugural moment of universal history.

John Esposito, an Islamologist, on the other hand, defends contemporary Islam's force and acumen in its redeeming traditions of awakening and revival (*Tajdeed*) and reform (*Islah*) inspired by a constant return to the fundamentals of the Book. In accordance with Esposito's reading, the list of 'Waldensian' revivalists is endless. Esposito urges the West to conceive Islam in the light of the dynamics of faith and history, and not on the basis of the prejudices and culturally specific values of post-enlightenment thought. However, is it possible to imagine an intellectual base for Islam outside the limits of its overly romanticized reformist traditions of revivalism of the Mahdis (1848–85), the Sanusis (1787–1859), the Wahabbis (1703–92) and the Fulanis (1754–1817), of their 'fundamentals of the Book', of orthodoxy, catholicity and the ensemble of deconstructible categories such as '*Dar al-Islam*' (the house of Islam), '*Dar al-Harb*' (the house of war), '*Jihad*' and '*Fatwa*'? Why should the issues of colonialism, neocolonialism, post-colonialism, and what Esposito attributes to Islamic realities as a condition of 'westoxification', always be discussed in eminent positive proximity with the West? What epistemological tools allow such conclusive assumptions? In short, why sublimate rupture for Islam?

Among many Anglo-American *new* Islamologists,[2] Islam is somehow immunized against a systematic dismantling of its core structures of belief because it is epistemically incommensurable with postmodernist/poststructuralist procedures of secular and negative self-reflexivity. 'Islam' is always locked in the medieval episteme characterized by the immutability of 'origin'. The majority who have rejected continental imports have adumbrated a concomitant reformulation of Islamic intellectual tradition. Even though the prominent Gayatri Spivak imagined and defended a 'progressive' Islam when she protested against Khomeini's *fatwa* on Rushdie, having not read the Qur'an, the fundamental bone of contention, she demonstrated that the category 'Islam' still belonged to the realm of abstractions located only in the post-colonial critic's imagination (*Harper's*, 1989, pp. 47–8).

The major determination of post-Saidian Muslim scholarship and post-colonial commentary on Islam is to divorce the notion of monotheism from its mythical procedures. Post-colonial theory is usually motivated by the exigency of historical immediacy and a desire to achieve political post-colonial effectiveness. As it may be argued in the case of the 'Rushdie Affair', many commentaries defended Islam's right to remain outside the 'secular paradigm' because many of them were consumed by the sentimentality of the sacred and the West's monolithic intolerance. The weakness of many post-colonial commentaries is to speak about Islam without attempting to understand its operations of writing and the ironic existence that its theological order breathes.

Heterodox Critiques

Mohammed Arkoun had broken new ground in his unassailable essay of 1972, 'Logocentrisme et Vérité Religieuse dans la Pensée Islamique' published a few years after Derrida's *De la grammatologie* and *L'écriture et la différence*, in 1967. In this essay, later reprinted as part of his series, *Islam d'hier et d'aujourd'hui*, he had initiated an important paradigm shift in Islamic studies, mesmerizingly dominated for centuries by empirical textuality and chrestomathy. Arkoun started his critique of Arabo-Islamic reason and orientalism much earlier in the 1960s and 1970s, with the publication of some short pieces, *Deux épîtres de Miskawayh* (1961), *Aspects de la pensée musulmane classique* (1963), *Traité d'éthique* (1969) and *La pensée Arabe* (1975). An Algerian Berber teaching at the Sorbonne University is indeed privileged by his theoretical proximity to Gallic poststructuralist thinking, and France, a neoteric allegedly heretic space for many Anglo-American academics.

Arkoun, in my view, is the first to have perceptively articulated a systematic need and outline of the implications of a radical 'rethinking' of Islamic thought.[3] As he explains:

> Modern rationality restores the psychological and cultural functions of myth and develops a global strategy of knowledge in which the rational and the imaginary interact perpetually to produce individual and historical existence. We must abandon the dualist framework of knowledge that pits reason against imagination, history against myth, true against false, good against evil, and reason against faith. We must postulate a plural, changing welcoming sort of rationality, one consistent with the psychological operations that the Quran locates in the heart and that contemporary anthropology attempts to reintroduce under the label of the imaginary. (Arkoun, 1994, p. 36)

His method of 'Applied Islamology' is inspired by philosophical hermeneutics that examines *the modes* of Qur'anic discourse including narrative, proverbs, mythology and poetics (drawing on Ricoeur). The purpose is to establish a mediation between the speech act and its content, to explore the dynamics and tensions between the oral utterance and the act of transmitting to reflect on the gap that exists between the utterance and its speaker, the discourse and its beginnings and its relationship with its immediate listeners. As Ricoeur puts it, 'The problem of interpretation is already started. It does not begin with written texts but with all these subtle dialectics of oral language that give a basis to the concept of modes of discourse' (Ricoeur, 1995, p. 37). Islamic reason has been imprisoned by the notion of classification. Being aware of this epistemological *cul de sac*, Arkoun has attempted to initiate a generative poetics that recognizes the multiplicity of meaning in the Qur'an, but most important, and this is where Arkoun moves ahead of many rationalist Qur'anic scholars such as Fazur, is the fact that the recovery of the event of revelation takes the form of slippery reconstructions starting from the structure of Qur'anic discourse. In other words, as Ricoeur explains, 'if hermeneutics is always an attempt to overcome a distance, it has to use distanciation as both the obstacle and the instrument in order to re-enact the initial event of discourse in a new event of discourse that will claim to be both faithful and creative' (ibid., p. 38).

Arkoun has invested so much patience in doing what orientalists relegated to the sphere of the unthinkable.[4] In *Lectures du Coran* (1982), he deconstructs dogmatic readings of sacred literature by exploring its interiority, including processes of doubling and dynamics between magic (*le merveilleux*), myth, language, anthropology and history. Arkoun's methodology is sensitive to the structure of mythical language because such structure allows us to understand the anthropological and cultural formations of sacred literature. For him, 'Le récit mythique est plus ou moins solidaire de la situation culturelle du groupe social où il est élaboré' (the mythical narrative is, more or less, in solidarity with the cultural situation or the social group where it is developed) (Arkoun, 1982, p. 10). Arkoun's distinct innovation is to have claimed a fundamental problem eclipsed by many critical studies of the Qur'an: the fact that the literary modes of the Book have to be reconceived outside the boundaries of religious and rational language. To understand them in these boundaries is to investigate the unthinkable (*L'impensable*)[5] – an inquiry into how religious language has lost its primitive roots of expression, and consequently how the question and very expression of revelation must not be approached as a problem to be resolved, but rather as a conceptual thinkable to be expanded. For Arkoun, religious experience is not born in a vacuum, but it comes to language through the richness and semantic density of modes of discourse.

One such perceptive analysis is of the commentaries of al-Suyûtî (m. 911/1505CE), a Muslim theologian, and A.T. Welch, an orientalist. Arkoun examines the aporias that inhabit both religious and secular or quasi-religious thinking. He is interested in 'les questions demeurées *impensables* et l'etendue de *l'impensé*' (The questions that have remained unthinkable, and the thread of the undecidable)[6] (Arkoun, 1982, p. vi). The nine centuries of classical scholastic commentary has been characterized, in addition to a rigorous knowledge of religious and grammatical organization, by what Arkoun describes as *le pensable* (the thinkable), *l'impensable* (the unthinkable) and *l'impensé* (the undecidable). Therefore medieval theological knowledge, as constructed by al-Suyûtî, Mâwardi, Juwaynî, Abû ya' lâ and F.D. Râzi has been a scholastic labour of 'filtrage, sélection, de condensation des données, des points de vue, des définitions, des explications, des types de savoirs' (filtration, selection, compression of particulars, of points of view, of definitions, of explications and types of knowledge) that constituted what we call Islamic orthodoxy (ibid., pp. ix–x).

By unveiling the unthinkable and undecidable spaces of scholastic commentaries, the determinations of the philologist orientalist, Arkoun concedes that these forms of knowledge are almost always ahistorical because the questions about circumstances of revelation, transmission, collection of the Book (*Mushaf*) or lexical evolution of Arabic have been reduced to scattered notations (ibid., x). The consistency in religious reason is its very construction of pragmatic coherence inside the theological closure.

A critical theory of Islam must interrogate the premises, presuppositions and convictions that allow the discourse to operate inside the closure. On this account, Akbar's Greco-Semitic divide belongs to this space of the unthinkable, as he would not imagine the rupture of Islamic logos. In spite of his rationalized insights and historically aware analysis, Akbar's interrogation has to stop at the level of the fundamentals (*usûl*) of Islamic discourse. His rejection of the implications of processes of translation and negative theologies in Islamic consciousness is based on the very historicist arguments that he despises in orientalists. In the final analysis, his interdisciplinary approach to Islam and postmodernism maintains one major closure, that of positive theology. When Akbar speaks about Islam's notion of balance between religion (*din*) and world (*dunya*), precepts that are not interior to postmodernist sensibility, he always refers to theological notions, aphorisms and Qur'anic verses that fit in the space of thinkable transcendentalism and unthinkable solicitation (emphasis added); '*the frame* of religion', '*the future* after-life', 'the divine *presence*' (ibid., pp. 48–9), '*the essence* of the Qur'anic message' (p. 264); 'There is a formula *central* to Islam which every Muslim recognises: no prophet, no Quran; no Quran, no Islam' (169–70). For him,

> The Quran … is at *the core* of Islamic belief, and few Muslims, however liberal, would suggest its re-interpretation. Even Fazlur Rahman, cited by Watt … considered modern by some Western scholars, notes: 'The Muslim modernists say exactly the same thing as the so-called Muslim fundamentalists say: that Muslims must *go back* to the *original* and *definitive* sources of Islam and *perform ijtihad* on that *basis*'. (Arkoun, 1982, p. 181; emphasis added)

The vast majority of Muslim scholars, particularly the Anglo-Indians, be they traditionalist, orthodox, radical, modernist or inhabiting some or all of these intellectual trends,[7] still manage to perceive Islam according to the credo; theological convictions dominate their perception, sensibility, meditation and action. This has remained cryptic primarily because of an enduring image of Islam's unthinkable self-reflexivity. Anglo-Indian Muslim scholarship, in spite of its subtle use of many critical theories and theoretical achievements in social sciences, submits to the *ex cathedra* of tradition. It is these *reliquiae* of the credo and a discourse of positive post-coloniality of diaspora that paralyse other meanings for the multi-layered construct of *Sub*mission. The UK-based Muslim commentator, having been undermined by the Rushdie Affair, stops building his arguments; he rejects the very notion of conceptual critique. Instead he narrates, describes, deprecates, procrastinates, or regresses into a retardant ancestral authenticity, imagining a reasoned tradition that absorbs the transformations of the global village.

The varying degrees of modern, at times progressive, theologization by Muslim scholars is a strategy of violent containment belonging in the realm of psychoanalysis and political ideology. Islamic epistemological archeologies are not critically analysed and reconstructed from outside Islamic phonocentrism but are always taken to constitute the eternal verities that must not be dismantled. This is the 'anxiolytic' that helps dismiss subversive fictionalized readings of tradition, *The Satanic Verses* and *Iranian Nights*, as *outré*. The theologizing of Islam by an Anglo-American scholarship appears to be no more than a system of the spectral commentator's megalomania; it also betrays insatiable paranoia and a pathological sense of tradition anxiety and boundary loss. This is due to a confusion over the subtle differences between, for example, postmodernism and poststructuralism, the widespread notion that all of postmodernist reflection ruins boundaries irreparably –

that it elides the difference between truth-oriented discourses of at least theology and classical philosophy, history, anthropology and discourses of a fictive and poetic nature where truth is not sought, circumferentially determined and accentuated.

The latter anxiety is residual of philosophical ontological determinations belonging to Islamic Aristotelian classical thought. The rejection of a thinkable poststructuralist perception of Islam is a traumatic trope, a chiliastic historical strategy of necessary solidarity, archetypal of the medieval strategy of containment through *Umma* consensus. Theologizing Islam is a compulsory gesture, disavowing the loss of tradition *bordure*, the effacement of the artificial geography of the *terra incognito*, the horror and intimidation of schism and conceptual denudation. Every reading, no matter how liberal, has to operate inside this closure, where the logos demonstrates its transcendence and ideality. 'The sign and divinity have the same place and time of birth. The age of the sign is essentially theological. Perhaps it will never *end*. Its historical *closure* is, however, outlined' (Derrida, 1976, p. 14). On this account, it is high time we recovered some of *Orientalism*'s blind spots (which have become the blinkers of a majority of the Anglo-American Muslim scholarship) such as poetics and mysticism as alternative spaces that negotiate and reconceptualize the possibility of difference in Islamic philosophy of religion.

Islam's Immediate Other: Reclaiming the Poet

Said refers to Dante's sympathetic yet violent positioning in the *Inferno* of the Muslim elite: Avicenna, Averroës and Saladin alongside Hector, Aeneas, Abraham, Socrates, Plato and Aristotle. In spite of Dante's phonocentrism, this may be read as a testimony to the humanist participation of Islam's intellectual tradition and the anxiety of influence involved in the fear and contempt that Dante injects into his poem. Dante's poem reflects more the schematic, overtheologized discourse of medieval Christianity than a fully-fledged view of Islam. Ironically, Dante's poetic inclusion of the refined and cultured other made mediation impossible and devalued poetic imagination to temptations of ignorance and amnesia. Dante's imagination has been eclipsed by a closed system of magic and mythology rooted in his own self-regulating religious reason. Yet Said's commentary on the role of poetics in informing the discourse of orientalism begs other questions about Islam's own repository of poetic imagination. Said passes in one sentence over the translation of the Persian poem, *Rubáiyát of Omar Khayyám* by Fitzgerald (Said, 1995, p. 193), which elucidates the subversive nature of Islamic poetics. In the light of Said's strategic reminders hidden in the devices of his applied poststructuralism, who is Islam's immediate other? Who is the marginal(ized) *heteros* that may have 'completed' (and may have deferred) the colonial narrative of oppression?

If the orientalist's blind spot was his own orthodox use of rational philology, Islamic reason's blind spot was its instrumental, interminable and paradoxical dependence and rejection of poetics and discourses of independent thinking. The fear of poetry across cultures stems from the ambivalent, subversive streak of poetic discourse. Plato's annexation of the poets from *The Republic* indicates an anxiety about the seduction and danger of untruth, deviance and falsehood. Taha Hussein's book, *Fi Al-shi'er Al-jahili* (In Jahili Poetry) (1926) remains the most influential and 'transgressive' examination of the anxiety of influence in Islamic philosophy of religion. Even though it was immediately censored by the official *Al-Azhar* Theological Seminary, it inspired many contemporary Arab poets, especially Adonis, the pen name of Ahmad Said.

Hussein's book was responding to the consistent official closure by religious orthodoxy of poetic rhetorics, myth and the imaginary since the official collection of the Qur'an by Caliph `Uthman. Hussein questions the official canon of Islamic literature by introducing his theory, *Intihal* (reproducibility). Being a product of a Western philosophical training, and influenced by Descartes' methodology on truth, he wanted to force the theologians of his time to negotiate the relations and dynamics between poetics and scriptures. According to his analysis, the transmitters of pre-Islamic poetry (the textual fabric that Islam came into and inhabited) built transformed sequences of *Jahili* (which etymologically means 'ignorant') verses through processes of elimination and theoliterary syncopation, thereby providing a 'cloned' version of pre-Islamic poetics that would validate the new Islamic architecture of Submission.

What Arabs had considered Jahili poetry for so many centuries was Islamic epidermal duplication, replicated alongside the Book after the rise of Islam by zealous theologians. Hussein argues that Islam's textual heritage must be understood in terms of its anthropological value. It portrays an Islamic identity, sensibility, passion and the vagaries of polytheism, and unhousedness, rather than monotheism and catholicity. He insists that the anthropology, linguistic features and politics of literary reproducibility can be easily outlined. To understand Islam, one must start by examining its immediate others and its internal anxieties, namely the religious sciences and methods of duplication of the time, and their conflicting ideologies. Most importantly, it must be read in the light of other histories, civilizations and textual practices. This is why Arkoun's 'poststructuralist' critique of Islamic metaphysics insists that the historical and intellectual realities of Islamic societies have always been plural, not because the idea of Submission as it appeared in the seventh century institutionalized the open system, but because the open system had always already enveloped and deeply inhabited external constructions of fixity. Arkoun consistently demonstrates the precedence of plurality in his strategic constant reference to the Arabo-Indo-Turko-Persian Islamic tradition. This is Arkoun's safeguard against reductionist criticism that he is eradicating memory, dehistoricizing history and destabilizing certainties.

Hussein's controlling argument may be summed up as an 'inter-Jahilia-lock'; if the Qur'an redoubtably describes Jahileens' poetic licence, their intellectual life in terms of monomaniacal ferocious interlopers always de-claiming the prophets' ideas, it is inconceivable that these muses, the *effendis* of their time, could have been caitiff, obtuse, violent and insolent. This is why the Qur'an describes the poet as a magician who lures his audience with the military force of his composition, rhyme and rhythm. Hussein's scrupulous scrutiny of Jahili poetry concludes that the obscurity, demureness and privation of religious passion that characterize this closed and infallible canon have nothing to do with alternative poetry produced by 'Amrou Qayes, 'Antara or Tarafa. Alternative readings, based on the Qur'an's unmistakable commentary on Jahili religious dissent, are indicative of Jahileens' magnanimous faith, chider and cynicism. This is what explains the subversive character of

Qur'anic discourse. The polemical climate of the time is always interior to the self-interpretative life of the Book.

Hussein concedes that medieval compilers of poetry were sciolists, motivated by the necessary theophilosophical urge to construct an anthology of pre-Islamic literature that would reflect the solid boundary lines between isolation and expansion, ignorance and effulgence, division and unity. The literary compiler – also a theologian – attempted to categorize poetic imagination as a sensibility of hebetude and obdurateness in order to suppress the very notion of myth that contradicted his logocentric spatiality. Early Muslim theologians abnegated irregular unmathematical methods of oral transmission in order to produce an accurate, purified and regulated history of transmissions and their authenticity. Adonis reiterates the same anxiety about the impact of the inquisition on Islamic consciousness:

> Those in power designated everyone who did not think according to the culture of the caliphate as 'the people of innovation' (*ahl al-islah*), excluding them with this indictment of heresy from their Islamic affiliation. This explains how the terms *ihdath* (modernity) and *muhdath* (modern, new), used to characterise the poetry which violated the ancient poetic principles, came originally from the religious lexicon. Consequently we can see that the modern in poetry appeared to the ruling establishment as a political or intellectual attack on the culture of the regime and a rejection of the idealised standards of the ancient, and how, therefore, in Arab life the poetic has always been mixed up with the political and religious, and indeed continues to be so. (Adonis, 1990, p. 76)

This historicist methodology of triage and elimination has to be understood within the context of *the limits* and determinations of writing history in medieval times. Writing for the classical officiant was an oblatory exercise: an act of obeisance to God, who is the originator of thought. The Book is overlaid with the collator's rationality; its principles become his, but he has found in the invisible absent God a pedagogical usefulness that shields him from the thinkability of error. On this account he had to deny the transgressive verse of the poet, the fable and the notion of imagination. In many ways, like the orientalist philologist, the theologian concentrated on facts, schemes and a drive for canonicity. We are accustomed, as a result of the work of Islamologists, sociologists and anthropologists, to think that the phenomena of Islam exist in written documents and in collective consciousness – the *consensus communis*. This is *only* the eternal Islam constructed by the official theologians for over fourteen centuries reducing its complex multiplicity to an essentialist category. Is there perhaps an aporetic connection between the orientalist enlightened reason and Islam's fundamental orthodox reason that has shaped a number of post-colonial Islamic regimes? Or have I now implicated myself in the dangerous game of what Said has termed 'self-orientalization' by interrogating Islamic reason at its theological base?

The Paralysis of Magic or the Magic of Paralysis?

Hussein's book, marginalized especially by Anglo-American Islamologists and Anglo-Indian Muslim scholars (perhaps because it has never been translated into

English), breaks an old methodological taboo: the notion that pre-Islamic poetry of the Book is evidence for the Qur'an's inimitability. It is rather the opposite: Jahili poetry, fragmentary, mordant and aesthetically magical, must interpret the Book, its immediate and interior *host*. Hussein destabilizes a fundamental thought pattern that dominated Islamic theology of metaphysics because he asserts that the Qur'an, by reverting to what one may call 'locations of eternal credibility', has effaced itself, turning against its own infinite character of immutability (*Al-I'jaz*).[8] The dogma of a magical character, inimitable, stems from the challenge levelled at Jahili poets to produce an utterance (*énoncé*) as clear, coherent and charged with sense (*sens*) as the message communicated by the Prophet. 'What, do they not ponder the Qur'an? If it had been from other than God surely they would have found in it much inconsistency' (Women, 4: 82). Reproduction is fundamentally circumvention; it displays an aporia about the notion of the transcendence of the Arabic sacred letter itself. Orthodoxy constituted by the *Ulama*, the collators and theologians of the text as a closed eternal system, has elevated the paramountcy of memorization of the Word, and considered writing to be a sign of the inferiority of a nation's memory and its inherent mendacity (Abu al-Faraj Ibn al-Jawzi (d.597), 1985). Ibn al-Jawzi emphasizes that orality, or voice with its mnemonic rectitude, represents the very authority of Tradition.

This hermeneutic decidability about the state of the Arabic Letter has to be understood within the context of medieval theological reasoning. Classical theologians and historians were working through a crisis of collecting the Book in its written form.[9] They therefore selected texts that coincided with the procedures of *Shari'a*, an officialese regulated by their predecessors. Hence the establishment of a special science of abrogation, a point of order that fed on Islamic jurisprudence. The disputation became invincible, a historical necessity, since theologians had to use writing itself to invent an alternative methodology to solve the variance in the collected Book by Caliph `Uthman which was written down on the basis of a complex system of self-regulating correction, verification, dormatization and approval. Hence an inexhaustible literature of Reasons of Revelation (*asbab al-nouzoul*) appeared to ease the tensions of abrogation – this science assumed that every verse had a justifiable *primum mobile* that must explain any redundant configurations of sameness within the content or form of Scriptures. This system of categorization, called *Isnad*, sought also to periodize the sequence of verses to avoid unnecessary overlapping or ungrounded operations of cross-reference between diverse, fragmented or feeble verses. No matter how unbridgeable the inconsistencies might be, the technique of abrogation for the theologian could only make the Word of God clear and reasonable.

This notion has been systematized in a linguistic and literary sense dominated by Aristotelian logic. The Qur'an has become a totality, impermeable, whose immutability is itself the centre of its structurality. It has been rendered as a self-enclosed system whose signifiers originate and refer to a transcendental signified. The *idée fixe* of the Book privileges the spoken voice (truth, presence) above the corruptibility of Jahili poetic writing. *Al-I'jaz* (from *A'jaza*) means to become paralysed – indicating the incommunicable nature of the sacred. Tradition, however, gives the word the meaning of incapacitating imitation of the Qur'anic letter, of *plus ça change, plus c'est la même chose*, influencing the study of grammar, logic, rhetorics and prosody.[10] Scholastic methodology necessitated accurate sciences of usage of grammatical rules and Arabic lexicon to secure permanent validity of significations. *Ijtihad*, which literally means studiousness/discipleship, from the verb *Ijtahada* (to work hard), demanded from the scholar to formulate and *construct* an architecture of (*ilm al-usul*) (Baqillani (d.403/1013CE), 1963), the 'Science of Foundations'. This science rusticated theology, logic, linguistics and ethics, producing a Systematic Theology called *Fiqh*. The closing of the Qur'anic canon by Caliph `Uthman has played the role of delimiting movements of play and undecidability between the Book's modes of discourse, and has paralysed the potential of every literary mode to negotiate the literary contradictions and tensions inside its structures. Instead, this ideological closure has created an anxiety about canonical bonification since the eleventh century.

The Limits of Reproducibility

Hussein's limitation, however, is perhaps the same as Said's, albeit pertaining to different results. Whilst Hussein's insight that such a theory of reproducibility as constructed by his reasoning may be questionable since a final truth (as Descartes himself envisaged of Western thought) is untenable, Said's explicit allusion to having captured the *real* violences of orientalist knowledge is close to an illusion. Hussein's blindness is to have conceived of Cartesian reason as a uniform philosophy in a sense that, when it comes to truth claims, it is the only legitimate grammar capable of unravelling the excessive falsehood and manipulation of tradition. Said's exclusion of Islam's immediate others, from poetics to mysticism and discourses of independent thinking, suggests that he did not need to take further 'measures' to test and verify his own self-regulating concepts that may have suppressed the possible reciprocal interrelations between the two rationalities. Furthermore, reproducibility, lies and falsehood may be the very fulcrum on which relations of power and ideological proximities swing.

Hussein's dissection of the structurality of the Islamic theory and practice of duplication, its suppression of poetic figural language and his deep suspicion about the alleged perdurability and integrity of the celestial Book, represent some cardinal insights into a 'deconstruction' *avant la lettre*. Hussein's modernist critique seems to suggest another reading: that, in order to overturn the theologian's phonocentric perception of the miraculous Book, it is important to look at the importance of metaphorical organization, the mythical narrative of the Qur'an and other elements of dream works and eschatological consciousness that inhabited poetic expression. These can be examined as sites of incongruent beliefs, fantasy and dreams produced by Muslim consciousness in its history and psychocultural formations. On this account, Hussein's 'intercolonial knitting' suggests that colonial reason, obsessed by a space of fixity, had already interwoven itself into a history of alterity already anxious about its latent fears and suppressions, or, as Mernissi suggests,

> The Muslims did not think of the phenomenon of modernity in terms of rupture with the past, but rather in terms of a renewed relation with the past ... In the majority of cases the Muslim approach, the approach of political and religious thinkers, was just the reverse of

the principles implied by a correct understanding of enlightenment thought. (Mernissi, 1993, p. 118)

To question the most revered, apotheosized Book in Arabo-Islamic consciousness in a debilitating condition of colonial subjugation indicates that processes of orientalizations may not have discouraged Muslim thinkers from uncovering procedures by which the ideology of official Islam was maintained. The trinitarian (*Mushaf*, *Umma*, *Ulama*) circumvolution that Hussein explicitly articulates remained until the very time of his writing as unassailable, semiotic, holy, natural; a part of the evolution of consciousness itself. The ultimate expediency of these syndromic values was the faith in them as unchanging realities, as the truth *in itself*.

The Horizons of the Unspeakable

Concomitantly, an anxiety over mysticism inhabits Said's reflection. An analysis of orientalism must be subject to those suppressed elements of myth and about myth, of negative theologies and the imaginary that have been systematically dichotomized, essentialized and de-authenticized by both secular and religious reason. When Said insists that all knowledge is fictional, that truth is not achievable, that a 'real Orient' does not exist, I take him to mean that the orientalist tradition has a fictional object at its core, but has suppressed it through another more fictional inquiry – perhaps, of all rational fictions, its textual primness, utilitarian categorization and ideological commitments. Orientalists have not constructed natural sites from which truth can be administered, but have characteristically spoken a wisdom they themselves did not see or understand since they could not envisage that such wisdom was indeed wise. They meant to present contingency, but betrayed it by resorting to an already ephemeral pervasiveness, collaboration and coercion. The case of orientalist textuality is one of Barmecide, like the wealthy man in *Arabian Nights* who gave a beggar a feast featuring lavishly embellished, filigreed, empty dishes.

Louis Massignon, 'the mature symbol', the one presenting 'the unorthodox view of Islam', who 'is willing to cross disciplinary and traditional boundaries in order to penetrate to the human heart of any text', has seen in Islamic mysticism an indication of subjective participation with the divine, has considered the great Muslim mystic al-Hallaj, condemned to death in 922CE, as evidence for rejecting the 'limiting consensus imposed ... by the orthodox Islamic community, or Sunna' (Said, 1995, pp. 266–8). If Said himself freely admits 'that his mystifying erudition and almost familiar personality sometimes make him appear to be a scholar invented by Jorge Luis Borges', Massignon's reflections on mysticism may be extended to indicate how the Muslim has constructed himself plurally and has always conceptualized alternatives to Submission's logos, *arche* or *telos*. Al-Hallaj, the 'scientist' of hearts, claimed the 'agoras' (*souks*) of Baghdad by preaching God as the only Truth, the very Desire (*'ishq*) that is yet to come. He was a product of a reading and critical civilization that encouraged the mastery of all sciences; Nazzam, Ibn al-Rawandi, Jahiz, Tawhidi, abu Nuwas, Sirafi, Mubbarad,

Razi, Ibn al-Rumi, Mutanabbi and Battani were the architects of Arabo-Islamic renaissance.

The memory and traces of this miscommunicated mystic are still legendary in many parts of Arabia and Persia. While Said alleged that 'Massignon's al-Hallaj was intended literally to embody, to incarnate, values essentially outlawed by the main doctrinal system of Islam' (Said, 1995, p. 172) this may not *necessarily* be the basis of Massignon's perverseness, but the fact that his writing was paradoxically detecting a marginal space, an institutionalized rationality that al-Hallaj rejected. On this account, the notion of ambivalence, shuttle effect and interdeterminacy indicate that processes of desire, translation, exoticism and fear have, more often than not, been subtle, deeply nuanced and obscure. In this spirit, Massignon admits,

> It is with lowered eyes, *markhiya 'aynayya*, that I hail from afar this lofty figure, always veiled for me, even in his tortured nakedness: then snatched up from the ground, borne away, covered with blood, torn completely to pieces with fatal wounds, carried by the jealousy of the most ineffable Love. (Massignon, 1994, p. xxvii)

Islamic literature of mysticism (Sufism), with its metaphorical readings, secret codes and Gnostic allegories, highlights more the figural life of the Book/book (this being Arkoun's configuration to show the interrelationships between the sacred and the profane text). For this reason, Arkoun urges a systematic rereading of the Islamic tradition of textual practice. Reading Arkoun's reflection about this historical (epistemic) necessity itself requires patience because there is a risk of seeing his deconstructive gesture, inscriptionalist mode and mood as a total rupture from the reasoned continuities of metaphysics' concerns for truth, representation and ethics. Patience, which means 'a prudent, differentiated, slow, stratified' (Derrida, 1981, p. 33) reading, is when the reader and commentator are able to conceive of the space of radical self-reflexivity for Islam. Islam, as Abdullah al-Qusaimi urges, must be understood outside the legacy of 'a faith that has always searched for the ultimate Divine Culprit/Victim of all crimes and sins' (Abdullah al-Qusaimi, 2001, p. 5). For Arkoun, as Ricoeur would concede, 'faith is the limit of all hermeneutics and the non-hermeneutical origin of all interpretation' (Ricoeur, 1995, p. 46). Faith has a prelinguistic and hyperlinguistic characteristic; it is a feeling of 'absolute dependence', 'unconditional trust', because 'it is inseparable from a movement of hope' (ibid., p. 47). The term *Sufi* itself, which etymologically means 'wool' indicates that the Sufi, a polyhistor, was meditating upon the secrets of the Book/book through the inspiration of the texture he perceived in his garment that reminded him that his wool gathering meant seclusion, and a readiness to be filled, even if full-fil(*a*)ment is only always to come. The notion of imagination, 'ce pouvoir de médiation' and of 'synthèse entre le sens et la lettre' is the arcane point of departure for structure and scheme. Imagination in Derrida's view represents a certain friendship or fidelity between 'La forme et le fond'; it is art itself, as Kant conceded (Derrida, 1978, pp. 15–16). The Book/book that drinks from the wells of imagination invites a perception of myth outside religious dogma and scholastic philology that dominated the study of religion and language for many centuries.

The political malaise of Islam in relationship to the West has become, following Said's influential book, incontrovertibly pregnable. Post-colonial theory, positive

Muslim scholarship and 'post-orientalist' commentaries have pervasively 'named and shamed' the limits of the Western humanist tradition, but in relationship to its theological sign, Islam may have already begun to lose its prehensibility. The modern Anglo-American establishment of Islamic studies is yet to examine the challenges of critical theories of Islam that dare to indulge in the indispensable question of the boundary of the Muslim mind, the *closure* of its own logos and the incarceration of Islamic reason's trace of heterodoxy.

Notes

1. Abdullah Aroui concentrated on the archaeology of Arab thought, Mohamed 'Abid Jabiri focused on the history of Muslim ideology and a critical re-reading of Iberian Muslim philosophy, especially the philosophy of Ibn Rushd, and Fatima Mernissi and Nawal El-Saadawi concentrated on the image and construction of woman in Islamic theology and history. More recently, Naser 'Abu Zaid has worked on the critical interpretation of the Qur'an, among many others.
2. Michael Fisher, Theodore Wright, Hastings Donnan, Norman Daniel, Francis Robinson, Pnina Werber, Henry Munson, Michel Gilsenan, Barbara Metcalf and William Chittick trained in the orientalist tradition of influential scholars such as Bernard Lewis, Claude Cahen and Gustav Von Grunebaum.
3. The word 'rethinking', as translated by Robert Lee in *Rethinking Islam* (1994), as Arkoun points out, falls 'short of the critical force and programmatic approach suggested by the French, *penser Islam*'.
4. *Arabica*, a scholarly periodical founded by MohammedArkoun, has long initiated the most noteworthy example of the epistemological treatment of Islam. To encourage discussion towards this end, the editorial board initiated an edition called *Méthodes et Débats* to open up debates on the relationship between epistemology and history among traditional orientalists. See especially the contributions of P. Crone (1992), A. Cheikh-Moussa and D. Gazagnadou (1993). A more recent interdisciplinary critical periodical, *Fiqr wa Na'qd* (Thought and Criticism), founded by Mohammed 'Abid al-Jabiri, has been published by Express, Casablanca, since 1997.
5. *L'impensable* also means the thing that cannot be envisaged or grasped by thought.
6. The translation of *l'impensé* as the 'undecidable' remains inadequate because in French the word really means that which cannot be made clear or precise.
7. For example, Fazlur Rahman, Sir Sayyed Iqbal, Ismail Faruqi, Hossein Nasr, Khurshid Ahmad, Ali Shariati, Parvez Manzoor, Ziauddin Sardar, Shabbir Akhtar, Ali Ashraf, M.W. Davies, Kalim Siddiqui, Yasmin Alibhai and Rana Kabbani.
8. According to Muslim tradition, the Qur'an transformed into *mushaf* was assembled immediately after the death of the Prophet in 632 by the third caliph, 'Uthman (645–56CE). It was written down based on memorization by the Companions of the Prophet, many of whom were dying. His collection was declared final, complete and closed; dubious compilations were destroyed to avoid dissent. Hence the notion of Closed Official System as elaborated by Arkoun's 'Applied Islamology'.
9. This major controversy in Classical Qur'anic exegesis is known as *A-nassihk WA almansoukh* (The Abrogated Verses). Much of the early debate centred on the difference between 'clear verses' in the Quran (*ayat muhkamat*), which were the backbone of the Book, and 'ambiguous verses' (*ayat mutashabihat*) which were to be interpreted in accordance with the clear ones.
10. The word 'Qur'an' derives from the verb '*qara'a*', to read. The root, q-r-' has the sense of recitation more than reading. The first Arabic grammatical treatise by Sibawayhi is

called *Kitab*, 'the book', or 'Sibawayhi's book'. This is considered to be the first comprehensive description of the Arabic language at every level (phonetics, phonology, morphology, syntax and semantics). According to medieval Arabic sources, grammar was first established by Abu-Aswad al-Du'ali (d. 69/688CE?); another source claims the emergence of this science with 'Abd Allah ibn Abi Ishaq (d. 117/734CE).

References

Adonis, (1990), *An introduction to Arab Poetics*, trans. Catherine Cobban, London: Saqi.

Akbar, S. Ahmed (1992), *Postmodernism and Islam: Predicament and Promise*, London: Routledge.

Al-Qusaimi, Abdullah (2001), *Pharaoh writes the Book of Exodus* (*Phir'awn yaktub sifr al khorouj*), Beirut: Mouassasat Al-Intishar Al-Arabi.

Arkoun, Mohammed (1972), 'Logocentrisme et Vérité Religieuse dans la Pensée Islamique', *Studia Islamica*, **15**.

Arkoun, Mohammed (1975), *La Pensée Arabe*, Paris: Presses Universitaires de France.

Arkoun, Mohammed (1982), *Lectures du Coran*, Paris: Maisonneuve & Larose.

Arkoun, Mohammed (1984), *Essais Sur La Pensée Islamique, Islam d'hier et d'aujourd'hui*, 3rd edn, Paris: Maisonneuve & Larose.

Arkoun, Mohammed (1994), *Re-thinking Islam*, trans. Robert D. Lee, Oxford: Westview Press.

Baqillani (1963), *I'jaz al-Quran* (The Inimitability of the Quran), ed. A. Saqr, Cairo: Dar al-Ma`asif

Derrida, Jacques (1976), *Of Grammatology*, trans. G. Spivak, Baltimore: Johns Hopkins University Press.

Derrida, Jacques (1978), *Writing and Difference*, trans. A. Bass, London: Routledge & Kegan Paul.

Derrida, Jacques (1981), *Positions*, trans. Alan Bass, London: Athlone Press.

Esposito, John L. (1992), *The Islamic Threat: Myth or Reality?*, Oxford: Oxford University Press.

Harper's (September 1989), 'Who needs the Great Works?'

Hussein, Taha (1926), *Fi Al-shi'er Al-jahili* (In Jahili Poetry), Cairo: Mattbaât Dar al-Kittab.

Ibn al-Jawzi, Abu al-Faraj (1985), *Al-Hatt Ala Hifz Al-'ilm Wa dthikr Kibbar Al-Huffaz* (The Imperative of Memorizing Science and Messages of the Greatest Memorizers), Beirut. Dar al Da`wah.

Lewis, Bernard (1993), *Islam and the West*, New York: Oxford University Press.

Massignon, Louis (1994), *The Passion of Al-Hallaj: Mystic and Martyr of Islam*, trans. Herbert Mason, Princeton: Princeton University Press.

Mernissi, Fatima (1993), *Islam and Democracy: Fear of the Modern World*, trans. Mary Jo Lakeland, London: Virago Press.

Pasto, James (1998), 'Islam's "Strange Secret Sharer": Orientalism, Judaism and the Jewish Question', *Comparative Study of Society and History*, **40** (1).

Ricoeur, Paul (1995), *Figuring the Sacred: Religion, Narrative and Imagination*, trans. David Pellauer, Minneapolis: Fortress Press.

Said, Edward (1981), *Covering Islam*, New York: Pantheon.

Said, Edward (1995), *Orientalism*, London: Penguin Books.

Sardar, Ziauddin (1991) 'The Postmodern Age', in Ahmad Anees Munawar, Syed Z. Abedin and Ziauddin Sardar (eds), *Christian–Muslim Relations Yesterday, Today, Tomorrow*, London: Grey Seal Books, pp. 54–91.

Sardar, Ziauddin (1993), 'The Rushdie Malaise: A Critique of Some Writings on the Rushdie

Affair', in M.M. Ahsan and A.R. Kidwai, (eds), *Sacrilege Versus Civility: Muslim Perspectives on The Satanic Verses Affair*, Leicester: The Islamic Foundation.
Sarder, Ziauddin (1999), *Orientalism*, Buckingham: Open University Press.
The Koran Interpreted (1982), trans. Arthur J. Arberry, Oxford: Oxford University Press.

IV
LOCATING EXPERIENCE IN CULTURE

Chapter 10

Fantasy, Imagination and the Possibility of Experience

Paul Fletcher

Unshakeable Confidence towers over the valley.
Its peak offers an excellent view of the Essence of Things. (Wisława Szymborska, 'Utopia')

1973 or the Hypermodern Narcissus

Vaughan's fantasy was to kill Elizabeth Taylor in a head-on collision at Heathrow airport. With a fervent devotion he observed her daily routine (from a Lincoln identical to the one in which John F. Kennedy was killed) so that he would know exactly where the impact would need to occur if he was to realize this fantasy of celebrity martyrdom, where their bodies would be entwined with the harsh chrome of the automobiles and their bodily fluids – semen, blood and tissue – would be mixed in an offertory preparation for erotic sanctification. Such is the desire of a central character in J.G. Ballard's (in)famous novel *Crash*, a book that includes, in its 1995 reprint – the book was first published in 1973 – an 'introduction' that places the narrative's significance in the realm of prophetic warning: 'Do we see, in a car crash,' asks Ballard, 'a sinister portent of a nightmare marriage between sex and technology?' (Ballard, 1995, p. 6) The psychopathologies of everyday life in a Ballardian universe can be read in terms of the symptom that is the fantasy life of atomistic characters and the unrealizability of the promise of these fantasies, a promise mirrored by the insatiable thirst and destruction of technology.

Experience in Ballard's novel is only real or authentic when it reaches out – ad-ventures – to the extreme and the extraordinary, risking life and limb in the high speed collision (whether atomic or vehicular). Whatever the merits of Ballard's prose and plot, his work stands as a testament to an age for whom the habitat of the everyday is banal and the repetitive is death. Experience is divorced from place and purpose, identity and relation and is only 'authentic' if it mirrors the moves and fulfils the mores – that is, if it replays – the composition of a fantastic, interior dramatic production. The 'real' is a simulacrum of the phantasm (see Butterfield, 1999). Subjects undergo, but never have, experiences. Experience in this mode signifies the alienation of the world from a self who is lost in the midst of the 'dream world' that constitutes contemporary existence.[1] The effect, according to Giorgio Agamben, is thus:

Modern man makes his way home in the evening wearied by a jumble of events, but

however entertaining or tedious, unusual or commonplace, harrowing or pleasurable they
are, none of them will have become experience. It is this non-translatability into
experience that now makes everyday existence intolerable – as never before – rather than
an alleged poor quality of life or its meaninglessness as compared with the past. ... For
experience has its necessary correlation not in knowledge but in authority – that is to say,
the power of words and narration; and no one now seems to wield sufficient authority to
guarantee the truth of an experience, and if they do, it does not in the least occur to them
that their own authority has its roots in an experience. On the contrary, it is the character
of the present time that all authority is founded on what cannot be experienced, and
nobody would be inclined to accept the validity of an authority whose sole claim to
legitimation was experience. ... Hence the disappearance of the maxim and the proverb,
which were the guise in which experience stood as authority. The slogan, which has
replaced them, is the proverb of humankind to whom experience is lost. (Agamben, 1993,
p. 13)

We, the affluent, soporific inhabitants of the Ballardian text, who live in the midst of
slogans and sociopolitical 'spin', can be likened to those cartoon characters who
walk out from a cliff into the nowhere or thin air and can continue to walk as long
as we do not notice our vacuous condition (ibid., p. 16). There is no ground, whether
it be a cosmic ontology, repetitive performances and cycles or stories, upon which
experience is possible.

This transformation in the status of experience was vividly portrayed by Walter
Benjamin who, in a number of essays of the 1920s and 1930s, attempted to consider
the consequences of the loss of tradition in modern life. In 'The Storyteller',
published in 1936, Benjamin reflected on the poverty of experience that arose as a
result of the catastrophic events of the First World War:

men returned ... grown silent – not richer, but poorer in communicable experience ... What
ten years later was poured out in the flood of war books was anything but experience that
goes from mouth to mouth. And there was nothing remarkable about that. For never has
experience been contradicted more thoroughly than strategic experience by tactical
warfare, economic experience by inflation, bodily experience by mechanical warfare,
moral experience by those in power. A generation that had gone to school on a
horse–drawn streetcar now stood under the open sky in a countryside in which nothing
remained unchanged but the clouds, and beneath the clouds, in a field of force of
destructive torrents and explosions, was the tiny, fragile human body. (Benjamin, 1973,
p. 84)

What Benjamin diagnoses is a sickness in which experience has been fundamentally
transformed: it is not that there can be no experience *as such*, but that the conditions
of the possibility of experience are no longer extant. The subject who gazes at the
grey sky above is dislocated from his or her environment, not simply in organic
terms but in a more fundamental manner. There are no shared places to bear (and
bare) the significance of experience; sacred or symbolic texts are no longer read or
authoritatively heard; the translatability of reminiscences is dead in the age of the
'perpetuating remembrance' of the novel and the decontextualized memorial that is
the museum (see ibid., p. 97). In their place have come the inventions of the
phantasm: a world of technology and surveillance to which we are subjected and a
sublime, spectral world of the imagination that generates the real. Schiller is as

illustrative here as Ballard, even if the disinterestedness of the former's heroic figures is related to different (though still immanent) ends.

What Benjamin and Agamben remind us is that, in generating, constituting and desiring a world of our imagining, we simultaneously lose it. My aim here is not to lament this ruin but to chart its incipience and its ramifications for the religious thinker. In other words, this chapter might be characterized as a walk amongst the debris of those religious possibilities that are dependent on located experience – or *cultura* – rather than a desiring ego that constructs the world and consumes the other. Calculation, implementation and the realization of the representations of consciousness characterize an ontological shift in which the subject takes leave of a cultural milieu where the social is an *a priori* given. In its place come the fragmented elements (Man, citizen) that make up the social contract and civil society, in the view of which local and cultural particularisms are primitive and unreliable. In a similar vein, faith is discarded as untrustworthy and indeterminate by a sovereign subject who forges (and is forged by) the modern.

1641 or the Modern Narcissus

In his dedicatory letter to the Sorbonne, written to obtain the approval of the 'Dean and Doctors of the sacred Faculty of Theology' for the publication of the *Meditations on First Philosophy* (a response to which never materialized), René Descartes makes a quite remarkable claim for his project. He suggests that it is not reasonable to expect unbelievers to accept the truths of Christianity on the basis of faith when they do not possess such a 'gift of God'. As a necessary surrogate of this supernatural donation, Descartes offers an alternative yet secure route to the acceptance of these truths, especially the existence of God and the immortality of the soul, which does not depend on authority or revelation – the medium of human thought. Drawing on Romans 1, 'that which is known of God is manifest in them', he claims that 'everything that may be known of God can be demonstrated by reasoning which has no other source but our own mind' (Descartes, 1984, p. 3). Uncertainty has been banished, along with tradition, faith and experience. Not even God is safe from the omnipotent and omniscient pretensions of the Cartesian method. Indeed, in placing theology and philosophy on the (un)questionable ground of the *cogito*, Descartes has constructed anew the problem of difference. Faith, tradition and experience all depend on ties that are material, historical and singular. Consequently, they are by definition and determination outside the parameters of certitude unless – and this is Descartes' genius – they can be objectified and subjected to scientific enquiry. Mistrusted, traditional experience must be tamed and made to work for its new master – knowledge (see Agamben, 1993, p. 17). Hence experience is moved as far as possible outside the subject: on to scientific instruments and the abstractions of mathematics and calculation (Shapin and Schaffer, 1985, pp. 36–7).

As Jan Patočka demonstrates, this modern transformation, that affects 'politics, economics, faith and science' (Patočka, 1996, p. 83), renders vacuous any attempts to reassert the authority of cultural connectivity and plurality, and the importance of experience. Modern epistemological and cultural shifts, in which power overtakes grace as the foremost attribute of God,[2] and in which 'Man' becomes sovereign within the natural realm while God is either reduced to an object of intelligibility or exiled to the (unknowable) domain of super-nature and metaphysics, radically transformed fundamental questions that bear on the identity of both philosophy and theology. To quote Patočka: 'Not a care *for the soul*, the care to *be*, but rather the care to *have*, care for the external world and its conquest, becomes the dominant concern.' The concerns of Christian practices and '*motifs* of life which had originally constrained this care to have, the will to rule' are subdued – if not destroyed – with the modern invention of 'religion' (ibid.).

And this religion has its own (historical and etymological) 'ties' broken by an autonomous subject for whom (as Kant puts it) '*Religion is conscientiousness (mihi hoc religioni).*' The cultivation and realization of a certain kind of moral subjectivity is sufficient for religion to be religious. Religion is, Kant continues, 'The holiness of the acceptance [*Zusage*] and the truthfulness of what man must confess to himself. Confess to yourself. To have religion, the concept of God is not required (still less the postulate: "There is a God")' (Kant, 1993, p. 248). Religion is possible without any true experience of the other, let alone the divine. Indeed, if one considers the role and status of sex and marriage in Kant's thought, it becomes clear that it is the fate of the modern subject to wander disengaged from existence and the vicissitudes of experience. The bond between two people that is consummated sexually is intelligible only in terms of utility and objectification: sexual union is a 'reciprocal use' of sexual organs in which 'a human being makes himself into a thing' (Kant, 1991, pp. 96–7). The self as a bodily, love-making entity is classified as an object which in turn appropriates the 'thing' that lies beyond it as it comes back to itself and its own self-consciousness. The other (which now includes the loving body) is rendered utile and an experience with (and of) the other is accounted for only in terms of its value to an autonomous, atomized self. It nonetheless remains outside, exiled from that which is authentic and most real.

German Idealism marks the apotheosis of this sceptical repositioning of experience and the celebration of the alienation of the ego from the world. In post-Kantian philosophy, the polarities of existence are framed, on the one hand, by the finite and divided self and, on the other, by a finite and divided world that is rendered significant only as non-self. It is the imagination which produces the world of knowledge, or, in Fichte's terms, 'produces reality' (Fichte, 1970, p. 207). Although Kant attempted to control the imagination by subordinating its creative role to the restraining guidelines provided by the understanding – the imagination works (apprehends or re-presents) for reason (which posits totality)[3] – his Idealist pupils and critics turned the tables on him. As George Seidel demonstrates, with regard to Fichte's positing of the imagination as that which brings self and non-self into identity, 'The imagination is a capacity or power (*Vermögen*) that swings (*schwebt*, or oscillates) in the middle between determination and nondetermination, between the finite and the infinite' (Seidel, 1993, p. 12).[4] Truth and actuality are realized within the realms of the imaginative alone, where a dynamic oscillation occurs between the centrifugal projections of the phantasm and the centripetal demands of self-determination (see Makkreel, 1994, p. 11). The world is created by an imagination which gives rise to the desire to strive for an infinity or absolute that is within, not beyond (see Seidel, 1993, p. 80). That which is outside the self is a product of the self and its negation as limitation simply serves to affirm the self. Consequently, as Jean Starobinski avers, the world is left behind in this solipsistic revel: 'To imagine no longer means to participate in the world, it means to haunt one's own image in terms of the indefinitely variable illusions this image can fashion for itself. Imagination conforms to the myth of Narcissus' (Starobinski, 1970, p. 189).

The Religion of Narcissus

The journey from Ballard to Descartes via Fichte is, as it were, the uneven textual itinerary of a pilgrim moving towards his own deification, in the name of which religion itself is required to change. The common thread which adjoins – even if fairly loosely – the Fichtean (progenitive) imagination and the Ballardian (perverse) fantasy is provided by Friedrich Heinrich Jacobi. In the second edition of his (in)famous Spinoza book, Jacobi claimed to 'believe that one must never put the *sum* after the *cogito*' (Jacobi, 1789, p. xv). It is the *sum*, and its dramatic realization, rather than the *cogito* as indubitable ground, that serves as the supreme tenet of the rise and rise of Narcissus. The 'I' creates the universe and the Absolute is resituated in a seamless identity of being. The Spinozist shift announced by Jacobi, and his grafting of monistic substance onto a substantial Kantian ontological host, provided an opportunity for religious thinkers of the late eighteenth and early nineteenth centuries to revivify religious discourse after the mauling it had received from the critical turn in philosophy.

On a positive note, the emergence of the imagination and its creative possibilities provided a route to the infinite that bypassed the arid temper of the moral and placed the religious within the realms of what had come to be seen as the most productive and fecund of faculties. Moreover, even in a more defensive key, it also allowed religion to be reconstituted for apologetic purposes. Indeed, it is Schleiermacher who is commonly seen as the figure within religious Romanticism who most thoroughly transformed the status of religion to fit this new context and sensibility. Of course, the imagination is central to his project. And, as is demonstrated in the second of his celebrated *Speeches*, Schleiermacher's work conforms to, and follows in the wake of, the Fichtean delineation of the imagination as productive. Therefore the imagination is not to be understood as 'something subordinate or confused'. No, it is

> the highest and most original faculty in man. All else in the human mind is simply reflection upon it, and is therefore dependent on it. Imagination in this sense is the free generation of thoughts, whereby you come to a conception of the world; such a conception you cannot receive from without, nor compound from inferences. From this conception you are then impressed with the feeling of omnipotence. (Schleiermacher, 1958, p. 98)

The apologetic tone of the *Speeches* is not accidental. Schleiermacher is attempting to illustrate to those closest to him – his fellow Jena Romantics – the compatibility of religion with their Romantic quest for purity, beauty and the infinite (see Forstman, 1977, pp. 65–80). He is, as it were, making an ethical decision – that is, concerning a way of life (*ēthos*) – regarding the inheritance of the religious past and the shape of its modern 'after-life', its transmission, reception and polarization. In the midst of the impressionistic rhetoric and reasoning of the *Speeches* lies a difficult and demanding project. To the question 'What is to be the dwelling place (*ēthos*) of the Christian who is at risk of slipping into the interstices between the old and the new?', Schleiermacher responds unequivocally. The old must conform to the new or, more specifically, what is considered to be outdated is in fact *the* core element of the new. In offering this rejoinder to those cultured despisers who happened to be his closest friends and colleagues, especially Novalis and the Schlegels, Schleiermacher provided the groundwork for the most thoroughgoing innovation within religious thought and practice since the Reformation. Indeed, it was Friedrich Schlegel, with whom Schleiermacher collaborated on the *Athenäum* journal at the end of the eighteenth century, who offered the most radical and revolutionary reconstitution of religion in the light of Fichte's *Wissenschaftslehre*, the French Revolution and Goethe's *Wilhelm Meister*. This threefold historico-dramatic constellation constitutes what Schlegel calls 'the great tendencies of the age' (Schlegel, 1991, p. 46).[5]

What this trinity of cultural possibilities demonstrates, according to Schlegel, is that 'there is in man a terrible, unsatisfied desire to soar into infinity' (Berlin, 1999, p. 15). The only means to any possible satisfaction of this unsatisfied desire is to move beyond the quest for understanding – that ceaseless oscillation between the polarities of understanding and not understanding – to a form of becoming, self–production and formation in which the absolute and the unconditioned might be 'experienced and realised in an unmediated, immediate fashion' (Lacoue–Labarthe and Nancy, 1988, p. ix). So reminiscent of the arduous task of self–composition undertaken in the Ignatian *Spiritual Exercises* (except that is, for the immediate satisfaction of desire), this production of the self is not the result of a commitment to a brute mastery of the world (as with, say, Francis Bacon). It is a more effete and disengaged dynamic that requires the mediation and incarnation of a given truth. For Schlegel this 'subject–work' (as Lacoue–Labarthe and Nancy call it) is only possible in the subject of and as art. Art *is* religion, and 'religion is a matter of the unveiling of truth (in other words, of the subject)' (Lacoue–Labarthe and Nancy, 1988, p. 76).

Religion here is neither the dry moralism of Kant's *Religion* book nor a traditional configuration of thought, revelation, authority and practice. Indeed, Novalis commented to Schlegel in the margin of a manuscript of the latter's *Ideen* of 1799 that whenever religion is described or delineated by Schlegel what is meant is 'enthusiasm in general.' (Novalis, 1960b, p. 489). In what is an almost alchemical intermingling of philosophical reflection, gnosticism and sentimentalism, Schlegel gives birth to a religion that is – indeed, must be – utterly distinct and particular: 'Only someone who has his own religion,' claims Schlegel, 'his own original way of looking at infinity, can be an artist' (Schlegel, 1991, p. 35). And to be an artist is *the* vocation of freedom for which one must die. Religion is, then, little more than an inspiration or ecstasy that is made possible by the imaginative aestheticization of existence: 'God is everything that is purely original and sublime, consequently the individual himself taken to the highest power. But aren't nature and the world also individuals?' (ibid., p. 98). What Schlegel effects is the fusion of the divine and the human, super-nature and nature in a pantheistic orgy in which the human imagination reigns supreme. This is no incarnation of the Christian tradition. It is, on the contrary, a Promethian elevation of the artist (that is, the one who works on his or her very self) to the status of God: 'Man frees himself by bringing forth God or making him visible' (ibid., p. 96). The notion that there is one mediator between God and humanity is the product of 'prejudice and presumption': 'For the perfect Christian – whom in this respect Spinoza probably resembles most – everything would have to be a mediator' (ibid., p. 50).

There is, nevertheless, a contradiction in the 'theology' (if one can give this form of religious reflection a name) of Schlegel. While his ecstatic pronouncements on mysticism and sublime possibility disclose an aesthetic religion, lived within the limits of its vocation, yet unrestrained by the artistic substance of that vocation, Schlegel is still determined to rigidly define and delimit the divine. God is literally formulated by dividing imagination, sentiment and myth – the building blocks of religion as art – by zero again and again until the quantity of these elements is 'infinitely infinitesimal' (Forstman, 1977, p. 34). Religion, or more accurately, the divine is the object of the subject (and his or her imagination) who can gain access to and measure the infinite. The religious individual observes and works upon the construction of the divine, the self and the work of art. Unification and totality are realized through a constitution of the divine by the subject's imagination. The subject is, as it were, the one who begets God: in the beginning was the imagination and the imagination was divine and the divine was the product of the imagination.

The imagination creates a religion within the bounds of the aesthetic alone which endeavours to fracture and eliminate boundaries: Romantic poetry, as with all strands of art, aims to unite all that is divided (Schlegel, 1991, p. 31). A pivotal feature of this poetic formation of this religio–aesthetics is a quest for unity and harmony in the infinite *and* in the beginning: 'The revolutionary desire to realize the kingdom of God on earth is the elastic point of progressive civilization and the beginning of modern history. Whatever has no relation to the kingdom of God is of strictly secondary importance' (ibid., p. 48).

In other words, the Romantic anthropotheology of art was at the same time a philosophy of history that looked to the realization of a sublime utopia, a re-envisioned kingdom of god, in which divisions will be dissolved.[6] It was a cosmic history that was tripartite in character (Szondi, 1986, p. 57). Paradise preceded the fall and the return to paradise follows the trials of disunity and sin. The paradigmatic figure of heaven is the androgyne in whom the polarities and distinctions of a post–lapsarian existence are healed in consummate wholeness. With its dependence on a theory of nature as an organic whole, the Romantic model of human possibility and potentiality was given philosophical and cultural credibility by Schelling's *Naturphilosophie*. Schelling proposed that the polarities within the natural world – which he termed male and female – must exist in a dynamic tension so that headway towards their synthesis might be maintained. Again, the Fichtean emphasis on the oscillation of polarities (reworked by Schelling) is central to unification, harmony and identity. Human beings, as a microcosm of nature, were to strive to bring about perfection both within themselves and throughout the natural world through the formation of a synthesis (or a reconstitution of their pre-lapsarian condition) that could be initiated in the coupling of the sexes. Sexual intercourse was an expression of the desire for the infinite, a realization of the indifferentiation of identities.

Indeed, Franz von Baader (a colleague of Schelling at Munich) declared that 'the division of the sexes, as well as the fall, could be attributed to Adam's sexual desire for the woman within him. And only sexual union could restore the image of the divine on earth' (Friedrichsmeyer, 1983, p. 59). Baader even went as far as to profess that the arms were an extension of the ribs. Consequently, when a man embraced a woman he was drawing her once more into the rib-cage from which she had earlier been expelled (Baader, 1856, p. 236; see also Betanzos, 1998, pp. 167–207). Religious activity, allied with the satisfaction of primordial desire, is actualized in the violent consumption of the other who becomes a building block to the completion of the self. She is a commodity, a whore whose very existence is to return from whence she came. The hollowed out subject must draw in this woman in order to overcome alienation and to achieve satisfaction in the insatiability of the imaginative subject.

The harmonious facade of the romantic world reveals little more than the poverty–stricken status of worldly inhabitants; that is, inhabitants who clamour for experience that is lost. The modern obsession with the grounds of subjectivity, for which the *cogito* is a potent emblem, and the compulsive default to the experiential by the Romantics, for whom the *sum* stands as the principle of formation of meaning, constitute the framework within which the contemporary loss of, and quest for, experience must be understood. This setting might be designated the New Age by some and a catastrophe by others. However we understand these times, religion is defined by the preferences and predilections of subjects and the 'supernatural arts' that *they* decide to practise. Religion *qua* religion is dead. In its place comes Ovid's narcissistic nightmare: being 'in love with an insubstantial hope, mistaking a mere shadow for a real body' (Ovid, 1955, p. 85). Back to Schlegel: in 1808, he became a Catholic. This was a man who proclaimed himself a pagan and asserted that pure religion could be found in alchemy and astrology owing to their immanent conjoining of the sacred and the profane. Indeed, he was honest enough to declare to many of his correspondents that he believed little if anything of Catholic dogma and doctrine. It was the aesthetic and decorative performativity of Catholicism – bells and smells – that awakened his excitement and provoked his conversion (see Hellerich, 1995, pp. 219–36).

Capital Religion

The significance of this step is that religion is the *parasite* of the quest for experience and the consumption of the aesthetic. There is no negotiation of cultural and political inheritance and there are no prerequisites for the satiability of desire except the renewal of the promise (or illusion) of satisfaction. Religion invests in this illusory economy in its search for a meaningful place in the market place. In its own way, religion has become Ballardian in its acceptance of the terms of relevance: that a desire for the infinite can be sated through erotic or artistic totality. Nevertheless, while this modern configuration of desire fulfils the neo-Romantic quest for the conflation of the sacred and the profane in the immediacy of an experience, it does so by giving itself over to the guardian of its realization – consumption. And the latter's means, as a pure means, is capital. It is this immaculate logic that is examined by Benjamin in his fragment, 'Capitalism and Religion', written in 1921 but unpublished in his lifetime.

Benjamin offers an uncompromising analysis of a phenomenon which 'serves essentially to allay the same anxieties, torment, and disturbances to which the so–called religions offered answers' (Benjamin, 1996, p. 288). There are, according to Benjamin's analysis, three distinctive characteristics intrinsic to this religiosity that 'may be discerned in capitalism': the purely cultic nature of this religion, the permanence of this cult, and the pervasive nature of guilt engendered by the purely cultic form of capital. Capitalism as pure cult implies that 'things only have a meaning in their relationship to the cult; capitalism has no specific dogma, no theology'. In other words, capitalism is *the* religion devoid of any content, the religion sought after by Friedrich Schlegel (and, I would argue, one that has a family resemblance to all religions without religion, but that is just a controversial digression). Moreover, in relation to Benjamin's second point, capitalism 'is the celebration of a cult *sans rêve et sans merci* [without dream or mercy].' It is the impalpable nature of capital, its status as unqualified system, that yields both its success and its consequence – guilt. This third distinguishing mark of capitalism as religion has, in its wake, even engulfed God:

> A vast sense of guilt that is unable to find relief seizes on the cult, not to atone for this guilt but to make it universal, to hammer it into the conscious mind, so as once and for all to include God in the system of guilt and thereby awaken in Him an interest in the process of atonement. This atonement cannot then be expected from the cult itself, or from the reformation of this religion (which would need to be able to have recourse to some stable element in it), or even from the complete renouncement of this religion. (Benjamin, 1996, pp. 288–9)

God is no longer transcendent, nor the possible point of reference for an authentic form of existence: God is inscribed and incarcerated within the immanent demands of a system that claims that desire can be satisfied. 'God's transcendence is at an end. But he is not dead; he has been incorporated into human existence' (Benjamin, 1996, p. 289). What Benjamin proposes, then, is a religion in which measure is not something that stands to be so thoroughly comprehended or grasped but is an excessiveness in which the human being is located (in fact, dis-located) in the context of the 'absolute loneliness of his trajectory'.

More importantly, at least for what concerns us here, there is a second central characteristic of 'capital' religiosity. Benjamin suggests that, while (following Weber) one can reiterate the fact that capitalism's development was parasitic upon Christianity, a point has been reached 'where Christianity's history is essentially that of its parasite – that is to say, of capitalism'.[7] The logic of infinite love is always indebted to the restrictive benevolence of *Schuld* – guilt and debt. The barometer of the possible is the level of anxiety that is inculcated by capitalist religiosity: '"Worries" are the index of the sense of guilt induced by a despair that is communal, not individual and material, in origin' (ibid., p. 290). And then comes Benjamin's warning. 'Capitalism is entirely without precedent, in that it is a religion which offers not the reform of existence but its complete destruction.' Despair is the fulfilment of religion as capital, its *telos* which has no end, no goal: capitalism is the religion of nihilism, of mourning without end.[8] Desire can never be sated, even though that is the immanent promise of the commodity. Desire is rather produced and reproduced in the empty promise of fulfilment. In other words, desire is a lack which is 'created, planned and organized' by capital (Deleuze and Guattari, 1983, p. 28). This mode of desiring, contra Weber, re-enchants the social world and, through it, brings about a 'reactivation of mythic powers' upon which religion is now dependent. Revelation and lost traditions are displaced onto relations among things (commodity fetishism) in a desiring economy that is a process of unknowing. Redemption, in our empty lives, is the ability to consume.

Conclusion

In the face of this account, where the prospects for contemporary existence are seen in unremittingly gloomy terms, is there a rejoinder that can be both responsible and concrete? For Benjamin, the only possible retort is Messianic. That is, divine (bloodless) violence is posited in the face of the mythic violence of the law, and the sovereignty of God dispels the illusions of the present (Benjamin, 1996, pp. 236–52). This mixture of pessimism and utopianism, while it reflects the desolation of politics after liberalism, fascism and communism, does point to an ineluctable, if immense, set of demands. Nevertheless, Benjamin's eschatological desire for the overcoming of the present profane order shares the same logic as the solipsistic and insubstantial religion that is born of the modern and Romantic transmutations of religious life and practice. Both approaches to the religious and the religiopolitical are born of the demand for immediacy and refuse a way of life that is institutionally or legally substantial, even if the latter is to be understood in preliminary and provisional terms. The repudiation of mediation is an abandonment of the world, a retreat from collectivity and representation and an immature desire for instant fulfilment. Indeed, just as Novalis could claim (in the *Athenäum*) that the failure of the French Revolution was the 'crisis of the ensuing puberty' (Novalis, 1960a, p. 459), so one could suggest that the predicament of Romanticism and its bequest is the continuing inability to depart from this immaturity.

To renounce the seductive claims for immediacy is not to suggest that the loss of utopia institutes an extreme and irredeemable pessimism but, rather, is to intimate that resolution and fulfilment, if at all possible, must be understood as process. Two examples may help to illustrate what I mean.

First, in Martin Scorsese's controversial filmic adaptation of Nikos Kazantzakis's classic novel, *The Last Temptation of Christ* (1988), we are presented with a problematization of the circumscription of desire and its satisfaction. Following his encounter with the Baptist and his immersion in the Jordan, Jesus (Willem Defoe) departs for the wilderness. There he draws a circle in the sand and sits and awaits his enticer(s). Three temptations come his way mediated by a cobra, a lion and an immense and blinding flame: the satisfaction of erotic desire; the fulfilment of the dream of absolute power; to join Satan himself in usurping God. As in the Christian scriptures, the temptations are rebutted. They nonetheless return, and return again, at different stages of the narrative and under different guises. The *pan rema* of Matthew's gospel (4:3–4), the every word (that proceeds from the mouth of God), is presented in the film as received by Jesus but never dispensed with. These words are lived in the constitution of a community and all that such a mediated existence entails with regard to interpretation and risk is intrinsic to their embodiment.

The second example comes from Gregory of Nyssa's integration of the Hebrew scriptures and fourth-century Neoplatonism in *The Life of Moses* (1978). There Gregory outlines a theory of eternal progress. Perfection comes in neither achievement nor the satisfaction of desire. That is because perfection is unattainable because of its status as limitless (ibid., p. 117). 'Thus, no limit would interrupt growth in the ascent to God, since no limit to the good can be found nor is the increasing of desire for the good brought to an end because it is satisfied' (p. 116). There is always a new summit to which one must climb but its horizon is only disclosed in the midst of satiety that is revealed as partial and conditional. One is nomadic in the sight of God, always on the (perpetual) move towards a satisfaction that can never be attained. Desire, for Gregory, is increased with each progression towards God and yet satisfaction is real and attainable in the motion along the stages on life's way.

In contrast to Vaughan's vision and to the expectations of a Romantic or utopian messianism, the visions that Scorsese and Gregory offer take seriously a process of accomplishment that requires re-vision and re-construction. To borrow a term from Malcolm Schofield, we might propose that they present 'an anti-*o*utopian *e*utopia'. In this enigmatic phrase, Schofield is suggesting that 'the good society is not a mirage fit for a never-never-land, but something people can achieve by practising virtue in whatever place they live – turning it into a "good place"' (Schofield, 1999, p. 205, n. 29). Nonetheless, the major challenge that is presented here concerns the meaning and significance of 'virtue' and 'good' in the midst of the loss of authoritative renderings of these terms. That is where religion as life and practice questions the insubstantial fantasies of the imagination and capital.

Notes

1. Indeed, the thrust of Walter Benjamin's *Passegenwerk* is to show how capital and the culture of the commodity – contra Weber – systematically re-enchant the world through a mythopoeisis that lays claim to eternity. See Benjamin (1999, pp. 388ff).
2. See Gillespie (1996, pp. 1–32) for a succinct account of the emergence of 'power' as the *leitmotif* of modernity.
3. There is, of course, a development in Kant's theoretical reflection on the place and role of the imagination, but there remains a significant amount of continuity on the imagination's relation to understanding. See Kant (1933, p. 165; 1952, p. 134) for a comparison of the status of the imagination in the First and Third Critiques.
4. See also Fichte (1970, p. 193).
5. See also the comment of Schlegel in a letter to Novalis (of 2 December 1798): 'Can the synthesis of Goethe and Fichte produce anything other than religion?' (Schlegel, 1957, p. 140).
6. Benjamin calls this feature of Romanticism 'Romantic Messianism'. See his doctoral dissertation, 'The Concept of Criticism in German Romanticism', in Benjamin (1996, p. 185, n.3) and the letter of Novalis to Schlegel of 20 January 1799 in Schlegel (1957, pp. 151–2).

7. Benjamin actually argues against Weber and Troeltsch in that he maintains what Howard Caygill calls 'a more radical thesis': 'The Christianity of the Reformation period did not favour the development of capitalism, but transformed itself into capitalism' (1996, p. 290). See Caygill (1998, p. 56).
8. Caygill calls Benjamin's study of the Baroque *Trauerspiel, Origin of the German Mourning Play* (1977) an analysis of 'the culture of nascent capitalism'. See Caygill (1998, p. 57).

References

Agamben, G. (1993), *Infancy and History: the Destruction of Experience*, trans. L. Heron, London: Verso.

Baader, F. von (1856), *Sämmlichte Werke*, vol VII, Leipzig: Bethmann.

Ballard, J.G. (1995), *Crash*, London: Vintage.

Benjamin, W. (1973), 'The Storyteller: Reflections on the Works of Nikolai Leskov', *Illuminations*, ed. H. Arendt, London: Fontana, pp. 83–107.

Benjamin, W. (1977), *Origin of the German Mourning Play*, trans. J. Osborne, London: Verso.

Benjamin, W. (1996), *Selected Writings, Vol 1: 1913–1926*, ed. M. Bullock and M.W. Jennings, Cambridge, MA: Harvard University Press.

Benjamin, W. (1999), *The Arcades Project*, trans. H. Eiland and K. McLaughlin, Cambridge, MA: Harvard University Press.

Berlin, I. (1999), *The Roots of Romanticism*, ed. H. Hardy, London: Chatto & Windus.

Betanzos, R.J. (1998), *Franz von Baader's Philosophy of Love*, Vienna: Passagen Verlag.

Butterfield, B. (1999), 'Ethical Value and Negative Aesthetics: Reconsidering the Baudrillard-Ballard Connection', *PMLA*, **114** (1), 64–77.

Caygill, H. (1998), *Walter Benjamin: The Colour of Experience*, London: Routledge.

Deleuze, G. and F. Guattari (1983), *Anti–Oedipus: Capitalism and Schizophrenia*, trans R. Hurley, Mark Seem and Helen R. Lane, London: Athlone.

Descartes, R. (1984), *Meditations on First Philosophy*, in J. Cottingham, R. Stoothoof and D. Murdoch (eds), *The Philosophical Writings of Descartes*, vol. II, Cambridge: Cambridge University Press, pp. 1–62.

Fichte, J.G. (1970), *Science of Knowledge* (*Wissenschaftslehre*) ed.and trans. P. Heath and J. Lachs, New York: Meredith.

Forstman, J. (1977), *A Romantic Triangle: Schleiermacher and Early German Romanticism*, Missoula: Scholars Press.

Friedrichsmeyer, S. (1983), *The Androgyne in Early German Romanticism: Friedrich Schlegel, Novalis and the Metaphysics of Love*, Berne: Peter Lang.

Gillespie, M.A. (1996), *Nihilism Before Nietzsche*, Chicago: University of Chicago Press.

Gregory of Nyssa (1978), *The Life of Moses*, trans. A.J. Malherbe and E. Ferguson, New York: Paulist Press.

Hellerich, S.V. (1995), *Religionizing, Romanizing Romantics: The Catholico-Christian Camouflage of the Early German Romantics: Wackenroder, Tieck, Novalis, Friedrich & August Wilhelm Schlegel*, Frankfurt am Main: Peter Lang.

Jacobi, F.H. (1789), *Über die Lehre des Spinoza in Briefen an den Herrn Moses Mendelssohn* 2nd edn, Breslau: Lowe.

Kant, I. (1933), *Critique of Pure Reason*, trans. N. Kemp Smith, London: Macmillan.

Kant, I. (1952), *The Critique of Judgement*, trans. J. Creed Meredith, Oxford: Clarendon Press.

Kant, I. (1991), *The Metaphysics of Morals*, trans. M. Gregor, Cambridge: Cambridge University Press.

Kant, I. (1993), *Opus Postumum*, trans. E. Förster and M. Rosen, Cambridge: Cambridge University Press.

Lacoue-Labarthe, P. and J-L. Nancy (1988), *The Literary Absolute: The Theory of Literature in German Romanticism*, trans. P. Barnard and C. Lester, Albany, NY: SUNY Press.

Makkreel, R.A. (1994), 'Fichte's Dialectical Imagination', in D. Breazedale and T. Rockmore (eds), *Fichte: Historical Contexts/Contemporary Controversies*, Atlantic City: Humanities Press, pp. 7–16.

Novalis (1960a), *Schriften*, vol II: *Das philosophische Werk I*, 2nd edn, ed. R. Samuel and P. Kluckohn, Stuttgart: W. Kohlhammer.

Novalis (1960b), *Schriften*, vol III: *Das philosophische Werk II*, 2nd edn, ed. R. Samuel and P Kluckohn, Stuttgart: W. Kohlhammer.

Ovid (1955), *Metamorphoses*, trans. M. Innes, Harmondsworth: Penguin.

Patočka, J. (1996), *Heretical Essays in the Philosophy of History*, trans. E. Kohák, Chicago: Open Court.

Schlegel, F. (1957), *Friedrich Schlegel und Novalis: Biographie einer Romantiker-freundschaft in ihren Briefen,* ed. M. Preitz, Darmstadt: Wissenschaftliche Buchgesellschaft.

Schlegel, F. (1991), *Philosophical Fragments*, trans. P. Firchow, Minneapolis: Minnesota University Press.

Schleiermacher, F.D.E. (1958), *On Religion: Speeches to its Cultured Despisers*, trans. J. Oman, New York: Harper.

Schofield, M. (1999), *Saving the City: Philosopher-Kings and Other Classical Paradigms*, London: Routledge.

Seidel, G.J. (1993), *Fichte's Wissenschaftslehre of 1794: A Commentary on Part 1*, West Lafayette, IN: Purdue University Press.

Shapin, S. and S. Schaffer (1985), *Leviathan and the Air-Pump: Hobbes, Boyle and the Experimental Life*, Princeton, NJ: Princeton University Press.

Starobinski, J. (1970), *La relation critique: essai*, Paris: Gallimard.

Szondi, P. (1986), 'Friedrich Schlegel and Romantic Irony, with Some Remarks on Tieck's Comedies', *On Textual Understanding and Other Essays*, trans. H. Mendelsohn, Manchester: Manchester University Press, pp. 57–73.

Chapter 11

Religious Materialism: Bataille, Deleuze/Guattari and the Sacredness of Late Capital

Jim Urpeth

> In reintroducing the experience of the divine at the centre of thought, philosophy has been well aware since Nietzsche ... that it questions an origin without positivity and an opening indifferent to the patience of the negative. (Michel Foucault)

For one strand of 'Continental philosophy' the main task for contemporary philosophy of religion lies in the formulation of a fully positive religious materialism. What for Kant, in the guise of 'hylozoism', was rejected summarily as the allegedly contradictory concept of 'living matter' (Kant, 1987, p. 276) is, given the 'death of God', conceived as the basis for a rethinking of the 'divine' by some of those who, following Nietzsche, undertake to complete the critique of metaphysics. This chapter will sketch some of the basic features of such a religious materialism based on the claim that, although not a term found in their texts, it is a key theme in the thought of Bataille and, more contentiously, Deleuze/Guattari.[1] From this perspective the 'return of religion' which some have detected in contemporary 'Continental' thought concerns the disconcerting emergence of the sacredness of 'late' capital.[2]

In contrast to both the reductive tendencies of the materialist accounts of religion given by Marx and Freud and the anti-naturalism of phenomenological approaches to it, the perspective outlined here rejects both anti-materialist religions and anti-religious materialisms. Both non-materialist conceptions of religion and materialist interpretations of it not premised upon a commitment to the inherently religious nature of the primary processes of matter itself are criticized from a non-reductive materialist perspective that aims to think beyond the matter versus spirit and nature versus culture and history oppositions.

Religious materialism insists that the critical unmasking of religion by Marx and Freud has been accepted, but argues that it only has application to anthropomorphic religion, to those faiths or aspects of them that have their origin in ideology or neurosis. Beyond anthropological accounts of religion, the religious materialists considered here explore the possibilities of non-anthropomorphic religion based on a recovery of the transcendences inherent in material life itself. Hence religious materialism is not hostile to religion *per se*, but only to 'reactive' forms of it or anthropomorphic 'projections' of human weakness, need and resistance which have, admittedly, all but monopolized the field. Religious materialism is the reassertion of the religious sensibility that grows, as Nietzsche would say, out of 'abundance' rather than 'hunger' (Nietzsche, 1967, p. 445).

The religious materialism to be sketched here represents a 'fusion' of the thought of Bataille and Deleuze/Guattari. The claim is that a synthesis of some of the fundamental claims of these thinkers generates a religious materialism that posits the sacredness of 'late' capital, a perspective not adopted explicitly by the thinkers individually. The reading of Bataille in the light of Deleuze/Guattari, and vice versa, makes possible a realization of the extent to which 'late' capital, as described by Deleuze/Guattari, exhibits features that qualify it as 'sacred' from the perspective of Bataille's economics. When read through the lens of Bataille's thought, Deleuze/Guattari can be said to identify a 'sacred' aspect to 'late' capital without acknowledging it as such. Alternatively, from the perspective of Deleuze/Guattari, Bataille's tendency to condemn capitalism as a predominantly 'restricted economy' of production and accumulation, and hence 'profane', misinterprets its underlying trajectory in which it increasingly emerges as an economy of consumption and 'expenditure', a possibility Bataille resisted. The challenge of a religious materialism based on such a combination of sources emphasizes the importance of the notion of *immanence* in the formulation of a credible contemporary religious outlook. Beyond the residual moralisms of 'pantheist' and 'pagan' religions of nature, the religious sensibility explored here requires a complete expulsion of all gestures of negation, a voiding of any appeal to a realm transcendent to, or 'outside' of, capital through a celebratory embrace of the 'divine' forces of contemporary life. This is a stance critically hostile to sociopolitical and religious perspectives, both 'right' and 'left', that resist a total identification with the synthetic dynamism of 'late' capital. The religious materialism suggested here insists that the only viable critique of capital available is immanent, an auto-critique inherent to capital that surpasses in radicality those critiques that merely oppose it.

Before exploring the aforementioned 'fusion' via a discussion of Bataille's and Deleuze/Guattari's thought, respectively, I shall clarify briefly some terminology and general themes relevant throughout. A conception of religious materialism will emerge as the autotransfiguration of dysteleological matter, an immanent sublimity registered intensively in impersonal affect. The 'divine' thus discloses itself affectively as the 'return' of self-differential material processes, as inherently sacred flows of life and capital that dissolve identity in desire. This makes possible a re-envisioning of critique in religious terms, an affirmative, rather than 'moral', politics and ethics of the sacred.

The Transcendence of Matter

The radicalizations of Kant's critique of metaphysics considered here tend towards a conception of primary synthesis as a material power of self-differentiation that culminates in a gesture of 'affirmation' inherently religious in nature. It is a materialism which offers a religious critique of religion on the basis of a becoming-religious of matter itself. In Kantian terms this amounts to a critique of religion by religion. Such a radicalization of Kant's critical project pursues an uncompromising deanthropomorphization of both the divine and nature based on a critique of the theologico-humanist values and interpretations underpinning them. This is an evaluative inheritance from the 'Platonic–Christian' tradition which eluded Kant's critique. Although Kant attained, to a remarkable extent, a largely desubstantialized and desubjectivized conception of being, he left intact, and even reinforced, a regime of value and an orientation of desire that were the very source of the 'dogmatic metaphysics' his critique was aimed at. This uncritical stance towards an inherited system of interpretation, value and desire is subjected to critique by Kant's successors considered here.

Rejecting the ontological and evaluative conspiracy of reactivity that characterizes the God–Man complex, the advocates of religious materialism argue that critique has an autosacrificial momentum that terminates in the affirmation of the intrinsic religiosity of a deanthropomorphized materiality. For religious materialists the 'death of God' is an unproblematically positive religious event in which unassimilable material intensities are liberated from theologico-humanist ontological categories and evaluations. Without metaphysical appropriations of transcendence in transcendent terms, non-determined material syntheses circulate and find their own religious expression. The possibility that so terrified Kant – a religious hylozoism – returns in the form of an autopoietic materiality, a self-sufficient material order that produces its own conditions of possibility and autotransfiguration from a differential process of origination without reference to a transcendent source (whether theological or anthropological) of intelligibility and sustenance. Such a transvaluation of 'this world' in terms of excess rather than lack makes possible a rethinking of spirituality in non-reductive materialist terms, of transcendence in terms of immanence.

The religious materialists considered below insist on the primacy of affectivity – the feelings that characterize 'religious experience'. Indeed, such thinkers stress the primacy of a 'religious' form of affectivity *per se*. They do not thereby resurrect the ontologically derivative notion of a transcendent personal deity but identify the 'divine' with a cluster of impersonal and intense affects conceived as the element within which the autoconsecration of material becoming discloses itself. Those fortunate to undergo such self-loss christen the desire flows possessing them 'divine love', and the referent produced, 'God'.[3]

The religious materialists discussed below radicalize Kant's conception of the sublime as, given the 'death of God', this is transcribed from a transcendent to an immanent terrain. The key claim here is that Bataille and Deleuze/Guattari do not exhibit a hostility to transcendence in the sense of the self-transcendence implicit in the notions of originary difference and exteriority found in many 'Continental' thinkers. They undertake their uncompromising critiques of the transcendent as, they argue, it represents an attempt to abort the irrecuperable movement of excess that characterizes transcendence as such.[4] Like many of their phenomenological contemporaries, Bataille and Deleuze/Guattari undertake an overcoming of the traditional transcendent/immanent opposition but, unlike them, they pursue this 'genealogically'. That is to say, their rethinking of transcendence in immanent terms identifies a hostility to materiality and a resistance to the fundamental continuity of 'man' and 'nature' as the source of the reduction of transcendence to the transcendent that sustains a reductive interpretation of the potentiality of matter and denies its intrinsic religiosity. On the basis of a materialist rethinking of transcendence, Bataille and Deleuze/Guattari undertake a thorough renaturalization of the discourse of religion, offering diagnostic critiques of the transcendent and affirmatively courting immanence, acknowledging its 'divinity'.

Hence a fundamental series of contrasts emerges in relation to the thematization of transcendence and the sublime. On the one hand, there is what can be termed the 'moral sublime', on the other hand, the 'tragic sublime'. The 'moral sublime' aligns transcendence with the transcendent and privileges the object rather than desire (conceived as 'lack'). It develops conceptions of the presentation and affectivity of the sublime in terms of negation and analogy. The 'tragic sublime', in contrast, conceives transcendence in terms of immanence as the ineffable powers of a fully positively conceived self-sufficient material order. It privileges desire (conceived as 'excess') over the object and explores affirmative, non-positive, conceptions of the presentation and affectivity of the sublime.[5]

The 'negative pleasure' through which Kant thematizes his critically disciplined account of the manifestation of the transcendent sublimity of reason is reconceived, in both its mode of manifestation and the affectivity that is its vehicle, in affirmative (rather than positive) terms for those of his successors intoxicated by the immanent sublimity of material life. To rethink religious affectivity is to provide an exposition of such an ineffably resurgent vitality that, insofar as it concerns an exchange with non-human forces or an 'overcoming of man', must be couched in radically anonymous terms. Hence for the religious materialists considered here a reconception of hierophany is necessary given the 'death of God'. The disclosure of the material immanent sublime, as a self-differentiation beyond presentation, is affective in nature. The autotransfiguration of matter 'occurs' as an intensity, it is felt rather than presented, whether positively or negatively.

Kant's valorization of 'negative pleasure' offers an overtly 'extramoral' defence of the pleasures of an affective–libidinal economy that went largely uncontested in philosophy until Nietzsche. In redefining philosophy as a comparative erotics, Nietzsche, and his successors considered below, challenge the affective–libidinal economy of Kant's sublime. In contrast to the transcendental *Schadenfreude* that reason has at the expense of the imagination in the Kantian sublime, Bataille and Deleuze/Guattari evoke a very different affective–libidinal sensibility drawn towards a sublimity in which the human *in toto*, rather than just its finite dimensions, is engulfed.

Bataille and the Sacred

More than any other thinker, Bataille realizes the intrinsically religious possibilities of Nietzsche's thought.[6] He insists that the 'sacred' is the pre-eminent theme contemporary thought is historically compelled to address.[7] Bataille's conception of the 'sacred' offers a striking fusion of materialist and religious perspectives. In contrast to both Marx and Freud, Bataille acknowledges a *first-order* material process of *autoconsecration* in which the sublimity of what he terms 'base matter' (Bataille, 1985, p. 51) is affirmed in a 'sacred instant' (ibid., p. 241). This interrupts the theoretical and practical functional circuits of self-preservation that constitute the 'human' hypostasized in the profane religions of the transcendent. For Bataille, the religiosity of a religion consists in the extent of its valorization of dysteleological material processes ('expenditure') resistant to idealist assimilation.

Bataille conceives the 'death of God' as a positive religious 'event'. As he states, 'what the love of God finally rises to is really the death of God' (Bataille, 1987, p. 141) and 'the absence of God is greater, and more divine, than God' (Bataille, 1994, p. 48). Following Nietzsche, Bataille rejects secularist responses to the collapse of reductive interpretations of transcendence and affirms instead a transfiguration of immanence thereby made possible. He writes in this respect of the 'passion of giving the world an intoxicating meaning' (Bataille, 1985, p. 245). Bataille, like Nietzsche, argues that this immanent sublimity is inaccessible to knowledge and is pre-eminently disclosed affectively.[8] This is thematized in Bataille's thought in terms of the notion of 'inner experience'.

Underpinning Bataille's thought is a conception of the accumulation and expenditure of energy that overturns the primacy traditionally accorded to the notions of utility, scarcity and lack. This 'accursed share' of excess energy has, ultimately, to be expended gratuitously without reference to productive ends. On the basis of this 'economics', Bataille develops a series of contrasts of which the most relevant here are those between the 'continuity' and 'discontinuity' of being and 'intimacy' and the 'order of things'. In relation to these distinctions, Bataille formulates his principal contrast between the 'sacred' and 'profane'. For Bataille 'continuity' and 'intimacy' are terms for the most fundamental plane of being, a material field of self-differentiation prior to negation, a domain in which the oppositions which make possible the field of 'discontinuity' and the 'order of things' are scrambled, blurred and self-identities returned to a realm of pre-oppositional, differential relation. It is this domain of 'continuity' and 'intimacy' that, for Bataille, characterizes the 'sacred'. In contrast, the realm of 'discontinuity' and the 'order of things' is the mode of being of distinct, spatiotemporal, causally related entities as conceived by representational and calculative thought. Bataille aligns the realm of 'discontinuity' and the 'order of things' with the 'profane' world of work and rational calculation, founded upon taboo, especially in relation to sexuality and death. His conception of religious affectivity in this context is stated thus:

> there are transitions from continuous to discontinuous or from discontinuous to continuous. We are discontinuous beings ... but we yearn for our lost continuity. We find the state of affairs that binds us to our random and ephemeral individuality hard to bear. Along with our tormenting desire that this evanescent thing last, there stands our obsession with a primal continuity linking us with everything that is ... This nostalgia is responsible for the three forms of eroticism in man ... physical, emotional and religious ... with all three ... the concern is to substitute for individual isolated discontinuity a feeling of profound continuity. (Bataille, 1987, p. 15)

The pre-individuated nature of the 'sacred' in Bataille's sense is clearly stated here. Also apparent is his radically impersonal conception of the ecstasies of the most intense religious feelings conceived in terms of affirmative self-annihilation. Recalling implicitly Nietzsche's notion of 'tragic joy', Bataille conceives the affectivity of the 'sacred', which occurs on the cusp of the contrasts described above, as intrinsically 'dual' in character. The 'anxiety' and 'horror' felt by the 'discontinuous' entity upon encountering the 'limit' vies with the 'ecstasy' and 'joy' of affirmative self-loss. Religious affectivity is necessarily ambiguous as it concerns the transvaluative surrender of individuation at the limits of the 'human' or the 'extreme limit of the possible' (Bataille, 1988b, p. xxxiii). Bataille writes in this respect that the 'mind moves in a strange world where anguish and ecstasy coexist' (ibid, p. xxxii).

Bataille develops a non-reductive notion of 'religious eroticism' or self-transcendence conceived as a first-order process of material expenditure, an autotransfiguration of impersonal energy rather than its 'sublimation'. Surpassing Nietzsche in this respect, Bataille identifies this process in the Christian mysticism, 'that ultimate in human potentialities' (Bataille, 1987, p. 221). Bataille, like Nietzsche, experienced mystical states 'missing a God' (Bataille, 1988b, p. 9). He conceives mysticism in non-reductive materialist terms as 'contagions of energy', a 'streaming of electricity' and as a 'celestial bacchanalia' (ibid., pp. 94–5). Bataille aligns mysticism with an immanent otherness, a state of enraptured fusion with a self-transfiguring world, an 'ecstasy before the void' (ibid., pp. 112–13). Christian mysticism is, for Bataille, the manifestation of a *becoming-religious of matter*. In energeticoeconomic terms, it is a process of intensificatory self-expenditure concerning a 'desire to live to the limits of the possible and the impossible with ever-increasing intensity ... to die without ceasing to live' (Bataille, 1987, p. 240). Unlike Nietzsche, therefore, Bataille pursues an immanent trajectory in both the rethinking of transcendence demanded by the 'death of God' and in his affirmative critique of Christianity.

Bataille and the Sacrifice of Capital

Bataille's critique of the modern world contains a conception of the historico-economic conditions of possibility for the reaffirmation of the 'sacred'. He argues that modern capitalism is characterized by a relation between 'surplus' and the limits of growth that compels it to address the issue of how to spend through 'useless consumption' (Bataille, 1988a, p. 23) and, in ways other than global conflagration, the 'accursed share' of excess energy which defines it.[9] Bataille indicates his conception of these present-day economic determinants thus:

> Henceforth what matters *primarily* is no longer to develop the productive forces but to spend their products sumptuously ... immense squanderings are about to take place after a century of populating and of industrial peace, the temporary limit of development being encountered, the two world wars organized the greatest orgies of wealth – and of human beings – that history has recorded. (Bataille, 1988a, p. 37)

Bataille depicts the modern world as one in which, as a result of the increasing hegemony of the interconnected processes of representational consciousness and the rise of capitalism, man has become 'more estranged from himself than ever before' (Bataille, 1989, p. 93). He writes of a 'world of complete reduction or the reign of things' (ibid., p. 92) which, owing to the 'reign of the autonomous productive operation' (ibid.) obliterates the economic condition of possibility of the overcoming of 'alienation', namely, the 'intense consumption ... of the excess resources produced' (ibid., p. 93) which are merely reinvested for productive ends. Bataille describes this as a process that

> in its complete success ... consummates man's estrangement from himself and realizes, in the case of the scientist, the reduction of all life to the real order ... Authority and authenticity are entirely on the side of things, of production and consciousness of the thing produced. (Ibid., pp. 96–7)

It is against this background that Bataille introduces his conception of the possibility of the acknowledgment of the 'sacred' in the modern world. In its most radical guise, Bataille interprets this as an *immanent* process of self-overcoming *within* capitalism itself such that critique consists in an affirmation of the 'essence' of contemporary capital rather than an 'oppositional' (that is, 'moral') stance towards it inevitably complicit with neo-humanist perspectives and reactionary religious gestures. The crucial historical axis Bataille discerns is stated thus:

> Doubtless ... [the] ... majority has let itself be *reduced to the order of things*. But this generalized reduction, this perfect fulfillment of the thing, is the necessary precondition for the conscious and fully developed posing of the problem of man's reduction to thinghood. Only in a world where the thing has reduced everything ... can intimacy affirm itself without any more compromises ... Only the gigantic development of the means of production is capable of fully revealing the meaning of production, which is the nonproductive consumption of wealth – the fulfillment of self-consciousness in the free outbursts of the intimate order. But the moment when consciousness, reflecting back on itself, reveals itself to itself and sees production destined to be consumed is precisely when the world of production no longer knows what to do with its products. (Ibid., p. 94)[10]

It is 'a question of tearing man away from the order of works' (ibid., p. 89) a point reiterated in the following terms: 'being reduced to thinghood by the operation, all that he can do is to undertake the *contrary operation*, a *reduction of the reduction*' (ibid., p. 99). Bataille hints at the religious interpretation of this conception of the contemporary situation and underlines the immanent nature of his critical stance when he writes of the 'principle of inner experience: to emerge through project from the realm of project' (Bataille, 1988b, p.46).

It is through such gestures that Bataille's thought surpasses the merely oppositional relation towards the contemporary world in which it is interpreted as having a solely negative or mutually exclusive relation to the 'sacred' which it often seems to have. He insists on the historical necessity for a self-overcoming rather than rejection of 'clear consciousness' through the advent of a 'self-consciousness' in which the limits of the 'order of things' are explicitly acknowledged. Without forgetting the radical incommensurability between the realms of 'intimacy' and 'things', Bataille nonetheless insists:

> It implies SELF-CONSCIOUSNESS taking up the lamp that science has made to illuminate objects and directing it toward intimacy ... this real world having reached the apex of its development can be destroyed, in the sense that it can be reduced to intimacy ... consciousness cannot make intimacy reducible to it, but it can reclaim its own operations, recapitulating them in reverse, so that they ultimately cancel out and consciousness itself is strictly reduced to intimacy ... consciousness will regain intimacy

only in darkness. In so doing it will have reached the highest degree of distinct clarity ... it will rediscover the night of the animal intimate with the world – *into which it will enter*. (Bataille, 1989, pp. 97, 100)

There is much that is contentious in Bataille's account of this autodestructive process, an 'eroticization' of consciousness (rather than its rejection) in which its operations are undone in a fusion with its conditioning limits. In 'self-consciousness' the 'sacred' conditions of possibility of 'consciousness' are explicitly acknowledged rather than negated.[11] For Bataille, the necessary economic preconditions for regaining the 'sacred' prevail in the present age when 'the world of production, the order of things has reached the point of development where it does not know what to do with its products' (Bataille, 1989, p. 101). The response he proposes is that the labour that produced the entity must be undone in order to liberate it and ourselves from the servility of utility and productive consumption.[12] Such affirmative destruction restores an irreducible self-excess beyond utilitarian determination and attains a 'clear self-consciousness' (ibid, p. 103) the economic meaning of which is described thus:

> The reduction of the reduction of the real order brings a fundamental reversal into the economic order. If we are to preserve the movement of the economy, we need to determine the point at which the excess production will flow like a river *to the outside*. It is a matter of endlessly consuming – or destroying – the objects that are produced. (Ibid.)

Bataille insists that this movement entails 'the destruction of the subject as an individual' (ibid., p. 104), a process distinguishable from 'war' to the extent that it is *consciously* undertaken. He clarifies the nature of a contemporary relation to the 'sacred' as a 'religious attitude that would result from clear consciousness' (ibid., p. 109). This process of perpetual self-destruction through the affirmation of the anti-teleological forces of life is the condition of a 'sovereign self-consciousness that ... no longer turns away from itself' (ibid., p. 111). Bataille suggests an identity between the recognition of the priority of 'general' over a 'restricted' economy and the advent of 'self-consciousness'. As he states,

> consciousness ... tries to grasp some object of acquisition, *something*, not the *nothing* of pure expenditure. It is a question of arriving at the moment when consciousness will cease to be a consciousness of *something*; in other words, of becoming conscious of the decisive meaning of an instant in which increase (the acquisition of *something*) will resolve into expenditure; and this will be precisely *self-consciousness*, that is, a consciousness that henceforth has *nothing as its object*. (Bataille, 1988a, p.190)

Bataille even gestures toward a radical mysticism at the heart of 'late' capital insofar as the dawning 'self-consciousness' possible at this juncture of economic history is likened to the 'experience of the mystics, to intellectual contemplation "without shape or form"' (ibid., p. 189). For Bataille, the 'religious' trajectory of the process of critique consists in the affinity between its self-radicalization and the theme of 'sacrifice', with, that is, the autodestruction of reason, knowledge, project, operation and agency which culminates in the 'death of God'.[13] He formulates this thus:

the supreme abuse which man ultimately made of his reason requires a last sacrifice: reason, intelligibility, the ground itself upon which he stands – man must reject them, in him God must die; … Man must find himself only on the condition of escaping, without rest, from the avarice which grips him. (Batatille, 1988b, p. 134)

Bataille therefore aligns the 'death of God' with the 'sacrifice of reason' (ibid., p. 155) and insists on the *religious* significance of this ultimate sacrificial moment which he contrasts favourably with a merely scientific atheism:

the atheist is satisfied with a world completed without God; the one who sacrifices is, on the contrary, in the anguish before an incompleted world, incompletable and forever unintelligible, which destroys him, tears him apart (and this world destroys itself, tears itself apart). (Ibid., p. 153)

It is clear that Bataille appreciated that the development of a religion of immanence based on the inherent sacredness of 'expenditure' also demanded a similarly affirmative, 'non-moral' critique of the contemporary world. This tantalizing prospect of a religious critique of capital based on its affirmation brings us to the thought of Deleuze/Guattari.

Deleuze/Guattari, Bataille and 'Romantic Anti-Capitalism'

The association of Deleuze/Guattari's thought with religious materialism will be highly contentious to many.[14] However, in lieu of a future justification I find much in their texts that resonates with the 'religious' elements in the thought of Bataille. The critique of transcendent conceptions of transcendence and the affirmation of the sublimity of an immanent domain of hyperdifferentiated, self-organizing and self-interpreting material life disclosed intensively, as well as the demonstration that both 'God' and 'Man' are derivative formations of a process not referred to any pre-given positivities, are key features of Deleuze/Guattari's conception of critique. Their texts frequently resonate a joy, often with a 'religious' inflection, that celebrates the resurgence of the anonymous creative process of 'becoming' that erodes the boundaries and fortifications of the 'human'. In addition to the 'deification' of 'deterritorialization', they also, like Bataille, contest genealogically the value of theologico-humanist values formulating an ethics and politics of material becoming based on the prioritization of conjunction over negation, difference in degree rather than distinction in kind.

The trajectory sketched here, building upon Nietzsche's radicalization of Kant's critical project, evokes a synthesis of Bataille's and Deleuze/Guattari's thought that combines the former's conception of the 'sacred' with the latter's affirmative critique of capitalism. On this basis the sacredness of 'late' capital can be discerned and religious materialism developed as the autocritique of the contemporary world.[15] I shall pursue this by considering a possible critique of Bataille's thought from the perspective of Deleuze/Guattari's.

Bataille's evaluation of the contemporary world, in contrast to the stance outlined above, often seems vulnerable to the charge of 'romantic anti-capitalism'. If correct, this would render its 'formal' critical stance merely 'moral' or oppositional.

Bataille's texts frequently condemn modern capitalism on the basis of a redundant conception of it in terms of utility, productive consumption and the profit motive. He thereby shies away from the recognition of what can, precisely on the basis of his own theoretical insights, be described as the *becoming-sacred* of capital. It is only insofar as Bataille's thought can be said to *affirm* the 'essence' of capital, as a recognition of its ever more apparent 'self-expending' nature, that it can claim to have thoroughly eliminated all 'moral' elements within its conception of the 'sacred'. It is only 'moral' forms of religion that seek to stand 'outside' capital. Religious materialists, by contrast, condemn capitalism affirmatively, and criticize its self-inhibition, for not becoming what it is. For Deleuze/Guattari, capital is an inherent accelerator of 'deterritorialization', an inciter of desire for its own sake. It is a global abstract flow of intrinsically undetermined desire operating in excess of any concept of 'need'. Capital increasingly inverts the relation of priority between desire and object which, arguably, characterized its earlier phases in which the 'necessary' and the 'superfluous', a distinction arguably crucial to Bataille's thought, were more readily distinguishable.[16]

Bataille's 'romantic' tendencies are evident in his valorization of pre- and non-capitalist societies which, he argues, exhibit a ritual acknowledgment of the priority of 'expenditure' over utility repressed by capital. The major historical axis Bataille examines is the transition from the pre-capitalist to capitalist eras, from the economics of 'potlatch' to the thrifty, bourgeois world and its profane spirituality of personal salvation. This historical process is frequently presented by Bataille as a narrative of decline, a terminal process of desacralization consummated in the present epoch which, at best, offers only the negative possibility of recognizing the absence of the 'sacred'. This falls short of the religious materialist possibility sketched here that contemporary capitalism, once liberated from profane, accumulative capitalists, can, on the basis of its relentless erosion of all forms of stable identity and reckless incitement of undetermined desire, be unequivocally affirmed as a *resacralization* of the world. The sacrilegious, reductive appropriation of capitalism by capitalists is what religious materialism seeks to undo, not capitalism *per se*.

Bataille's thought stumbles in the face of several key features of 'late' capital that cannot be accounted for in either 'classical' or 'Marxist' terms and for which – ironically – his own political economy provides the most advanced theoretical resources. Bataille often seemed to fail to appreciate the mutation of capital beyond its 'early' phase to its present 'post-bourgeois' form in which it manifests many of the features associated with 'potlatch'. Bataille mistakenly identifies capitalism *per se* with a historical stage of its development in which production was valorized over consumption. He seems to need to delimit capital to its 'reformation-bourgeois' stage and to be oblivious to the extent to which it conducts an autocritique of its 'restricted' beginnings.[17] Hence Bataille's analysis fails to acknowledge the increasingly manifest nature of capital as revealed in its incessant subversion of human self-determination and the dissolution of 'man' in anonymous desire flows. This surpassing of the human defines the religious or 'self-expending' essence of capital, its impersonality and amoralism. An example of Bataille's shortcomings in this respect is his description of archaic, pre-capitalist system of exchange as a 'cycle of generosity' (Bataille, 1987, p. 206) that is characterized as the 'opposite of capitalism which accumulates the profits of work and uses them to create further profits' (ibid.).[18] Similarly, noting the 'colossal waste' and 'squandering annihilation' (Bataille, 1987, p.60) that characterizes the engendering of life, Bataille contrasts 'the narrow capitalist principle, that of the company director, that of the private individual who sells in order to rake in the accumulated credits in the long run (for raked in somehow they always are)' (ibid.).[19]

This resistance on Bataille's part to the religious or 'self-expending' essence of capital is discussed by Jean-Joseph Goux, who gestures towards an emerging 'anti-bourgeois defence of capitalism' that appeals to the jettisoning, by capital itself, of the 'moral' bourgeois value system.[20] Goux notes the shift away from the 'puritan ideology of early capitalism' to the 'ethical liberation (even moral license) necessary to consumption' in a post-industrial phase of capitalism. An entrepreneurial–speculative mode of capital has emerged in which 'conspicuous consumption' rather than reinvestment is not only the response to surplus value but its source. As he states,

'postbourgeois' capitalism ... contradicts Bataille's sociological interpretation and confirms his ontological vision ... Perhaps Bataille's economic theory is explained not by his discovery of potlatch in primitive societies, but by his presentiment of what capitalism is becoming. (Stoekl, 1990, pp. 218, 223)

For Goux, contemporary capital is the realization of J.-B. Say's law that 'supply creates its own demand', as evident in the manner in which the guarantee of 'returns', on the basis of the satisfaction of identifiably pre-given 'needs', is recklessly suspended.[21] On this basis, Goux writes of a '*postmodern legitimation of capitalism*' (Stoekl, 1990, p. 213) which valorizes those aspects of 'late' capital which elude the 'rationalist' accounts of both Smith and Marx. Goux argues that Bataille's political economy offers the first alternative to these predecessors and, ironically, provides the theoretical resources required for the adequate analysis of contemporary capital in which 'only the appeal to compete infinitely in unproductive consumption ... allows for the development of production' (ibid., p. 219).

If it is plausible to interpret 'late' capital as a form of global 'potlatch' then it is possible to outline a radical 'religious' politics based on an affective–libidinal and affirmative, rather than rational–moral and oppositional, critique of it. Bataille outlined a revolutionary politics seeking to establish a social order based on 'expenditure', a process which, he claimed, required a proletarian revolution in order to seize the productive resources currently appropriated merely accumulatively by the bourgeoisie.[22] Yet this remains an essentially *anti-capitalist* stance. In contrast, a radical religious materialism affirms the sacredness, in Bataille's sense, of 'late' capital. Only such a critique of capital (by capital) sustains the radicality of Bataille's unique synthesis of political economy and religion.

Deleuze/Guattari: Traces of Religious Materialism

Having considered a possible religious materialist 'fusion' of the thought of Bataille and Deleuze/Guattari, I shall close by suggesting some implicitly 'religious' motifs in their thought, particularly with reference to the rethinking of religious affectivity, or what it feels like to be a 'late' capitalist.[23] Through their recovery and rethinking of Spinoza's notion of affect and development, from Scholastic sources, of the notion of 'haecceity' as the manifestation of their radical formulation of the ontological primacy of becoming, Deleuze/Guattari's texts contain powerful resources not only for the reinterpretation of the 'divine love' of the mystics but also for the deification of an infinite range of ontological explorations ('becoming-animal, becoming-woman, becoming imperceptible ...'). The contagious channels of communication that carry these 'molecular' material becomings are pre-eminently affective – 'affects are becomings' (Deleuze/Guattari, 1988, p. 256). Deleuze/Guattari develop a striking sense of affectivity in terms of the non-subjectified. They associate it with intensities of a becoming-other, a passage away from personal and organic integrity, a dysteleological process. Such becomings are sacred in that they indicate the suspension of the ontological and evaluative teleological categories of theologico-humanist thought and the encounter with an anonymous, impersonal fecundity of undetermined synthesis.

Deleuze/Guattari assert the priority of 'alliance' between heterogeneous types of 'assemblages' (ibid., p. 242) which they term 'blocks of becoming' (ibid., p. 237). These involve '*symbioses* that bring into play beings of totally different scales and kingdoms, with no possible filiation' (ibid., p. 238). This non-moral vision of nature is apparent in their valorization of 'unnatural participations' (ibid., pp. 241–2).[24] Deleuze/Guattari construct an ontology appropriate to the thoroughly impersonal molecular processes that precede the individuated subject or organism. It is on this primordial level that the symbioses of becoming operate far beneath the reach of intentionality. The key ontological criteria at this level of reality are 'intensity' and 'speed' or 'tempo'.

This realm of anonymity that the 'human' explores through becoming has its own mode of individuation which Deleuze/Guattari term 'haecceity'. This is a thoroughly impersonal mode of individuation that consists 'entirely of relations of movement and rest between molecules or particles, capacities to affect and be affected' (ibid., p. 261). As they state,

> you will yield nothing to haecceities unless you realize that that is what you are, and that you are nothing but that ... you are ... a set of nonsubjectified affects ... cease to be subjects to become events, in assemblages that are inseparable from an hour, a season, an atmosphere, an air, a life ... Climate, wind, season, hour *are not of another nature* than the things, animals, or people that populate them, follow them, sleep and awaken within them. (Ibid., pp. 262–3)

The material realm of becoming produces 'a natural play of haecceities, degrees, intensities, events and accidents that compose individuations totally different from those of the well-formed subjects that receive them' (ibid., p. 253). The realm of becoming is that of the 'anorganic', the 'asignifying' and the 'asubjective' (ibid., p. 279). Deleuze/Guattari demand that we 'try to conceive of this world ... peopled by anonymous matter, by infinite bits of impalpable matter entering into varying connections' (ibid., 1988, p. 255).

Somewhat akin to Kant, Deleuze/Guattari are wary of religious affectivity. They likewise develop a remarkably impersonalist account of the nature or art which contains much potential for a rethinking of religious affectivity. Art releases a '*bloc of sensations … a compound of percepts and affects*' (Deleuze/Guattari, 1994, p. 164) that induces '*nonhuman becomings of man*' (ibid., p. 169). Deleuze/Guattari thematize a sublimity of 'nonhuman becoming', the dissolution of the human through the affirmation of immanence. This is to follow a quite different trajectory from Kant. As Deleuze/Guattari state, 'its sensory transcendence enters into a hidden or open opposition to the suprasensory transcendence of religion' (ibid., p. 193). Nonetheless their account of the task of art as that of 'making the invisible forces visible in themselves … to make perceptible the imperceptible forces that populate the world, affect us, and make us become' (ibid., p. 182) is, perhaps, to borrow a phrase from Nietzsche, also a 'divine way of thinking' (Nietzsche, 1967, p. 15).

Deleuze/Guattari's conception of 'asubjective' affect provides important resources for rethinking 'religious experience' conceived as a becoming that is more primary than either the subject it possesses or the object it generates by investing with desire. Religious experience can, on such terms, be rethought as a nomadic cluster of radically autonomous, errant affects in which the priority, and divinity, of affectivity over both subject and object are acknowledged. For Bataille and Deleuze/Guattari, the 'death of God', in contrast to the predominant response of phenomenology and deconstruction, makes possible the formulation of a religious materialism, a 'return to religion' conceived as a 'left' deification of 'late' capital.[25]

Notes

1. In line with customary practice, I use the composite 'Deleuze/Guattari' to refer to their jointly authored texts.
2. For an interesting example and account of the phenomenon of the 'return of religion', in the sense implicitly contested here, see Vattimo (1999).
3. I explored this possibility in '"Health" and "Sickness" in Religious Affectivity: Nietzsche, Otto, Bataille', in Lippitt and Urpeth (2000, pp. 226–51).
4. Of course, many traditional discourses simply identify transcendence with the transcendent and regard the terms as synonymous. Indeed, the thinkers discussed here are often tacitly complicit in this regard insofar as they attack transcendence when they clearly mean the transcendent! I use the term 'immanent transcendence' to refer to 'this-worldly', indeed 'materialist' conceptions of irreducible self-difference, a dimension of 'otherness' entirely inherent to material life without transcendent reference. My claim is that there is such a notion of transcendence, with a religious hue, that the thinkers discussed in this chapter explore, albeit often implicitly.
5. It will have been noted that, throughout this clarification of different senses of transcendence, I have passed over the 'transcendental'. This is, partly, because the thinkers considered here pursue 'transcendental critique' but more importantly because the topics addressed in this chapter, surpassing as they do the 'limits of presentation' and its conditions of possibility, even when also acknowledged to be unpresentifiable, are not, strictly speaking, 'transcendental' in nature. I have pursued the issue of rethinking the sublime, in relation to the crucial Kant/Nietzsche axis, in 'A "Pessimism of Strength": Nietzsche and the Tragic Sublime', in Lippitt (1999, pp. 129–48) and 'A "Sacred Thrill": Presentation and Affectivity in the Analytic of the Sublime', in Rehberg

and Jones (2000, pp. 61–78).

6. For a brilliant elaboration of this claim, see Land, 'Shamanic Nietzsche', in Sedgwick (1995, pp. 158–70). I also explored this relation in Lippitt and Urpeth (2000, pp. 226–51).
7. See Bataille (1985, pp. 240–41).
8. See Bataille (1987, pp. 22–4).
9. See also Bataille (1988a, pp. 35–7; 1989, pp.87–104). Many commentators on Bataille's thought assume that he sustains an exclusively oppositional conception of the relation between capitalism and the 'sacred'. They thereby fail to appreciate the more complex sense of their relation he develops.
10. There is a striking affinity both in terms of form, content and even rhetoric between Bataille's conception of the sources and consummation of techno-capital and that found in Heidegger's texts. I discussed the extent to which Heidegger succeeded in overcoming a merely oppositional conception of the technology/'being' relation in 'Need, Abandonment and Denial: Heidegger and the Turn', *Irish Philosophical Studies*, **32** (1988–90, pp.176–96). The other 'voice' problematically present in the passage is, of course, that of Hegel, whose complex role in Bataille's thought cannot be addressed here.
11. See Bataille (1989, pp.101–4).
12. For a specific example of this process, see Bataille (1989, p. 102).
13. See Bataille (1988b, pp.130–34, 152–57).
14. In this respect it is interesting to reflect on the balance of papers contained in M. Bryden (2001). Although excellent in many respects, many contributors to this collection (including Albert, Ansell-Pearson, Poxon, Protevi and Smith) merely rehearse and clarify the nature of Deleuze's materialist critique of the transcendent (often, following Deleuze, aligning this with transcendence *per se*). Others (such as de Gaynesford and Goodchild) are more ambiguous. An exception, which detects what I term 'religious materialism' in Deleuze/Guattari's thought, is the paper by Goddard. To reiterate, a basic claim of this paper has been that 'ontotheological' metaphysics is not 'overcome' by either anti-materialist religions or anti-religious materialisms. It is only in their fusion that anthropomorphism is defeated and both 'state' or 'majoritarian' science and religion are equally offended by a critical process no longer compromised by human interests.
15. There are, it must be admitted, remarkably few references to Bataille in Deleuze/Guattari's texts and, even then, most are either inconsequential or, even, critical. For an example, see Deleuze and Parnet (1987, p. 47).
16. Clearly, I am basing these claims on some of the main arguments of Deleuze and Guattari (1984). For statements of this inherently radicalizing, autocritical trajectory of capital, as well as the play of 're–' and 'de–territorialization' within it, see Deleuze/Guattari (1984, pp. 33–5, 100–105, 223–5, 232–40, 245–7, 255–62, 299–305, 335–8, 344–9). Deleuze/Guattari emphasize the inherently 'decodifying' or 'deterritorializing' trajectory of capital which in their view has a historically manifest priority over its undeniably formidable ability to 'recodify' or 'reterritorialize'.
17. See Bataille (1988a, p. 153).
18. See also Bataille (1987, pp. 204, 211).
19. Deploying another reactive opposition, Bataille contrasts capital with 'nature regarded as a squandering of living energy and an orgy of annihilation' (Bataille, 1987, p.61).
20. See J-J Goux, 'General Economics and Postmodern Capitalism', in A. Stoekl (ed.) (1990, pp. 206–24). Strangely, Goux does not evoke the thought of Deleuze/Guattari, even though it seems very close to the perspective of his paper.
21. See Stoekl (1990, pp. 212–13). Arguably, Goux exaggerates here and mistakenly aligns the speculative nature of 'venture' capital with Bataille's conception of a *wilful* squandering that precludes profitable return by *guaranteeing* bankruptcy. Surely there is

still too much control exercised by nation states, central banks, multinationals and so on, resisting the sacred 'deterritorialized' flows of capital to describe it yet as predominantly anti-accumulative in nature? It is, however, only a matter of time.

22. See Bataille (1985, pp. 123–9).
23. That Deleuze/Guattari's last work (Deleuze/Guattari, 1994) is far less upbeat about capitalism than their early work, bemoaning its propensity to reduce the 'creation of concepts' to commodification and marketing, is important but does not, I suggest, represent a fundamental rejection of their earlier view of its autocritical, radical potential.
24. Perhaps it is possible to read certain biblical texts as 'traces' of such becomings. An example might be the 'creatures' evoked in Chapters 38 and 39 of the 'Book of Job'. This possibility is prompted by Otto's remarkable reading of this, and other Old Testament texts, in Otto (1958, pp. 72–81). Indeed, the broader alignment of such odd bedfellows as Deleuze/Guattari and Otto might be pursued in terms of their respective notions of the 'virtual' and the 'numinous'. Do not, following Nietzsche, Bataille and Deleuze/Guattari seek to recover the intrinsically 'numinous' nature of matter?
25. I am grateful to Philip Goodchild for his critical comments on an earlier version of this chapter. In particular, I have benefited from reading two of Goodchild's papers that address issues closely related to my concerns here, 'Spirit of Philosophy', *Angelaki*, **5**(2), 2000, 43–57 and 'The Value of Becoming: Capitalism and Schizophrenia' (unpublished manuscript).

References

Bataille, Georges (1985), *Visions of Excess: Selected Writings 1927–1939*, ed. Allan Stoekl, trans. Allan Stoekl, Carl R. Lovitt and Donald M. Leslie Jr., Minneapolis: University of Minnesota Press.

Bataille, Georges (1987), *Eroticism*, trans. Mary Dalwood, London: Marion Boyars.

Bataille, Georges (1988a), *The Accursed Share: Volume One*, trans. Robert Hurley, New York: Zone Books.

Bataille, Georges (1988b), *Inner Experience*, trans. Leslie Anne Boldt, Albany: State University of New York Press.

Bataille, Georges (1989), *Theory of Religion*, trans. Robert Hurley, New York: Zone Books.

Bataille, Georges (1994), *The Absence of Myth: Writings on Surrealism*, ed. and trans. Michael Richardson, London: Verso.

Bryden, Mary (ed.) (2001), *Deleuze and Religion*, London: Routledge.

Deleuze, Gilles and Felix Guattari (1984), *Anti-Oedipus: Capitalism and Schizophrenia*, trans. Robert Hurley, Mark Seem and Helen R. Lane, London: Athlone Press.

Deleuze, Gilles and Felix Guattari (1988), *A Thousand Plateaus: Capitalism and Schizophrenia*, trans. Brian Massumi, London: Athlone Press.

Deleuze, Gilles and Felix Guattari (1994), *What is Philosophy?*, trans. Graham Burchell and Hugh Tomlinson, London: Verso.

Deleuze, Gilles and Claire Parnet (1987), *Dialogues*, trans. Hugh Tomlinson and Barbara Habberjam, New York: Columbia University Press.

Kant, Immanuel (1987), *Critique of Judgment*, trans. Werner S. Pluhar, Indianapolis: Hackett.

Lippitt, John (ed.) (1999), *Nietzsche's Futures*, London, Macmillan.

Lippitt, John and Jim Urpeth (eds) (2000), *Nietzsche and the Divine*, Manchester: Clinamen Press.

Nietzsche, Friedrich (1967), *The Will to Power*, ed. Walter Kaufmann, trans. Walter Kaufmann and R.J. Hollingdale, New York: Vintage Books.

Otto, Rudolph (1958), *The Idea of the Holy*, trans. John W. Harvey, Oxford: Oxford University Press.

Rehberg, Andrea and Rachel Jones (eds) (2000), *The Matter of Critique: Readings in Kant's Philosophy*, Manchester: Clinamen Press.

Sedgwick, Peter R. (ed.) (1995), *Nietzsche: A Critical Reader*, Oxford: Blackwell.

Stoekl, Allan (ed.) (1990), *On Bataille*, *Yale French Studies*, **78**, New Haven: Yale University Press.

Vattimo, Gianni (1999), *Belief*, trans. Luca D'Isanto and David Webb, Cambridge: Polity Press.

V
POLITICAL DIFFERENCE

Chapter 12

Politics, Pluralism and the Philosophy of Religion: an Essay on Exteriority

Philip Goodchild[1]

1. The Exterior Within

What happens when religious people meet? Courtesy, disengagement, companionship, curiosity, translation, assimilation, dialogue, proselytization, prayer, comprehension, conversion, syncretism, multiple participation, secularization, toleration, persecution, conflict, war: these are just a few possibilities. But what should happen when religious people meet? This is a question concerning religious and moral authority, a question that religious people may find answered for them by their existing traditions and authorities. Yet they may find many answers. For each strategy encountered in practice in the histories of religions may have received some degree of authoritative legitimation from within relevant traditions. Then the plurality of authoritative approaches – plurality within each tradition – yields responsibility to religious people to select the most appropriate response from within their traditions, according to the principles and practices which seem most fundamental to them. Again, the diversity of effective fundamental principles and practices within a tradition indicates that there is a diversity of modes of conceiving and acknowledging the fundamental, the ultimate, within any religious tradition. Thus traditions contain a diversity of religions, and the problem of encounter between religions takes place within traditions themselves – and perhaps, if people respond to more than one fundamental principle, within people themselves.

Although the terms and stages for such encounters have traditionally been set by religions, if such encounters occur between people committed to different ultimate principles or practices then the religions will be incommensurable. The religion of the other may be comprehended in the categories of the same, but with one vital modification: when I understand another religion, I do not share its commitment, or its relation to its ultimate principle. Where what concerns me is the 'religion' of the other, what may concern the other is its ultimate principle or practice (Cantwell Smith, 1978, p. 19). I have little knowledge of this relation. Then encounters between religions may in fact be non-encounters, non-relations – and thus not comprehended under existing traditions and authorities.

Nevertheless, such encounters do indeed take place, and while the mode of conduct of religious people may be shaped by their religions, the course of the encounter itself, as a non-relation, may be exterior to both religions. Then what happens when religious people meet, within or between traditions? We cannot say in advance. There may be a contest of power (see Foucault, 1986). There may be a confluence of interests. There may be construction of a new form of life. There might even be attention given to the exterior that divides yet relates them.

For everywhere, in the actual course of life, the exterior is within.

2. Philosophy of Religion

In north-western Europe through the sixteenth, seventeenth and eighteenth centuries, the meeting of religions was all too frequently a contest over authority. Under such conditions of diversification, it became essential to consider whether authority succeeded in advancing religious truth, or whether it succeeded in advancing the personal interests of those in power. The evidence of the division of Europe suggested to observers that authority could be used to establish a false religion just as easily as a true one. Arguments from divine authority, or revelation, could not be entirely trusted unless it could be shown that revelation was indeed revelation. Into this interval between faith and authority, because of the fact of plurality, there emerged a site of autonomy, exterior to tradition, for modern reason to enter. Dissension demanded epistemology: a rational legitimation of religious truth claims. Thus arose modern philosophy of religion.

John Locke, in his *Letter on Toleration*, argued against the use of authority in religion on the grounds of the fact of plurality, the princes of the world being as divided over religious opinions as they were over secular interests. Since religious conviction could not be commanded, but could only be arrived at by 'light and evidence', then reason is essential to produce a conviction of conscience (Locke, 1977). Locke's argument depended on his conception of reason which, abstracting evidence from its situation within experience, tradition, community, performance or territory, constructs ideas in the neutral space of a *tabula rasa*. The result is a justification for secularization, separating a commonwealth as a society to promote civil interests from a church as a voluntary society for the worship of God. Once abstracted from the 'civil' realms of experience, tradition, community, performance and territory, all religious authority appeared to be an arbitrary imposition of a divine will.

Then philosophy of 'religion', in its very formulation of 'religion' as a category, abstracted religion from the authoritative claims of experience, tradition, community, performance and territory, so as to recast it in propositions, and submit it to the neutral, disinterested and exterior judgment of reason. Such a deformation of the object of study, as frequent today as then, was only possible insofar as religion leant itself to abstraction as a set of propositions, or belief claims, which could become the object of reason. The fact that England at the end of the seventeenth century was filled with pamphlets and tracts claiming to present in propositional form the essence of true religion is no coincidence (Harrison, 1990, p. 25).

By such moves, a revolution in religion is enacted. Authority, along with the whole swathe of political and civil interests, is yielded to the neutral realm of reason, while religion becomes essentially a private matter of conscience. Thus philosophy of religion changes religion itself. Moreover, instead of settling once and for all the question of religious truth claims, the peace it brings has simply been the prolongation of religious warfare by other means: for many a contemporary philosopher of religion will hold that 'basic beliefs' are unquestionable, or else they will not entertain questions about them. Philosophy of religion becomes a justification of 'basic beliefs', and is no more successful in solving the problems of religious diversity that gave rise to it than any other means.

On this issue today, opinion in modern Western philosophy of religion is divided into two broad opposing camps: 'pluralists', who wish to unify religions through reason, dialogue or collaborative practice, on a neutral stage that takes precedence over all religious commitments or authorities, and 'particularists', who wish to maintain the integrity and authority of their own tradition and its reasoning, over and above the modern construction of reason. Neither succeeds in separating religion from the claims of authority. Thus religious encounter takes place as a contest of power. Neither addresses the problem of the exterior within. Then could there be a third alternative, beyond tradition and modernity? Let us situate the current alternatives in order to move on.

3. The End of Dialogue?

Religious pluralists have been heavily criticized for propagating a new imperialism under the form of the 'myth of Western universalism'. One seminal essay, frequently cited by those who maintain a tradition-specific, particularist approach, is by John Milbank (1990a), entitled 'The End of Dialogue'.[2] The fundamental challenge Milbank offers to pluralism is to question its secularizing agenda: the tendency to see religions as separable from wider cultures and social projects, so that religions can then be brought together under a universal social framework of pluralism, dialogue or praxis. Yet religions already offer universal frameworks themselves. Here Milbank maintains that religion is not a genus, a realm within culture, for religion involves the 'basic organizing categories for an entire culture: the images, word-forms, and practices which specify "what there is" for a particular society' (Milbank, 1990a, p. 177). Then, 'from such a perspective the entire agenda concerning the "problem", or "the challenge of other religions", simply evaporates' (ibid.). Milbank's position, here, depends on his broader theological project, and in particular his concession that theology is a 'contingent, historical construct emerging from, and reacting back upon, particular social practices conjoined with particular semiotic and figural codings' (Milbank, 1990b, p. 2). The pluralist position, likewise, reflects the globalizing social project of 'the West-inspired nation-state and the West-inspired capitalist economy' (Milbank, 1990a, p. 175). Thus Milbank shows:

> One can only regard dialogue partners as equal, independently of one's valuation of what they say, if one is already treating them, and the culture they represent, as valuable mainly in terms of their abstract possession of an autonomous freedom of spiritual outlook and an open commitment to the truth. In other words, if one takes them as liberal, Western subjects, images of oneself. (Ibid., pp.177–8)

The fundamental conflict between pluralists and particularists occurs when particularists refuse to accept that subject position, and refuse to renounce the universal authority of their own tradition.

One has to accept the force of this critique, yet it would be foolish to regard this as a complete account of 'what there is' in religious encounter. Milbank exemplifies the ways in which particularists ward off the exterior. To begin with, insofar as a religion is a cultural logic specifying 'what there is', or the a priori conditions of possible experience, it restricts encounter to translation into its own terms (ibid., p. 189). Furthermore, Milbank's description of religions as different accounts of 'what there is' is itself culturally particular, and is hardly applicable in the case of non-abhidharmic forms of Buddhism, for example. Thus Milbank provides an encompassing framework of religion as a 'cultural logic' which itself excludes any exterior conceptions of religion. Moreover, this is an essentially Kantian and modern move, even if it follows the cultural–linguistic turn or is dubbed 'postmodern'. It falls into two philosophical illusions clearly identified by Kant (which, it must be said, Kant failed to escape himself).

Firstly, it commits the paralogism of pure reason: by taking the principles of the mode of representation (the 'cultural logic') as conditions of the represented content (the object of a religious project), one constructs a concept of truth out of the mode of representation itself (religion as social project) (see Kant, 1929, pp. 328–67).[3] Secondly, if it is impossible to locate the unconditioned within the object without contradiction, it is equally impossible to locate the unconditioned within a cultural logic without contradiction, for culture is itself conditioned. Milbank's 'aesthetic turn', essential to his postmodern recovery of the politics and ontology of Augustine and Aquinas, deliberately repeats both of these philosophical illusions insofar as the unconditioned is specifically identified as participating in a particular mode of representation (through incarnation and ecclesiology). The effect is not only an *a priori* exclusion of other modes of representation, but also an exclusion of that which escapes representation, such exclusions being enacted under the self-absorbed rubric of a 'beauty' that wishes to know nothing of the ugliness that constitutes actual life. For the fundamental yet unfounded assumption of postmodernists, culturalists and the new particularists is that a cultural logic or mode of consciousness is constructed within consciousness (by, for example, reflection or interpretation or *convenientia*), instead of being a resolution in consciousness of purely exterior forces that form thought as such.

The subsumption of 'religion' into 'culture' – the latter term itself being a reification of experiences, traditions, performances, communities and territories of questionable solidity – that specifies 'what there is', subsuming nature as well into a purely theological construct, means that there is never any encounter. Yet, to the extent that religion is propagated through symbols, it has a life of its own apart from the social project which gives rise to it, enabling not only the re-creation of the same social project elsewhere, but a fundamental transformation of the order of symbols and the subsequent order of society. Postmodernists acknowledge this; yet diversity seems to prevent any symbol from gaining universal currency (in practice, there is already a universal currency, the US dollar). A retreat into a cultural ontology evades exteriority, which can only be encountered in the present, by means of a retreat into the past: where a culture is assumed to have its source alongside a social project, where that source determines cultural identity, where that identity determines all present manifestations, and where that identity is expressed only in narratives, semiotic or figural codings.[4]

Under such conditions, the theologico-political problems of the present age are not allowed to determine the shape of religion, and philosophy of religion becomes impossible. Yet for those who maintain the possibility that life involves encounter with something exceeding culture – whether conceived as 'natural' or 'supernatural' – religion may stand in need of urgent revision insofar as it turns its attention solely to recreating an imaginary past or future.[5] For in present experience, 'dialogue' may not only be a formal position respecting 'dialogue partners as equal, independently of one's valuation of what they say' (the formal position of the market, not the cut and thrust of religious discussion) but it may include an encounter with the forces that shape religious consciousness, whether 'natural' or 'supernatural'.

4. Epistemology

Let us trace the pluralist position back to some of its historical and philosophical roots. In conditions of religious plurality, once the authority of one religious grouping is checked by that of another, diversity requires epistemology: how can religious truth claims be justified? Lacking the authority of experience, tradition, community, performance and territory, it becomes possible to doubt everything. Yet, while one may disregard authority, and disengage from experience, tradition, community, performance and territory, one can only doubt a truth claim. The corrosive effect of methodological doubt is that it is necessarily accompanied by disregarding and disengagement (even if this is only for the sake of an argument on the neutral territory of reason), in order to convert religious ways of life into truth claims. For such truth claims, constructed in a space of representation maintained by methodological doubt, existence can no longer be a predicate, nor can it inform the form of representation itself. For existence must be bracketed out, in order to be rediscovered through reason. When it comes to constructing a concept of truth that will explain what it means for a given proposition that 'it is the case' (that is, the existent), then, paradoxically, existence can play no part in this.

The paralogism of pure epistemology is as follows: by taking the principles of the mode of representation as conditions of the represented content, one constructs a concept of truth out of the mode of representation itself. For information to be represented as true, the form of truth presupposes the characteristics of information: an unconditioned unity of relation (that is, that truth is self-subsistent), an unconditioned unity of quality (that truth is not composite but simple), an unconditioned unity of plurality in time (that truth is identical to itself at different times) and an unconditioned unity of existence (that truth is knowledge of the existence of itself only, and of other things merely as representations) (see Kant, 1929, p. 366). Truth, here, is represented as one, unconditioned, self-subsistent, simple, eternal being. Moreover, one could infer that, bearing these properties, truth cannot be limited in respect of either its power of being true or its power of knowing its truth: it is thus a being of infinite power and knowledge. It is no coincidence that epistemological approaches to the philosophy of religion are primarily concerned with the God of classical theism, for such a God is the form of representation of knowledge, once abstracted from experience by methodological doubt. Religion is simply replaced by the cultural frame of the proposition itself.

Now, whatever one decides about the existence of such a God of classical theism, or the truth of religious claims, the form of this truth and the nature of this God have been decided in advance by the way of constructing propositions through doubt. The fundamental difference between the modern 'God of classical theism' and a Thomistic 'classical theism' is that, for the latter, the form of the proposition itself participates by analogy in Being, so that existence informs representation. Then modern attempts to test the truth claims of religious propositions can only do so hypothetically, in abstraction, in an absence of a relation to an existence that is merely represented. Those who merely assert religious truth claims as their subjective opinions are modern liberal, democratic subjects, who meet for the discussion of mere representations which derive value from their degree of exchangeability, and thus their degree of deterritorialization from a tradition. Thus modern philosophy of religion takes place in the absence of religion, suspending in advance the judgment that religious truth claims are true, and thus suspending the one relation that could enable one to decide the issue with certainty.

Finally, we should note that to regard a religion as a 'culture' is to subsume religion entirely into a form of representation. For even if the fundamental logic of a culture is 'inscribed in a people's mode of habitual action and social organization' (Milbank, 1990a, p. 178; see further Bourdieu, 1990 for substantiation of this claim), such an inscription remains a mode of representation. The unity and identity of a culture, its 'fundamental logic', remains a theological construct, the effect of constituting an object (in this case, a culture) through the 'theorization effect' of our propositional means of representation. The result is forced synchronization of the successive, fictitious totalization, neutralization of functions and substitution of products for the system of principles of production (see Bourdieu, 1990, p. 86). Then if 'truth claims' are regarded as products in isolation of their principles of production, of what might make them 'true', there will be no secure access to truth. An epistemological approach to religious encounter is simply a translation of the 'religion' of the other into a questionable set of truth claims or propositions, devoid of the religious relation to existence that determines whether or not they are true, under the guidance of the God of classical theism who will only recognize himself in the form of his own mirror. Can there be another way of being true and being religious?

5. Ontology

The particularist position derives historically from a philosophy that begins with ontology. Let us distinguish two ontological approaches to philosophy of religion which begin by exploring the relation between thought and existence. A first, broadly characterized as 'neoplatonic' (although it has relevance from Plato to the late Middle Ages), is where thought shares in existence by imitation, participation or analogy. The thought of being is subordinated to the One insofar as it is organized by a transcendent plan or cosmology. Here there is a philosophical and theological danger: if the transcendent plan is fully knowable, then the One or unconditioned will itself be conditioned by the intellect which is capable of grasping that plan, even though such an intellect has only been illuminated with such a capacity by the One itself. The divine becomes a graven image. The solution to this problem is some degree of apophasis: either the One withdraws from all revelation, or else it is eschatologically suspended, for example in Christianity to a beatific vision when the intellect will be taken up into the self-conditioning life of the Trinity. In both cases, faith in the existence of such a transcendent plan is required.

The key point is as follows: reasoning, here, is faith seeking understanding, requiring methodological trust. It is accompanied by an ascetic spirituality that wishes to take leave of current imperfections in order to approach the eternal ideal. Its ethos is essentially hierarchical, in that only those who have performed the self-transforming work of reason gain a greater access to the truth. Its politics is essentially exclusivist, in that those who elevate a heterodox vision of the One above that received by the hierarchy must be excluded from the community of reason, lest their pride and self-assertion corrupt the spirituality that aims at the One. Most significantly for our purposes, attention here is directed primarily towards the One (in intellection and contemplative prayer, for example), in relation to which the accidents, imperfections and deviations of life are mere distractions having no true being. This is the essence of a tradition-constituted, ontological approach to the philosophy of religion (here, I must mention in passing, in spite of the fact that the Christian theological tradition is largely located here, I find this ontology fundamentally incompatible in ethos, politics and piety with the message of Jesus as recorded in the Gospels).

A second ontological approach, broadly characterized as 'modern' (although Polka derives it from Anselm, through Descartes, Spinoza, Kant and Hegel), passes through modern critical theory, as opposed to the purely epistemological approach of modern analytic philosophy. Here thought itself has an existence insofar as it is thoughtful, and is not mere idle banter. Access to existence is no longer mediated via the True as an essence or aesthetic form, but is given simply insofar as thought engages with that which matters. Then the aim of modern critical thought is to separate the existence of thought from its idle representations that would require a methodological trust to attain an essence. Instead of encouraging complicity in common and authoritative representations of an essence, critical thought practices methodological suspicion. The historical actuality of the thinker is of greater significance than what the thinker proposes; such propositions may be treated as symptoms of the temporal processes which determine thought, including historical, social, linguistic, psychological, sexual, economic and biological. The ethos of this thought is critique and suspicion, while its politics consists of affirming and welcoming difference, since the existence it encounters is a multiplicity irreducible to a One. One may call this 'democratic', 'multiculturalist' and 'pluralist', but it is not the same democracy as that of representation and rights, which merely has a nominal relation to existence. Instead, the politics are inclusivist, rather than acceding to the hegemony of a democratic majority. The aim is to enhance the temporal existence of all, rather than give a nominal recognition to all, or to attain the ideal.

Critiques of pluralism are usually insensitive to these two discrete sources of modernity, one epistemological, paradigmatically represented by Locke, and the other ontological, paradigmatically represented by Spinoza, which coexist in varying mixtures and alliances. Beneath the philosophical roots of pluralism, particularism and secularism we discover the grounds of three different political models of religious encounter: a pluralist, democratic and dialogical model, which gives a limited authority and authenticity to the self-representation of religious persons, and facilitates an exchange between these representations (exemplified by Hick, 1989; Swidler, 1990); a traditional, ontological model, which has an exclusivist commitment to its own truth, and will only recognize the divine light that shines through the other insofar as it illuminates some aspect of the same (exemplified by Heim, 1995; D'Costa, 2000); and a modern, critical model, which does not take the self-representation of the other at face value, but constructs a knowledge of their existence through a synthesis of the historical, social, linguistic, psychological, sexual, economic and biological processes that shape such an existence (exemplified by the scientific study of religion). The latter approach tends to appear as essentially secular, since it can offer no account of specifically 'religious' relations and processes, if such matters are meaningful at all.

None of these models lends itself to a religious encounter with the religion of the other, its bond to its source, should it have one. Before we propose a different political model of religious encounter, let us ask, what makes such a source inaccessible?

6. Monotheism

> Whoever desires to be saved should above all
> hold to the catholic faith.
> Anyone who does not keep it whole and unbroken
> will doubtless perish eternally.
> Now this is the catholic faith:
> That we worship on God in trinity ...
> (Athanasian creed, in Plantinga, 1999, p. 87)

How could such a statement – that one's eternal destiny should depend on one's belief – become possible? How have eternal matters become so identified with temporal ideas? It has not been uncommon in the history of religions that one's devotion to one's deity should lead to the usage in praise of the epithet 'almighty'. From this, one naturally infers 'uncreated', 'immeasurable', 'eternal' and 'one' by negating the contrary – being 'created', 'measurable', 'temporal', and 'multiple' being incompatible with 'almightiness' – and one arrives at monotheism, well on the way to classical theism. Now, if God is not to be identified with the actual order, then there must be some differentiation of divine from natural order, yet if God is to remain powerful, then there must be some connection: the classic solution is that God's almightiness is expressed as *authority*, in legislation.[6] In the words of the Athanasian creed, 'truth *compels* us to confess ... catholic religion *forbids* us to say' (Plantinga, 1999, p. 88; emphasis added). Thus monotheism emerges as a protest against the social or natural order, claiming that the true king is not tangible.[7] The fundamental monotheistic legislation is against worship of other gods and powers, so that there will be one, almighty source of meaning and power in public and private life. Yet legislation also requires judgment, else its power would be ineffectual, and that judgment must be enacted primarily against the unbelievers who worship prohibited gods:

> If you hear it said about one of the towns that the Lord your God is giving you to live in, that scoundrels from among you have gone out and led the inhabitants of the town astray, saying, 'Let us go and worship other gods', whom you have not known, then you shall inquire and make a thorough investigation. If the charge is established that such an abhorrent thing has been done among you, you shall put the inhabitants of that town to the sword, utterly destroying it and everything in it – even putting its livestock to the sword. All of its spoil you shall gather into its public square; then burn the town and all its spoil with fire, as a whole burnt offering to the Lord your God. It shall remain a perpetual ruin never to be rebuilt. (Deuteronomy 13:12–16)

The ban follows logically from monotheism, legislation and judgment. It is simply the actualization of infinite authority. Ultimately, even if sinners are granted mercy, no opposition to the sole authority can be allowed to survive. Then eschatological judgment, of the kind repeated by all the main New Testament writers as well as in the Qur'an, re-enacts this apocalyptic drama of the ban, now become universal. Genocide is a divine privilege. This is the repressed side of monotheism, concealed within the self-image of monotheistic religions, yet evident in history. The ban is re-enacted whenever the truth of other religions is rejected in advance, except insofar as that truth reveals the one, true God. It is re-enacted whenever religious identity is formed, in covenant with and in the image of a single God, by means of an exclusion of other identities (see, further, Schwartz, 1997). It is re-enacted whenever the claims of one tradition take precedence over all others. It is re-enacted whenever words drawn from the social form of empire are used to describe God: 'almighty', 'Lord', 'messiah', 'Christ', 'kingdom'. It is re-enacted in all forms of practice, devotion and belief that worship a single God. It is re-enacted whenever a utopian social vision of peace is projected that excludes and replaces prior social orders. Every exodus has its Egyptians and Canaanites. Every Buddhist wheel-turning emperor establishes his empire first by conquest, before publicly repenting and establishing peace.

The logic of monotheism is a logic of religious identity. It is re-enacted, not only in monotheistic religions to whom identity is particularly important, but whenever religious devotion passes a threshold of intensity where it begins to exclude all other devotions. Such devotion renders exteriority inaccessible.

7. Modernity

Modern critical thought that challenges the effects of religious authority, as in the preceding section, is fundamentally incompatible with a strong sense of religious identity and commitment. It does not lead to a peaceful coexistence of a plurality of perspectives: few monotheists could tolerate the above assertions. The modern strategy of directing attention away from eternal truths to temporal existence is a violent act: where modern reason inserts an interval between faith and authority, modern critique inserts an interval between the self-consciousness of faith and its actual, historical existence and conduct. The religious are deceived about who they are; only secular outsiders can read this from actual conduct. Now, to the extent that scientific knowledge of such conduct is possible, the existence of the other is recast in the form of propositions – albeit somewhat unflattering ones. Here one repeats the paralogism of pure reason once more: the mode of representation of the other is taken as the mode of existence of the other, as if there were one, eternal truth about who the other really is. Monotheism is reduced to a 'fundamental logic'.

Modern critical thought risks insensitivity to ambivalence: there may be an excess in monotheism that cannot be reduced to the form of being inscribed within a proposition. Such excess is already expressed within monotheism through concepts of 'transcendence', 'the infinite' and 'mystery', where the divine functions as a critical resource that may exceed the claims of the current order. Transcendence is always the excess of the divine over the self-image of the religious.

Modern thought must therefore turn its critical gaze on itself (for example, Adorno and Horkheimer, 1997); it must inquire into the meaning of Being (for example, Heidegger, 1962), the distribution of power in its own discourse (for example, Foucault, 1972), or else explore a relation to the other that cannot be reduced to thematization in a proposition (for example, Levinas, 1991). It may explore the logic of writing as such (for example, Derrida, 1976) and may despair of ever escaping its own artificially constituted nature (for example, Lyotard, 1984); alternatively, it may construct an ontology of difference that can never be reduced to the same (for example, Deleuze, 1994). In whatever way one approaches existence, there remain limits internal to knowledge itself, insofar as the space of thought can never be expanded to grasp the whole of existence itself. Nor can thought be expanded to fence in the infinite, locating it in one privileged site of encounter.

Encounter with mystery, should there be such a thing, cannot be restricted to the terms of a tradition and identity, no more than it can be delimited to a medium through which existence may be thought. It occurs in the experience of encounter with exteriority.

8. The Contemporary Predicament

If truth remains withdrawn and transcendent, how may it be encountered? The problem of contemporary reason is its lack of potency. For if the True and the Good no longer speak unequivocally in thought, what will lend careful, critical thought substance? Moreover, the crisis in contemporary ontology is less epistemological than political: deprived of all authority, existence, were it to speak in thought, would claim little attention. In a mass-media society, whatever interest there may be in philosophical and religious questions, the voices of philosophers of religion remain all but inaudible. For the common coin of 'truth' can only be achieved by extensive critical labour; even then, the specialist labourers dispute over where truth is to be found. There is no credibility or authority in philosophy of religion, whatever the quality of its argumentation.

Instead, competing for attention, thoughts survive that attract attention. The validity of a thought is determined less by its essential truth than by the conditions of its actual existence: whether it is accessible, communicable, exchangeable and interesting. The transcendent remains inaudible here, except as a figure of an unattainable desire. Religion collapses into accessible identities, into idolatry. Thoughts prosper which gratify desires or which justify, whether through flattery or infantile dependence, the complacency of the religious subject. Thoughts prosper which devalue alternatives, asserting the self-importance of their own light by surreptitiously darkening the lights of others. Thoughts prosper which are disconnected from existence, and 'verified' solely by the attention they attract. In contemporary religion as in civil society, consciousness is built upon greed, hatred and delusion. For it is our base instincts that find gratification in the market of thought, where reason is simply a servant of the passions (see Hume, 1946, p. 415.).

This is in direct contrast to all traditional forms of thought, which, whether they emphasize activity or contemplation, whether they are 'ethnic religions' or 'world religions', whether they are 'Semitic religions' or 'Asian religions', whether they are 'religions' or 'philosophies', invoke determinate practices of directing attention.

Each contemporary person is left with a profound dilemma: whether to follow the ways of spiritual discipline (including reason), directing attention towards a source that is authoritatively given, while knowing that a modern wedge has been driven between such attention and its goal, as well as a critical wedge between such attention and its actual practice; or whether to expose oneself to encounter with the exterior, while knowing that one's attention will be distracted by the passions of greed, hatred and delusion. Under such conditions, what prospects are there for religious encounter?

9. Encounter with Exteriority

All religions and philosophies share the common character of having determinate practices of directing attention. Where they differ over essence, and differ in existence, they may share a common experience that attracts their attention. Moreover, to insert an interval of distracted attention into religious life does not undermine the essence of religion, nor does it substantially change its existence (although this may follow). It requires neither methodological trust nor methodological suspicion, but methodological attention to that which matters. It does not require identifying religions with cultures, identities or authorities. In distracted attention, we might participate in a common space of encounter, without undermining or reducing any degrees of difference.

Where might we find a universal horizon of experience? Two or three decades ago, such a horizon was only visible to the far-sighted (for example, Bookchin, 1982). Now it rushes to meet us. In the present century, the global mean temperature will rise by between 1·5°C and 5·5°C, with several models finishing somewhere near 2·7°C (IPCC, 2001). The temperature only rose by half a degree between 1900 and 1990, yet, by 2025, after only another half a degree rise, it is predicted that five billion people, some two-thirds of the world's population, will live in water-stressed countries (IPCC, 2001). This is a matter of some import to the philosophy of religion. For while such scientific predictions may be culturally-specific, Hurricane Mitch was not. Neither will the heat waves be, nor rising sea levels, droughts, floods, hurricanes, cyclones, soil erosion, desertification, forest fires and deforestation that will affect us all in very different ways. The disturbances that are likely to follow from such a destabilization of the global environment, including pollution, poor health, depletion of resources including agricultural land and ground water, droughts and famines of an unheard of scale, collapse of infrastructure, collapse of ecosystems, loss of over 50 per cent of plant and animal species, mass migrations, wars and the collapse in the credibility of national and international institutions and boundaries, will bring all cultures into a direct relation with the exterior. Whether or not religion originated from fear of the forces of nature, it will have to respond to them. An encounter with the exterior – a nature that can never be reduced to a culture – is the universal horizon that limits human experience.

There is another universal horizon which has also emerged in the past two or three decades, but has been approaching for much longer and is much more apparent. This is the emergence of global free market capitalism which increasingly penetrates all spheres of material life. Now this one seems to be highly culturally specific, and its spread seems to be a quest for domination of one form of life over others – a form of life that emerged in England. This is not entirely true, for economic growth is exterior in one respect to all cultures. For although a price records a conventional ascription of value within a culture, trade takes place between incommensurable cultures with the intention of increasing that value through transactions. Then, although the quantity of one's assets may depend on past accumulation, the value of them in currency is dependent on their creditworthiness, the anticipated rate of return on investment, a future projection. Such projections, expressed as a pure quantity, belong to no culture. Moreover, in order to interact with exterior social groups, I require a universally accepted currency, and in order to realize my own values, insofar as these involve production or consumption drawing from exterior social groups, I must value currency as a means to my end. Whatever my own values, the value of money, which is measured solely against itself as a rate of increase, must come first. In this respect, all who deal in money encounter an exterior, the value of money itself, that must now be treated as beyond and before all material cultural achievements.

Finally, in any contractual arrangement between those who seek the necessities of life and those who seek a rate of return on their investment, the conditions favour the investor who could enter all sorts of alternative and external transactions instead. Then since the conditions always favour finance capital, it profits from all exchanges (except those that collapse) and value is extracted from particular social groups and cultures so as to accumulate outside as a stock of finance capital. In such transactions, the needs of subsistence and sustainability are structurally subordinated to the need of capital to increase; transactions only occur when the latter condition can be satisfied. Thus, although dominant, global finance capital, aiming at its own expansion through competition, belongs to no one. It is an autonomous process, an exterior within, which, through its predomination over subsistence and sustainability, is of intimate concern to us all.

It is quite evident that the ecological crisis has been triggered by the expansion of modern and industrial consumer lifestyles. It is also quite evident that this expansion is driven by economic growth, as well as personal preference. Then these two exteriors, the ecological and economic, as universal limits of experience, are profoundly linked. These two futures – the speculative future of a rate of return on investment, and the predicted future of ecological catastrophe – are manifestations of that which is exterior or transcendent to all religions and philosophies, while having an increasingly determining effect on human life. They are worthy of attention, and constitute a common space of encounter with two universal horizons of exteriority.

10.   A Triple Apocalypse

Many religious worldviews have an eschatological vision that encompasses such apocalyptic predicaments within a cosmology. Thus nature is subsumed into culture, responsibility is alleviated by justification and attention reverts to an ideal essence. A lack of attention to experience, even in the form of mining the resources of one's tradition for its ecological credentials so that one can learn to value nature and take responsibility for it, is a failure to respond, to be responsible, for it replaces good attention with the idea of good intentions. Directing attention to the past, to tradition, to identity, to an eternal essence, unless it enhances one's ability to experience and to respond to the future, is quite simply *irrational*, a disproportionate distribution of attention.

Nevertheless, it is important to consider what claims attention. Why does the future matter if, as mortal beings, we are all going to die anyway, and a short life may be as worthwhile as a long one? What are the fundamental values of life? The ecological crisis matters because it will produce man-made human suffering on an unheard-of scale, and that scale could still be significantly reduced by present action. Economic globalization matters because, in spite of the beneficial effects of the prosperity it brings, it also uproots and destroys other ways of life, excludes many from its success, and it produces preventable present and future suffering (see Khor, 2001, Mander and Goldsmith, 1996, Burbach *et al.*, 1997). For some, the apocalypse has already happened. For others, it continues to happen, day by day. Finally, a central lesson of, especially, Buddhism, Judaism and Christianity, as well as other religions, is that the experience of suffering matters. Here we have a third universal horizon of human experience. Again, religious practices and beliefs involve attempts to give meaning to suffering, to subsume nature into culture, to ward off its apocalyptic effects. Yet in subsuming suffering under an eternal essence or ideal, one is in danger of naturalizing and justifying it, and thus colluding with it. By contrast, modern critical thought may aim at the alleviation of suffering, to end its existence. This is very much to be welcomed; yet it does little to enhance further awareness of suffering, and its significance. Finally, the experience of suffering – awareness of the dissolution of the composition of one's physical, emotional, personal, social and cultural identity – may itself bring an apocalypse, the dissolution of one's self and meaningful world, an encounter with exteriority within.

11.   The Meeting of Religions

What should happen when religious or non-religious people meet? All meeting of incommensurable perspectives, principles and practices takes place in a space exterior to any of them. If attention is directed primarily to a particular authority, out of methodological trust, then a group may inoculate itself against all encounter: one speaks within a community, for a community, to construct a shared point of view. This viewpoint is also complicit in the disavowal of the significance of the difference between the community's actual historical conduct and its shared viewpoint – if the actual community is imperfect, it is supposed that this is because it falls short of submission to its founding authority. By contrast, if attention is directed to the significance of such differences, out of methodological suspicion, then all become strangers to each other, requiring indubitable evidence to guarantee the value of other perspectives. Failing to reach such cast-iron guarantees, interaction and exchange may only be facilitated in the market place of modern thought, where what counts as truth for the public consensus is the sole currency giving value to what is said. Truth, here, is reduced to the lowest common denominator, becoming a function of the interests of those 'consumers of truth' who possess sufficient cultural capital to determine what is acceptable.

The approaches of methodological trust and methodological suspicion both assume that the exterior space of encounter is an inert space to be mastered, possessing no characteristics of its own. Yet encounter is also time spent together, where time, far from requiring the mutual impenetrability of bodies in space, is composed through relation as a 'mutual penetration, an interconnection and organization of elements' (Bergson, 1910, p. 101). Encounter involves mutual attention during time spent together. Moreover, the experience of time is not that of an inert space to be mastered: events happen to us. Our attention is demanded. Where we differ over essence, and differ in existence, we may share a common experience that attracts our attention. The exterior within becomes a temporal interval, a hesitation, which, whatever our tradition, gives us a degree of freedom in how we synthesize time by bringing our past to meet our present, in order to address the future. Within this degree of freedom, there are many prospects for cooperation.

No encounter is pure and unmediated. Each encounter takes place within a framework provided by nature, society and subjectivity. Under contemporary conditions of ecological and economic globalization, the dominant forces shaping nature, society and subjectivity are external to all, yet shared by all. We have at last arrived in the age of universal conditions of experience. We are each affected, to a much greater or lesser extent, by a triple apocalypse. Then any adaptive reconstruction of political relations must be post-apocalyptic: we all dwell in an exterior site now, but we dwell there together. We all have to come to terms with the unthinkable, and find a new life together – for as long as humanity is able to endure. How will we spend this time together? What shall we speak of? This is the fundamental political problem of dialogue and difference.

Two modes of collective inquiry demand our attention. One is to address the three universal limits of experience. What is required above all is inquiry into and action in relation to the exterior limits of nature, society and self, in the form of the ecological crisis, economic globalization and suffering.[8] Now, where each religion or philosophy might have established patterns of inquiry and action for nature, society and self, such patterns are developed from subsuming nature, society and self into a cosmology and culture, a meaningful world. What is usually overlooked is the way in which our actual forms of life directly impinge upon each other, whether through ecological, economic or symbolic violence, and contribute to each other's apocalyptic experience. Moreover, what have never properly been addressed are the contemporary forms of exteriority that emerge in experience, outside of any cosmology or culture. Then we require a new constructive, collective, natural, social and personal project, situated within the experience of exteriority, drawing on any resources brought from the religions and philosophies that may be of use.

A second mode of inquiry complements this. For our experiences, traditions, communities, performances and territories have real conditions of emergence. Even if such emergence takes place outside the conscious subject, even so, insofar as the life of the subject is shaped by them, it senses them directly. Human thought is thus fissured in temporal experience: in our 'innermost core' we find the 'living witness of all truth', the one who acts but does not understand, the forgotten past; in our conscious mind, we find the one who seeks to understand, but who does not perceive, the living present. In human experience, then, there is one thing that must be recalled, and another that recalls it. In the words of the great German philosopher F.W.J. Schelling:

> This separation, this doubling of ourselves, this secret intercourse between the two essences, one questioning and one answering, one ignorant and seeking to know and one knowledgeable without knowing its knowledge; this silent dialogue, this inner art of conversation, is the authentic secret of the philosopher from which the outer art (which for this reason is called 'dialectic') is only a replica and, if it has become a bare form, is only empty appearance and shadow. (Schelling, 1997, p. 115)

Such a dialogue, across the borders of spatial exteriority, is an attempt to think the unthinkable potencies that affect us, while exceeding the powers of our thought. The aim is no longer to simply trust or suspect the past, but to carry its resources forward to address the universal horizons of experience. This move is not likely to be popular. Many, of course, may prefer to remain in the past, where they trust that the eternal has a prior claim on their attention. Others, by contrast, might wish to liberate the present from the past and determine themselves, suspicious of any exterior claims of attention. Only those who attend to experience will feel the claim of being as it speaks, demanding our attention, determining our modes of thought and action. This third ontological approach to thinking, which inquires into what matters most while not remaining constrained by the authority of any particular tradition, is nothing less than a new constitution of the philosophy of religion.

Notes

1. In addressing the question of pluralism today, it is often assumed that one should situate oneself within one's own tradition and cultural identity, so as to avoid giving the appearance of claiming a universal perspective. So here goes: white, Anglo-Saxon, male, Protestant, heterosexual, employed at a major British university, adult, English-speaker, educated at an independent school and Cambridge, able-bodied – in short, all the qualifications for cultural privilege. In terms of religion and philosophy, I am primarily shaped by a political reading of the Gospels, Zen Buddhism, a eucharistic reading of Pauline theology, a Judaism of radical transcendence read from the Book of

Job, the philosophy of Deleuze, the anti-capitalist politics of Deleuze and Guattari, and the philosophies of Spinoza, Schelling, Kierkegaard, Marx, Nietzsche and Bergson. Such eclecticism of incommensurable sources sounds postmodern. So there you have it: a culturally privileged postmodernist – and thus a perspective one can discount with a label (a label I repudiate). But I have said nothing of the experiences, the inadequacies, the people (especially female) and the genetic inheritance that have shaped me, and the way in which the whole history of the world affects me and is enfolded in my skin. So do not ask for a cultural identity when you are presented with a person, else you will receive a ridiculous reduction. I am exterior to all cultural labels, however well they fit. Simply read my words.

2. One should also note the significance of Surin (1990), in pioneering this approach.

3. While this is a 'paralogism' according to Kant, there is a harmony between form of intellection and form of object, according to Milbank's reading of Thomist epistemology, that is guaranteed by God (see Milbank and Pickstock, 2000). Kant would thus appear to be a 'nominalist'. Here we have a case of incommensurability between Thomist and Kantian epistemologies. From a modern perspective, it would be extremely difficult to justify the assertion that the intellect can conform to the object (by Thomist means; there is an alternative in Bergson), or to describe the spiritual process of transformation of the intellect, and the mode of knowledge that it attains that is capable of knowing the object; this has to be taken on faith. Then, in arguing that Thomist epistemology is thoroughly theological, Milbank effectively concedes the incommensurable religious difference between Aquinas and Kant. We are then left with the problem of the plurality of religions, once more. Milbank's position is effectively this: if Thomism is true, then there is no problem of religious pluralism. But Thomism is true, because it is beautiful. To which a modern critic can rejoin: a theology which ignores actuality in the name of actuality, because it is obsessed with its own beauty, is vain, ugly and thus false by its own standards. For Thomist ontology, there is nothing outside the purposeful order of divine creation *ex nihilo*; this is a claim for universal relevance and comprehension and, apparently, an arbitrary assertion of megalomaniacal power. We are left with two questions: whether an ontology constructed from Christian doctrine is separable from the imperial (that is, messianic) ambitions manifest in its formulation; and whether there is an exterior within, an actuality irreducible to total comprehension by the Same.

4. The origins of such a postmodernity can be found in an alliance between a theological piety before an originary revelation and Heidegger's piety before an epochal revelation of Being in Greek thought which can only be expressed in the narrative of the history of metaphysics. This unwarranted piety is then misread into Foucault's genealogical method so that the past is taken to entirely determine the present, and adopted by Lyotard in his conversion of all modes of thought into narrative. Once such narratives are recognized as unverifiable, the postmodern conclusion follows naturally. Yet the history of this philosophical error can be avoided simply by refusing piety before any originary revelation, and adopting another ontology.

5. Milbank acknowledges the deterritorializing effect of a theoretical ideal of the Church which has never existed in practice (Milbank, 1990a, p. 179).

6. It would seem that monotheism emerged largely in areas where there had been imperial city-states. See Swanson (1968).

7. The emergence of monotheism as a protest against a dominant political order is especially clear in the cases of Zarathustra, the early Hebrew prophets and Mohammad.

8. In this respect, we rehabilitate the 'praxis solution' (see Hick and Knitter, 1987; Knitter, 1996), now shorn of its modern, liberal agenda and frame of thought (as in Küng, 1991, 1996; see the alternative political model developed in Goodchild, 2002).

References

Adorno, T. and M. Horkheimer (1997), *Dialectic of Enlightenment*, trans. J. Cumming, London: Verso.

Bergson, H. (1910), *Time and Free Will*, trans. F. Pogson, London: Swan Sonnenschein.

Bookchin, M. (1982), *The Ecology of Freedom*, Palo Alto: Cheshire Books.

Bourdieu, P. (1990), *The Logic of Practice*, trans. R. Nice, Cambridge: Polity.

Burbach, R., O. Núñez and B.Kagarlitsky (1997), *Globalization and its Discontents*, London: Pluto Press.

Cantwell Smith, W. (1978), *The Meaning and End of Religion*, London: SPCK.

D'Costa, G. (2000), *The Meeting of Religions and the Trinity*, Edinburgh: T.&T. Clark.

Deleuze, G. (1994), *Difference and Repetition*, trans. P. Patton, London: Athlone.

Derrida, J. (1976), *Of Grammatology*, trans. G. Spivak, Baltimore: Johns Hopkins University Press.

Foucault, M. (1972), *The Archaeology of Knowledge*, trans. A. Sheridan Smith, London: Tavistock.

Foucault, M. (1986), 'Nietzsche, Genealogy, History', in Paul Rabinow (ed.), *The Foucault Reader*, London: Penguin.

Goodchild, P. (2002), *Capitalism and Religion: The Price of Piety*, London: Routledge.

Harrison, P. (1990), *'Religion' and the Religions in the English Enlightenment*, Cambridge: Cambridge University Press.

Heidegger, M. (1962), *Being and Time*, trans. J. Macquarrie and E. Robinson, Oxford: Blackwell.

Heim, S. (1995), *Salvations: Truth and Difference in Religion*, Maryknoll: Orbis.

Hick, J. (1989), *An Interpretation of Religion*, Basingstoke: Macmillan.

Hick, J. and P. Knitter (eds) (1987), *The Myth of Christian Uniqueness*, Maryknoll: Orbis.

Hume, D. (1946), *A Treatise of Human Nature*, ed. L. Selby-Bigge, Oxford: Clarendon.

IPCC (2001), *Climate Change 2001*, Report of the Working Group of the Intergovernmental Panel on Climate Change, Cambridge: Cambridge University Press.

Kant, I. (1929), *Critique of Pure Reason*, trans. N. Kemp Smith, Basingstoke: Macmillan.

Khor, M. (2001), *Rethinking Globalisation*, New York: Zed Books.

Knitter, P. (1996), *Jesus and Other Names*, Maryknoll: Orbis.

Küng, H. (1991), *Global Responsibility*, London: SCM.

Küng, H. (ed.) (1996), *Yes to a Global Ethic*, London: SCM.

Levinas, E. (1991), *Otherwise than Being or Beyond Essence*, trans. A. Lingis, Dordrecht: Kluwer.

Locke, J. (1977), 'Letter on Toleration', in John Yolton (ed.), *The Locke Reader*, Cambridge: Cambridge University Press, pp. 245–74.

Lyotard, J.-F. (1984), *The Postmodern Condition*, Manchester: Manchester University Press.

Mander, J. and E. Goldsmith (eds) (1996), *The Case Against the Global Economy*, San Francisco: Sierra Club.

Milbank, J. (1990a), 'The End of Dialogue', in Gavin D'Costa (ed.), *Christian Uniqueness Reconsidered*, Maryknoll: Orbis, pp. 174–91.

Milbank, J. (1990b), *Theology and Social Theory*, Oxford: Blackwell.

Milbank, J. and C. Pickstock (2000), *Truth in Aquinas*, London: Routledge.

Plantinga, R. (ed.) (1999), *Christianity and Plurality*, Oxford: Blackwell.

Schelling, F. (1997), *The Ages of the World*, trans. J. Norman, Ann Arbor: University of Michigan Press.

Schwartz, R. (1997), *The Curse of Cain: The Violent Legacy of Monotheism*, Chicago: University of Chicago Press.

Surin, Kenneth (1990), 'A Politics of Speech: Religious Pluralism in the Age of the McDonald's Hamburger', in Gavin D'Costa (ed.), *Christian Uniqueness Reconsidered*, MaryKnoll: Orbis, pp. 192–212

Swanson, G. (1968), *The Birth of the Gods*, Ann Arbor: University of Michigan Press.

Swidler, L. (1990), *After the Absolute: The Dialogical Future of Religious Reflection*, Minneapolis: Fortress.

Index